ATS-34   ADMISSION TEST SERIES

This is your PASSBOOK for...

AFT

Armed Forces Tests (AFT/ASVAB)

Test Preparation Study Guide
Questions & Answers

COPYRIGHT NOTICE

This book is SOLELY intended for, is sold ONLY to, and its use is RESTRICTED to individual, bona fide applicants or candidates who qualify by virtue of having seriously filed applications for appropriate license, certificate, professional and/or promotional advancement, higher school matriculation, scholarship, or other legitimate requirements of education and/or governmental authorities.

This book is NOT intended for use, class instruction, tutoring, training, duplication, copying, reprinting, excerption, or adaptation, etc., by:

1) Other publishers
2) Proprietors and/or Instructors of "Coaching" and/or Preparatory Courses
3) Personnel and/or Training Divisions of commercial, industrial, and governmental organizations
4) Schools, colleges, or universities and/or their departments and staffs, including teachers and other personnel
5) Testing Agencies or Bureaus
6) Study groups which seek by the purchase of a single volume to copy and/or duplicate and/or adapt this material for use by the group as a whole without having purchased individual volumes for each of the members of the group
7) Et al.

Such persons would be in violation of appropriate Federal and State statutes.

PROVISION OF LICENSING AGREEMENTS – Recognized educational, commercial, industrial, and governmental institutions and organizations, and others legitimately engaged in educational pursuits, including training, testing, and measurement activities, may address request for a licensing agreement to the copyright owners, who will determine whether, and under what conditions, including fees and charges, the materials in this book may be used them. In other words, a licensing facility exists for the legitimate use of the material in this book on other than an individual basis. However, it is asseverated and affirmed here that the material in this book CANNOT be used without the receipt of the express permission of such a licensing agreement from the Publishers. Inquiries re licensing should be addressed to the company, attention rights and permissions department.

All rights reserved, including the right of reproduction in whole or in part, in any form or by any means, electronic or mechanical, including photocopying, recording, or by any information storage and retrieval system, without permission in writing from the Publisher.

Copyright © 2025 by
National Learning Corporation

212 Michael Drive, Syosset, NY 11791
(516) 921-8888 • www.passbooks.com
E-mail: info@passbooks.com

PASSBOOK® SERIES

THE *PASSBOOK® SERIES* has been created to prepare applicants and candidates for the ultimate academic battlefield – the examination room.

At some time in our lives, each and every one of us may be required to take an examination – for validation, matriculation, admission, qualification, registration, certification, or licensure.

Based on the assumption that every applicant or candidate has met the basic formal educational standards, has taken the required number of courses, and read the necessary texts, the *PASSBOOK® SERIES* furnishes the one special preparation which may assure passing with confidence, instead of failing with insecurity. Examination questions – together with answers – are furnished as the basic vehicle for study so that the mysteries of the examination and its compounding difficulties may be eliminated or diminished by a sure method.

This book is meant to help you pass your examination provided that you qualify and are serious in your objective.

The entire field is reviewed through the huge store of content information which is succinctly presented through a provocative and challenging approach – the question-and-answer method.

A climate of success is established by furnishing the correct answers at the end of each test.

You soon learn to recognize types of questions, forms of questions, and patterns of questioning. You may even begin to anticipate expected outcomes.

You perceive that many questions are repeated or adapted so that you can gain acute insights, which may enable you to score many sure points.

You learn how to confront new questions, or types of questions, and to attack them confidently and work out the correct answers.

You note objectives and emphases, and recognize pitfalls and dangers, so that you may make positive educational adjustments.

Moreover, you are kept fully informed in relation to new concepts, methods, practices, and directions in the field.

You discover that you are actually taking the examination all the time: you are preparing for the examination by "taking" an examination, not by reading extraneous and/or supererogatory textbooks.

In short, this PASSBOOK®, used directedly, should be an important factor in helping you to pass your test.

PASSBOOK® SERIES

THE *PASSBOOK® SERIES* has been created to prepare applicants and candidates for the ultimate academic battlefield – the examination room.

At some time in our lives, each and every one of us may be required to take an examination – for validation, matriculation, admission, qualification, registration, certification, or licensure.

Based on the assumption that every applicant or candidate has met the basic formal educational standards, has taken the required number of courses, and read the necessary texts, the *PASSBOOK® SERIES* furnishes the one special preparation which may assure passing with confidence, instead of failing with insecurity. Examination questions – together with answers – are furnished as the basic vehicle for study so that the mysteries of the examination and its compounding difficulties may be eliminated or diminished by a sure method.

This book is meant to help you pass your examination provided that you qualify and are serious in your objective.

The entire field is reviewed through the huge store of content information which is succinctly presented through a provocative and challenging approach – the question-and-answer method.

A climate of success is established by furnishing the correct answers at the end of each test.

You soon learn to recognize types of questions, forms of questions, and patterns of questioning. You may even begin to anticipate expected outcomes.

You perceive that many questions are repeated or adapted so that you can gain acute insights, which may enable you to score many sure points.

You learn how to confront new questions, or types of questions, and to attack them confidently and work out the correct answers.

You note objectives and emphases, and recognize pitfalls and dangers, so that you may make positive educational adjustments.

Moreover, you are kept fully informed in relation to new concepts, methods, practices, and directions in the field.

You discover that you are actually taking the examination all the time: you are preparing for the examination by "taking" an examination, not by reading extraneous and/or supererogatory textbooks.

In short, this PASSBOOK®, used directedly, should be an important factor in helping you to pass your test.

HOW TO TAKE A TEST

I. YOU MUST PASS AN EXAMINATION

A. WHAT EVERY CANDIDATE SHOULD KNOW

Examination applicants often ask us for help in preparing for the written test. What can I study in advance? What kinds of questions will be asked? How will the test be given? How will the papers be graded?

As an applicant for a civil service examination, you may be wondering about some of these things. Our purpose here is to suggest effective methods of advance study and to describe civil service examinations.

Your chances for success on this examination can be increased if you know how to prepare. Those "pre-examination jitters" can be reduced if you know what to expect. You can even experience an adventure in good citizenship if you know why civil service exams are given.

B. WHY ARE CIVIL SERVICE EXAMINATIONS GIVEN?

Civil service examinations are important to you in two ways. As a citizen, you want public jobs filled by employees who know how to do their work. As a job seeker, you want a fair chance to compete for that job on an equal footing with other candidates. The best-known means of accomplishing this two-fold goal is the competitive examination.

Exams are widely publicized throughout the nation. They may be administered for jobs in federal, state, city, municipal, town or village governments or agencies.

Any citizen may apply, with some limitations, such as the age or residence of applicants. Your experience and education may be reviewed to see whether you meet the requirements for the particular examination. When these requirements exist, they are reasonable and applied consistently to all applicants. Thus, a competitive examination may cause you some uneasiness now, but it is your privilege and safeguard.

C. HOW ARE CIVIL SERVICE EXAMS DEVELOPED?

Examinations are carefully written by trained technicians who are specialists in the field known as "psychological measurement," in consultation with recognized authorities in the field of work that the test will cover. These experts recommend the subject matter areas or skills to be tested; only those knowledges or skills important to your success on the job are included. The most reliable books and source materials available are used as references. Together, the experts and technicians judge the difficulty level of the questions.

Test technicians know how to phrase questions so that the problem is clearly stated. Their ethics do not permit "trick" or "catch" questions. Questions may have been tried out on sample groups, or subjected to statistical analysis, to determine their usefulness.

Written tests are often used in combination with performance tests, ratings of training and experience, and oral interviews. All of these measures combine to form the best-known means of finding the right person for the right job.

II. HOW TO PASS THE WRITTEN TEST

A. NATURE OF THE EXAMINATION

To prepare intelligently for civil service examinations, you should know how they differ from school examinations you have taken. In school you were assigned certain definite pages to read or subjects to cover. The examination questions were quite detailed and usually emphasized memory. Civil service exams, on the other hand, try to discover your present ability to perform the duties of a position, plus your potentiality to learn these duties. In other words, a civil service exam attempts to predict how successful you will be. Questions cover such a broad area that they cannot be as minute and detailed as school exam questions.

In the public service similar kinds of work, or positions, are grouped together in one "class." This process is known as *position-classification*. All the positions in a class are paid according to the salary range for that class. One class title covers all of these positions, and they are all tested by the same examination.

B. FOUR BASIC STEPS

1) Study the announcement

How, then, can you know what subjects to study? Our best answer is: "Learn as much as possible about the class of positions for which you've applied." The exam will test the knowledge, skills and abilities needed to do the work.

Your most valuable source of information about the position you want is the official exam announcement. This announcement lists the training and experience qualifications. Check these standards and apply only if you come reasonably close to meeting them.

The brief description of the position in the examination announcement offers some clues to the subjects which will be tested. Think about the job itself. Review the duties in your mind. Can you perform them, or are there some in which you are rusty? Fill in the blank spots in your preparation.

Many jurisdictions preview the written test in the exam announcement by including a section called "Knowledge and Abilities Required," "Scope of the Examination," or some similar heading. Here you will find out specifically what fields will be tested.

2) Review your own background

Once you learn in general what the position is all about, and what you need to know to do the work, ask yourself which subjects you already know fairly well and which need improvement. You may wonder whether to concentrate on improving your strong areas or on building some background in your fields of weakness. When the announcement has specified "some knowledge" or "considerable knowledge," or has used adjectives like "beginning principles of..." or "advanced ... methods," you can get a clue as to the number and difficulty of questions to be asked in any given field. More questions, and hence broader coverage, would be included for those subjects which are more important in the work. Now weigh your strengths and weaknesses against the job requirements and prepare accordingly.

3) Determine the level of the position

Another way to tell how intensively you should prepare is to understand the level of the job for which you are applying. Is it the entering level? In other words, is this the position in which beginners in a field of work are hired? Or is it an intermediate or advanced level? Sometimes this is indicated by such words as "Junior" or "Senior" in the class title. Other jurisdictions use Roman numerals to designate the level – Clerk I, Clerk II, for example. The word "Supervisor" sometimes appears in the title. If the level is not indicated by the title, check the description of duties. Will you be working under very close supervision, or will you have responsibility for independent decisions in this work?

4) Choose appropriate study materials

Now that you know the subjects to be examined and the relative amount of each subject to be covered, you can choose suitable study materials. For beginning level jobs, or even advanced ones, if you have a pronounced weakness in some aspect of your training, read a modern, standard textbook in that field. Be sure it is up to date and has general coverage. Such books are normally available at your library, and the librarian will be glad to help you locate one. For entry-level positions, questions of appropriate difficulty are chosen – neither highly advanced questions, nor those too simple. Such questions require careful thought but not advanced training.

If the position for which you are applying is technical or advanced, you will read more advanced, specialized material. If you are already familiar with the basic principles of your field, elementary textbooks would waste your time. Concentrate on advanced textbooks and technical periodicals. Think through the concepts and review difficult problems in your field.

These are all general sources. You can get more ideas on your own initiative, following these leads. For example, training manuals and publications of the government agency which employs workers in your field can be useful, particularly for technical and professional positions. A letter or visit to the government department involved may result in more specific study suggestions, and certainly will provide you with a more definite idea of the exact nature of the position you are seeking.

III. KINDS OF TESTS

Tests are used for purposes other than measuring knowledge and ability to perform specified duties. For some positions, it is equally important to test ability to make adjustments to new situations or to profit from training. In others, basic mental abilities not dependent on information are essential. Questions which test these things may not appear as pertinent to the duties of the position as those which test for knowledge and information. Yet they are often highly important parts of a fair examination. For very general questions, it is almost impossible to help you direct your study efforts. What we can do is to point out some of the more common of these general abilities needed in public service positions and describe some typical questions.

1) General information

Broad, general information has been found useful for predicting job success in some kinds of work. This is tested in a variety of ways, from vocabulary lists to questions about current events. Basic background in some field of work, such as sociology or economics, may be sampled in a group of questions. Often these are principles which have become familiar to most persons through exposure rather than through formal training. It is difficult to advise you how to study for these questions; being alert to the world around you is our best suggestion.

2) Verbal ability

An example of an ability needed in many positions is verbal or language ability. Verbal ability is, in brief, the ability to use and understand words. Vocabulary and grammar tests are typical measures of this ability. Reading comprehension or paragraph interpretation questions are common in many kinds of civil service tests. You are given a paragraph of written material and asked to find its central meaning.

3) Numerical ability

Number skills can be tested by the familiar arithmetic problem, by checking paired lists of numbers to see which are alike and which are different, or by interpreting charts and graphs. In the latter test, a graph may be printed in the test booklet which you are asked to use as the basis for answering questions.

4) Observation

A popular test for law-enforcement positions is the observation test. A picture is shown to you for several minutes, then taken away. Questions about the picture test your ability to observe both details and larger elements.

5) Following directions

In many positions in the public service, the employee must be able to carry out written instructions dependably and accurately. You may be given a chart with several columns, each column listing a variety of information. The questions require you to carry out directions involving the information given in the chart.

6) Skills and aptitudes

Performance tests effectively measure some manual skills and aptitudes. When the skill is one in which you are trained, such as typing or shorthand, you can practice. These tests are often very much like those given in business school or high school courses. For many of the other skills and aptitudes, however, no short-time preparation can be made. Skills and abilities natural to you or that you have developed throughout your lifetime are being tested.

Many of the general questions just described provide all the data needed to answer the questions and ask you to use your reasoning ability to find the answers. Your best preparation for these tests, as well as for tests of facts and ideas, is to be at your physical and mental best. You, no doubt, have your own methods of getting into an exam-taking mood and keeping "in shape." The next section lists some ideas on this subject.

IV. KINDS OF QUESTIONS

Only rarely is the "essay" question, which you answer in narrative form, used in civil service tests. Civil service tests are usually of the short-answer type. Full instructions for answering these questions will be given to you at the examination. But in case this is your first experience with short-answer questions and separate answer sheets, here is what you need to know:

1) Multiple-choice Questions

Most popular of the short-answer questions is the "multiple choice" or "best answer" question. It can be used, for example, to test for factual knowledge, ability to solve problems or judgment in meeting situations found at work.

A multiple-choice question is normally one of three types—

- It can begin with an incomplete statement followed by several possible endings. You are to find the one ending which *best* completes the statement, although some of the others may not be entirely wrong.
- It can also be a complete statement in the form of a question which is answered by choosing one of the statements listed.

- It can be in the form of a problem – again you select the best answer.

Here is an example of a multiple-choice question with a discussion which should give you some clues as to the method for choosing the right answer:

When an employee has a complaint about his assignment, the action which will *best* help him overcome his difficulty is to
- A. discuss his difficulty with his coworkers
- B. take the problem to the head of the organization
- C. take the problem to the person who gave him the assignment
- D. say nothing to anyone about his complaint

In answering this question, you should study each of the choices to find which is best. Consider choice "A" – Certainly an employee may discuss his complaint with fellow employees, but no change or improvement can result, and the complaint remains unresolved. Choice "B" is a poor choice since the head of the organization probably does not know what assignment you have been given, and taking your problem to him is known as "going over the head" of the supervisor. The supervisor, or person who made the assignment, is the person who can clarify it or correct any injustice. Choice "C" is, therefore, correct. To say nothing, as in choice "D," is unwise. Supervisors have and interest in knowing the problems employees are facing, and the employee is seeking a solution to his problem.

2) True/False Questions

The "true/false" or "right/wrong" form of question is sometimes used. Here a complete statement is given. Your job is to decide whether the statement is right or wrong.

SAMPLE: A roaming cell-phone call to a nearby city costs less than a non-roaming call to a distant city.

This statement is wrong, or false, since roaming calls are more expensive.

This is not a complete list of all possible question forms, although most of the others are variations of these common types. You will always get complete directions for answering questions. Be sure you understand *how* to mark your answers – ask questions until you do.

V. RECORDING YOUR ANSWERS

Computer terminals are used more and more today for many different kinds of exams.

For an examination with very few applicants, you may be told to record your answers in the test booklet itself. Separate answer sheets are much more common. If this separate answer sheet is to be scored by machine – and this is often the case – it is highly important that you mark your answers correctly in order to get credit.

An electronic scoring machine is often used in civil service offices because of the speed with which papers can be scored. Machine-scored answer sheets must be marked with a pencil, which will be given to you. This pencil has a high graphite content which responds to the electronic scoring machine. As a matter of fact, stray dots may register as answers, so do not let your pencil rest on the answer sheet while you are pondering the correct answer. Also, if your pencil lead breaks or is otherwise defective, ask for another.

Since the answer sheet will be dropped in a slot in the scoring machine, be careful not to bend the corners or get the paper crumpled.

The answer sheet normally has five vertical columns of numbers, with 30 numbers to a column. These numbers correspond to the question numbers in your test booklet. After each number, going across the page are four or five pairs of dotted lines. These short dotted lines have small letters or numbers above them. The first two pairs may also have a "T" or "F" above the letters. This indicates that the first two pairs only are to be used if the questions are of the true-false type. If the questions are multiple choice, disregard the "T" and "F" and pay attention only to the small letters or numbers.

Answer your questions in the manner of the sample that follows:

32. The largest city in the United States is
    A. Washington, D.C.
    B. New York City
    C. Chicago
    D. Detroit
    E. San Francisco

1) Choose the answer you think is best. (New York City is the largest, so "B" is correct.)
2) Find the row of dotted lines numbered the same as the question you are answering. (Find row number 32)
3) Find the pair of dotted lines corresponding to the answer. (Find the pair of lines under the mark "B.")
4) Make a solid black mark between the dotted lines.

VI. BEFORE THE TEST

Common sense will help you find procedures to follow to get ready for an examination. Too many of us, however, overlook these sensible measures. Indeed, nervousness and fatigue have been found to be the most serious reasons why applicants fail to do their best on civil service tests. Here is a list of reminders:

- Begin your preparation early – Don't wait until the last minute to go scurrying around for books and materials or to find out what the position is all about.
- Prepare continuously – An hour a night for a week is better than an all-night cram session. This has been definitely established. What is more, a night a week for a month will return better dividends than crowding your study into a shorter period of time.
- Locate the place of the exam – You have been sent a notice telling you when and where to report for the examination. If the location is in a different town or otherwise unfamiliar to you, it would be well to inquire the best route and learn something about the building.
- Relax the night before the test – Allow your mind to rest. Do not study at all that night. Plan some mild recreation or diversion; then go to bed early and get a good night's sleep.
- Get up early enough to make a leisurely trip to the place for the test – This way unforeseen events, traffic snarls, unfamiliar buildings, etc. will not upset you.
- Dress comfortably – A written test is not a fashion show. You will be known by number and not by name, so wear something comfortable.

ARMED SERVICES VOCATIONAL APTITUDE BATTERY (ASVAB)

EXAM DESCRIPTION

The Armed Services Vocational Aptitude Battery (ASVAB) is a multiple-choice test battery that measures a candidate's strengths, weaknesses and potential for future success in various career fields. The ASVAB serves as an indicator of a candidate's success in civilian and military occupations. Results on certain subtests combine to form a separate Armed Forces Qualification Test (AFQT) score, which is used to determine if a candidate is qualified to pursue a career in military service.

The written ASVAB is three hours and thirty minutes long consisting of nine subtests totaling approximately 225 questions. The subtests are general science, arithmetic reasoning, word knowledge, paragraph comprehension, mathematics knowledge, electronics information, auto and shop information, mechanical comprehension, and assembling objects. Each of the nine subtests is timed individually, and all work must be completed in the allotted time. Guessing on exam questions is not penalized – test scores are based on the total number of items answered correctly.

The ASVAB is also available to be taken as a computer-adaptive test. The computer version of the test battery is 90 minutes long and consists of approximately 145 questions. Questions vary in difficulty depending on the candidate's performance on previous questions, and scores are determined using formulas that take into account the difficulty of questions answered correctly. Unlike the written ASVAB, the computer-adaptive version allows the candidate to finish subtests at his or her own pace but does not allow the candidate to change answers.

AFQT scores are determined based on test results in the arithmetic reasoning, mathematics knowledge, word knowledge, and paragraph comprehension subtests. This score predicts potential for training in military occupations. Each military service branch requires a different minimum score on the AFQT for candidate qualification.

The ASVAB is given at more than 14,000 schools and Military Entrance Processing Stations nationwide and is developed and maintained by the United States Department of Defense.

- Leave excess paraphernalia at home – Shopping bags and odd bundles will get in your way. You need bring only the items mentioned in the official notice you received; usually everything you need is provided. Do not bring reference books to the exam. They will only confuse those last minutes and be taken away from you when in the test room.
- Arrive somewhat ahead of time – If because of transportation schedules you must get there very early, bring a newspaper or magazine to take your mind off yourself while waiting.
- Locate the examination room – When you have found the proper room, you will be directed to the seat or part of the room where you will sit. Sometimes you are given a sheet of instructions to read while you are waiting. Do not fill out any forms until you are told to do so; just read them and be prepared.
- Relax and prepare to listen to the instructions
- If you have any physical problem that may keep you from doing your best, be sure to tell the test administrator. If you are sick or in poor health, you really cannot do your best on the exam. You can come back and take the test some other time.

VII. AT THE TEST

The day of the test is here and you have the test booklet in your hand. The temptation to get going is very strong. Caution! There is more to success than knowing the right answers. You must know how to identify your papers and understand variations in the type of short-answer question used in this particular examination. Follow these suggestions for maximum results from your efforts:

1) Cooperate with the monitor

The test administrator has a duty to create a situation in which you can be as much at ease as possible. He will give instructions, tell you when to begin, check to see that you are marking your answer sheet correctly, and so on. He is not there to guard you, although he will see that your competitors do not take unfair advantage. He wants to help you do your best.

2) Listen to all instructions

Don't jump the gun! Wait until you understand all directions. In most civil service tests you get more time than you need to answer the questions. So don't be in a hurry. Read each word of instructions until you clearly understand the meaning. Study the examples, listen to all announcements and follow directions. Ask questions if you do not understand what to do.

3) Identify your papers

Civil service exams are usually identified by number only. You will be assigned a number; you must not put your name on your test papers. Be sure to copy your number correctly. Since more than one exam may be given, copy your exact examination title.

4) Plan your time

Unless you are told that a test is a "speed" or "rate of work" test, speed itself is usually not important. Time enough to answer all the questions will be provided, but this does not mean that you have all day. An overall time limit has been set. Divide the total time (in minutes) by the number of questions to determine the approximate time you have for each question.

5) Do not linger over difficult questions

If you come across a difficult question, mark it with a paper clip (useful to have along) and come back to it when you have been through the booklet. One caution if you do this – be sure to skip a number on your answer sheet as well. Check often to be sure that you have not lost your place and that you are marking in the row numbered the same as the question you are answering.

6) Read the questions

Be sure you know what the question asks! Many capable people are unsuccessful because they failed to *read* the questions correctly.

7) Answer all questions

Unless you have been instructed that a penalty will be deducted for incorrect answers, it is better to guess than to omit a question.

8) Speed tests

It is often better NOT to guess on speed tests. It has been found that on timed tests people are tempted to spend the last few seconds before time is called in marking answers at random – without even reading them – in the hope of picking up a few extra points. To discourage this practice, the instructions may warn you that your score will be "corrected" for guessing. That is, a penalty will be applied. The incorrect answers will be deducted from the correct ones, or some other penalty formula will be used.

9) Review your answers

If you finish before time is called, go back to the questions you guessed or omitted to give them further thought. Review other answers if you have time.

10) Return your test materials

If you are ready to leave before others have finished or time is called, take ALL your materials to the monitor and leave quietly. Never take any test material with you. The monitor can discover whose papers are not complete, and taking a test booklet may be grounds for disqualification.

VIII. EXAMINATION TECHNIQUES

1) Read the general instructions carefully. These are usually printed on the first page of the exam booklet. As a rule, these instructions refer to the timing of the examination; the fact that you should not start work until the signal and must stop work at a signal, etc. If there are any *special* instructions, such as a choice of questions to be answered, make sure that you note this instruction carefully.

2) When you are ready to start work on the examination, that is as soon as the signal has been given, read the instructions to each question booklet, underline any key words or phrases, such as *least, best, outline, describe* and the like. In this way you will tend to answer as requested rather than discover on reviewing your paper that you *listed without describing*, that you selected the *worst* choice rather than the *best* choice, etc.

3) If the examination is of the objective or multiple-choice type – that is, each question will also give a series of possible answers: A, B, C or D, and you are called upon to select the best answer and write the letter next to that answer on your answer paper – it is advisable to start answering each question in turn. There may be anywhere from 50 to 100 such questions in the three or four hours allotted and you can see how much time would be taken if you read through all the questions before beginning to answer any. Furthermore, if you come across a question or group of questions which you know would be difficult to answer, it would undoubtedly affect your handling of all the other questions.

4) If the examination is of the essay type and contains but a few questions, it is a moot point as to whether you should read all the questions before starting to answer any one. Of course, if you are given a choice – say five out of seven and the like – then it is essential to read all the questions so you can eliminate the two that are most difficult. If, however, you are asked to answer all the questions, there may be danger in trying to answer the easiest one first because you may find that you will spend too much time on it. The best technique is to answer the first question, then proceed to the second, etc.

5) Time your answers. Before the exam begins, write down the time it started, then add the time allowed for the examination and write down the time it must be completed, then divide the time available somewhat as follows:
    - If 3-1/2 hours are allowed, that would be 210 minutes. If you have 80 objective-type questions, that would be an average of 2-1/2 minutes per question. Allow yourself no more than 2 minutes per question, or a total of 160 minutes, which will permit about 50 minutes to review.
    - If for the time allotment of 210 minutes there are 7 essay questions to answer, that would average about 30 minutes a question. Give yourself only 25 minutes per question so that you have about 35 minutes to review.

6) The most important instruction is to *read each question* and make sure you know what is wanted. The second most important instruction is to *time yourself properly* so that you answer every question. The third most important instruction is to *answer every question*. Guess if you have to but include something for each question. Remember that you will receive no credit for a blank and will probably receive some credit if you write something in answer to an essay question. If you guess a letter – say "B" for a multiple-choice question – you may have guessed right. If you leave a blank as an answer to a multiple-choice question, the examiners may respect your feelings but it will not add a point to your score. Some exams may penalize you for wrong answers, so in such cases *only*, you may not want to guess unless you have some basis for your answer.

7) Suggestions
    a. Objective-type questions
        1. Examine the question booklet for proper sequence of pages and questions
        2. Read all instructions carefully
        3. Skip any question which seems too difficult; return to it after all other questions have been answered
        4. Apportion your time properly; do not spend too much time on any single question or group of questions

5. Note and underline key words – *all, most, fewest, least, best, worst, same, opposite,* etc.
6. Pay particular attention to negatives
7. Note unusual option, e.g., unduly long, short, complex, different or similar in content to the body of the question
8. Observe the use of "hedging" words – *probably, may, most likely,* etc.
9. Make sure that your answer is put next to the same number as the question
10. Do not second-guess unless you have good reason to believe the second answer is definitely more correct
11. Cross out original answer if you decide another answer is more accurate; do not erase until you are ready to hand your paper in
12. Answer all questions; guess unless instructed otherwise
13. Leave time for review

b. Essay questions
1. Read each question carefully
2. Determine exactly what is wanted. Underline key words or phrases.
3. Decide on outline or paragraph answer
4. Include many different points and elements unless asked to develop any one or two points or elements
5. Show impartiality by giving pros and cons unless directed to select one side only
6. Make and write down any assumptions you find necessary to answer the questions
7. Watch your English, grammar, punctuation and choice of words
8. Time your answers; don't crowd material

8) Answering the essay question

Most essay questions can be answered by framing the specific response around several key words or ideas. Here are a few such key words or ideas:

M's: manpower, materials, methods, money, management
P's: purpose, program, policy, plan, procedure, practice, problems, pitfalls, personnel, public relations

a. Six basic steps in handling problems:
1. Preliminary plan and background development
2. Collect information, data and facts
3. Analyze and interpret information, data and facts
4. Analyze and develop solutions as well as make recommendations
5. Prepare report and sell recommendations
6. Install recommendations and follow up effectiveness

b. Pitfalls to avoid
1. *Taking things for granted* – A statement of the situation does not necessarily imply that each of the elements is necessarily true; for example, a complaint may be invalid and biased so that all that can be taken for granted is that a complaint has been registered

2. *Considering only one side of a situation* – Wherever possible, indicate several alternatives and then point out the reasons you selected the best one
3. *Failing to indicate follow up* – Whenever your answer indicates action on your part, make certain that you will take proper follow-up action to see how successful your recommendations, procedures or actions turn out to be
4. *Taking too long in answering any single question* – Remember to time your answers properly

IX. AFTER THE TEST

Scoring procedures differ in detail among civil service jurisdictions although the general principles are the same. Whether the papers are hand-scored or graded by machine we have described, they are nearly always graded by number. That is, the person who marks the paper knows only the number – never the name – of the applicant. Not until all the papers have been graded will they be matched with names. If other tests, such as training and experience or oral interview ratings have been given, scores will be combined. Different parts of the examination usually have different weights. For example, the written test might count 60 percent of the final grade, and a rating of training and experience 40 percent. In many jurisdictions, veterans will have a certain number of points added to their grades.

After the final grade has been determined, the names are placed in grade order and an eligible list is established. There are various methods for resolving ties between those who get the same final grade – probably the most common is to place first the name of the person whose application was received first. Job offers are made from the eligible list in the order the names appear on it. You will be notified of your grade and your rank as soon as all these computations have been made. This will be done as rapidly as possible.

People who are found to meet the requirements in the announcement are called "eligibles." Their names are put on a list of eligible candidates. An eligible's chances of getting a job depend on how high he stands on this list and how fast agencies are filling jobs from the list.

When a job is to be filled from a list of eligibles, the agency asks for the names of people on the list of eligibles for that job. When the civil service commission receives this request, it sends to the agency the names of the three people highest on this list. Or, if the job to be filled has specialized requirements, the office sends the agency the names of the top three persons who meet these requirements from the general list.

The appointing officer makes a choice from among the three people whose names were sent to him. If the selected person accepts the appointment, the names of the others are put back on the list to be considered for future openings.

That is the rule in hiring from all kinds of eligible lists, whether they are for typist, carpenter, chemist, or something else. For every vacancy, the appointing officer has his choice of any one of the top three eligibles on the list. This explains why the person whose name is on top of the list sometimes does not get an appointment when some of the persons lower on the list do. If the appointing officer chooses the second or third eligible, the No. 1 eligible does not get a job at once, but stays on the list until he is appointed or the list is terminated.

X. HOW TO PASS THE INTERVIEW TEST

The examination for which you applied requires an oral interview test. You have already taken the written test and you are now being called for the interview test – the final part of the formal examination.

You may think that it is not possible to prepare for an interview test and that there are no procedures to follow during an interview. Our purpose is to point out some things you can do in advance that will help you and some good rules to follow and pitfalls to avoid while you are being interviewed.

What is an interview supposed to test?

The written examination is designed to test the technical knowledge and competence of the candidate; the oral is designed to evaluate intangible qualities, not readily measured otherwise, and to establish a list showing the relative fitness of each candidate – as measured against his competitors – for the position sought. Scoring is not on the basis of "right" and "wrong," but on a sliding scale of values ranging from "not passable" to "outstanding." As a matter of fact, it is possible to achieve a relatively low score without a single "incorrect" answer because of evident weakness in the qualities being measured.

Occasionally, an examination may consist entirely of an oral test – either an individual or a group oral. In such cases, information is sought concerning the technical knowledges and abilities of the candidate, since there has been no written examination for this purpose. More commonly, however, an oral test is used to supplement a written examination.

Who conducts interviews?

The composition of oral boards varies among different jurisdictions. In nearly all, a representative of the personnel department serves as chairman. One of the members of the board may be a representative of the department in which the candidate would work. In some cases, "outside experts" are used, and, frequently, a businessman or some other representative of the general public is asked to serve. Labor and management or other special groups may be represented. The aim is to secure the services of experts in the appropriate field.

However the board is composed, it is a good idea (and not at all improper or unethical) to ascertain in advance of the interview who the members are and what groups they represent. When you are introduced to them, you will have some idea of their backgrounds and interests, and at least you will not stutter and stammer over their names.

What should be done before the interview?

While knowledge about the board members is useful and takes some of the surprise element out of the interview, there is other preparation which is more substantive. It *is* possible to prepare for an oral interview – in several ways:

1) Keep a copy of your application and review it carefully before the interview

This may be the only document before the oral board, and the starting point of the interview. Know what education and experience you have listed there, and the sequence and dates of all of it. Sometimes the board will ask you to review the highlights of your experience for them; you should not have to hem and haw doing it.

2) Study the class specification and the examination announcement

Usually, the oral board has one or both of these to guide them. The qualities, characteristics or knowledges required by the position sought are stated in these documents. They offer valuable clues as to the nature of the oral interview. For example, if the job involves supervisory responsibilities, the announcement will usually indicate that knowledge of modern supervisory methods and the qualifications of the candidate as a supervisor will be tested. If so, you can expect such questions, frequently in the form of a hypothetical situation which you are expected to solve. NEVER go into an oral without knowledge of the duties and responsibilities of the job you seek.

3) Think through each qualification required

Try to visualize the kind of questions you would ask if you were a board member. How well could you answer them? Try especially to appraise your own knowledge and background in each area, *measured against the job sought*, and identify any areas in which you are weak. Be critical and realistic – do not flatter yourself.

4) Do some general reading in areas in which you feel you may be weak

For example, if the job involves supervision and your past experience has NOT, some general reading in supervisory methods and practices, particularly in the field of human relations, might be useful. Do NOT study agency procedures or detailed manuals. The oral board will be testing your understanding and capacity, not your memory.

5) Get a good night's sleep and watch your general health and mental attitude

You will want a clear head at the interview. Take care of a cold or any other minor ailment, and of course, no hangovers.

What should be done on the day of the interview?

Now comes the day of the interview itself. Give yourself plenty of time to get there. Plan to arrive somewhat ahead of the scheduled time, particularly if your appointment is in the fore part of the day. If a previous candidate fails to appear, the board might be ready for you a bit early. By early afternoon an oral board is almost invariably behind schedule if there are many candidates, and you may have to wait. Take along a book or magazine to read, or your application to review, but leave any extraneous material in the waiting room when you go in for your interview. In any event, relax and compose yourself.

The matter of dress is important. The board is forming impressions about you – from your experience, your manners, your attitude, and your appearance. Give your personal appearance careful attention. Dress your best, but not your flashiest. Choose conservative, appropriate clothing, and be sure it is immaculate. This is a business interview, and your appearance should indicate that you regard it as such. Besides, being well groomed and properly dressed will help boost your confidence.

Sooner or later, someone will call your name and escort you into the interview room. *This is it.* From here on you are on your own. It is too late for any more preparation. But remember, you asked for this opportunity to prove your fitness, and you are here because your request was granted.

What happens when you go in?

The usual sequence of events will be as follows: The clerk (who is often the board stenographer) will introduce you to the chairman of the oral board, who will introduce you to the other members of the board. Acknowledge the introductions before you sit down. Do not be surprised if you find a microphone facing you or a stenotypist sitting by. Oral interviews are usually recorded in the event of an appeal or other review.

Usually the chairman of the board will open the interview by reviewing the highlights of your education and work experience from your application – primarily for the benefit of the other members of the board, as well as to get the material into the record. Do not interrupt or comment unless there is an error or significant misinterpretation; if that is the case, do not hesitate. But do not quibble about insignificant matters. Also, he will usually ask you some question about your education, experience or your present job – partly to get you to start talking and to establish the interviewing "rapport." He may start the actual questioning, or turn it over to one of the other members. Frequently, each member undertakes the questioning on a particular area, one in which he is perhaps most competent, so you can expect each member to participate in the examination. Because time is limited, you may also expect some rather abrupt switches in the direction the questioning takes, so do not be upset by it. Normally, a board member will not pursue a single line of questioning unless he discovers a particular strength or weakness.

After each member has participated, the chairman will usually ask whether any member has any further questions, then will ask you if you have anything you wish to add. Unless you are expecting this question, it may floor you. Worse, it may start you off on an extended, extemporaneous speech. The board is not usually seeking more information. The question is principally to offer you a last opportunity to present further qualifications or to indicate that you have nothing to add. So, if you feel that a significant qualification or characteristic has been overlooked, it is proper to point it out in a sentence or so. Do not compliment the board on the thoroughness of their examination – they have been sketchy, and you know it. If you wish, merely say, "No thank you, I have nothing further to add." This is a point where you can "talk yourself out" of a good impression or fail to present an important bit of information. Remember, *you close the interview yourself.*

The chairman will then say, "That is all, Mr. _____, thank you." Do not be startled; the interview is over, and quicker than you think. Thank him, gather your belongings and take your leave. Save your sigh of relief for the other side of the door.

How to put your best foot forward

Throughout this entire process, you may feel that the board individually and collectively is trying to pierce your defenses, seek out your hidden weaknesses and embarrass and confuse you. Actually, this is not true. They are obliged to make an appraisal of your qualifications for the job you are seeking, and they want to see you in your best light. Remember, they must interview all candidates and a non-cooperative candidate may become a failure in spite of their best efforts to bring out his qualifications. Here are 15 suggestions that will help you:

1) Be natural – Keep your attitude confident, not cocky

If you are not confident that you can do the job, do not expect the board to be. Do not apologize for your weaknesses, try to bring out your strong points. The board is interested in a positive, not negative, presentation. Cockiness will antagonize any board member and make him wonder if you are covering up a weakness by a false show of strength.

2) Get comfortable, but don't lounge or sprawl

Sit erectly but not stiffly. A careless posture may lead the board to conclude that you are careless in other things, or at least that you are not impressed by the importance of the occasion. Either conclusion is natural, even if incorrect. Do not fuss with your clothing, a pencil or an ashtray. Your hands may occasionally be useful to emphasize a point; do not let them become a point of distraction.

3) Do not wisecrack or make small talk

This is a serious situation, and your attitude should show that you consider it as such. Further, the time of the board is limited – they do not want to waste it, and neither should you.

4) Do not exaggerate your experience or abilities

In the first place, from information in the application or other interviews and sources, the board may know more about you than you think. Secondly, you probably will not get away with it. An experienced board is rather adept at spotting such a situation, so do not take the chance.

5) If you know a board member, do not make a point of it, yet do not hide it

Certainly you are not fooling him, and probably not the other members of the board. Do not try to take advantage of your acquaintanceship – it will probably do you little good.

6) Do not dominate the interview

Let the board do that. They will give you the clues – do not assume that you have to do all the talking. Realize that the board has a number of questions to ask you, and do not try to take up all the interview time by showing off your extensive knowledge of the answer to the first one.

7) Be attentive

You only have 20 minutes or so, and you should keep your attention at its sharpest throughout. When a member is addressing a problem or question to you, give him your undivided attention. Address your reply principally to him, but do not exclude the other board members.

8) Do not interrupt

A board member may be stating a problem for you to analyze. He will ask you a question when the time comes. Let him state the problem, and wait for the question.

9) Make sure you understand the question

Do not try to answer until you are sure what the question is. If it s not clear, restate it in your own words or ask the board member to clarify it for you. However, do not haggle about minor elements.

10) Reply promptly but not hastily

A common entry on oral board rating sheets is "candidate responded readily," or "candidate hesitated in replies." Respond as promptly and quickly as you can, but do not jump to a hasty, ill-considered answer.

11) Do not be peremptory in your answers

A brief answer is proper – but do not fire your answer back. That is a losing game from your point of view. The board member can probably ask questions much faster than you can answer them.

12) Do not try to create the answer you think the board member wants

He is interested in what kind of mind you have and how it works – not in playing games. Furthermore, he can usually spot this practice and will actually grade you down on it.

13) Do not switch sides in your reply merely to agree with a board member

Frequently, a member will take a contrary position merely to draw you out and to see if you are willing and able to defend your point of view. Do not start a debate, yet do not surrender a good position. If a position is worth taking, it is worth defending.

14) Do not be afraid to admit an error in judgment if you are shown to be wrong

The board knows that you are forced to reply without any opportunity for careful consideration. Your answer may be demonstrably wrong. If so, admit it and get on with the interview.

15) Do not dwell at length on your present job

The opening question may relate to your present assignment. Answer the question but do not go into an extended discussion. You are being examined for a *new* job, not your present one. As a matter of fact, try to phrase ALL your answers in terms of the job for which you are being examined.

Basis of Rating

Probably you will forget most of these "do's" and "don'ts" when you walk into the oral interview room. Even remembering them all will not ensure you a passing grade. Perhaps you did not have the qualifications in the first place. But remembering them will help you to put your best foot forward, without treading on the toes of the board members.

Rumor and popular opinion to the contrary notwithstanding, an oral board wants you to make the best appearance possible. They know you are under pressure – but they also want to see how you respond to it as a guide to what your reaction would be under the pressures of the job you seek. They will be influenced by the degree of poise you display, the personal traits you show and the manner in which you respond.

ABOUT THIS BOOK

This book contains tests divided into Examination Sections. Go through each test, answering every question in the margin. We have also attached a sample answer sheet at the back of the book that can be removed and used. At the end of each test look at the answer key and check your answers. On the ones you got wrong, look at the right answer choice and learn. Do not fill in the answers first. Do not memorize the questions and answers, but understand the answer and principles involved. On your test, the questions will likely be different from the samples. Questions are changed and new ones added. If you understand these past questions you should have success with any changes that arise. Tests may consist of several types of questions. We have additional books on each subject should more study be advisable or necessary for you. Finally, the more you study, the better prepared you will be. This book is intended to be the last thing you study before you walk into the examination room. Prior study of relevant texts is also recommended. NLC publishes some of these in our Fundamental Series. Knowledge and good sense are important factors in passing your exam. Good luck also helps. So now study this Passbook, absorb the material contained within and take that knowledge into the examination. Then do your best to pass that exam.

EXAMINATION SECTION

VERBAL ABILITIES TEST

DIRECTIONS AND SAMPLE QUESTIONS

Study the sample questions carefully. Each question has four suggested answers. Decide which one is the best answer. Find the question number on the Sample Answer Sheet. Show your answer to the question by printing the letter of the correct answer in the space at the right. If you have to erase a mark, be sure to erase it completely. Mark only one answer for each question. Do NOT mark space E for any question.

SAMPLE VERBAL QUESTIONS

I. *Previous* means MOST NEARLY I.____
   A. abandoned   B. former   C. timely   D. younger

II. (Reading) "Just as the procedure of a collection department must be clear cut II.____
and definite, the steps being taken with the sureness of a skilled chess player, so the various paragraphs of a collection letter must show clear organization, giving evidence of a mind that, from the beginning, has had a specific end in view."
The quotation BEST supports the statement that a collection letter should always
   A. show a spirit of sportsmanship   B. be divided into several paragraphs
   C. be brief, but courteous   D. be carefully planned

III. Decide which sentence is preferable with respect to grammar and usage suitable III.____
for a formal letter or report.
   A. They do not ordinarily present these kind of reports in detail like this.
   B. A report of this kind is not hardly ever given in such detail as this one.
   C. This report is more detailed than what such reports ordinarily are.
   D. A report of this kind is not ordinarily presented in as much detail as this one is.

IV. Find the correct spelling of the word and print the letter of the correct answer in IV.____
the space at the right. If no suggested spelling is correct, print the letter D.
   A. athalete   B. athelete   C. athlete   D. none of these

V. SPEEDOMETER is related to POINTER as WATCH is related to V.____
   A. case   B. hands   C. dial   D. numerals

EXAMINATION SECTION
TEST 1

DIRECTIONS: Each question or incomplete statement is followed by several suggested answers or completions. Select the one that BEST answers the question or completes the statement. *PRINT THE LETTER OF THE CORRECT ANSWER IN THE SPACE AT THE RIGHT.*

1. *Flexible* means MOST NEARLY
   A. breakable   B. flammable   C. pliable   D. weak

2. *Option* means MOST NEARLY
   A. use   B. choice   C. value   D. blame

3. To *verify* means MOST NEARLY to
   A. examine   B. explain   C. confirm   D. guarantee

4. *Indolent* means MOST NEARLY
   A. moderate   B. happiness   C. selfish   D. lazy

5. *Respiration* means MOST NEARLY
   A. recovery   B. breathing   C. pulsation   D. sweating

6. PLUMBER is related to WRENCH as PAINTER related to
   A. brush   B. pipe   C. shop   D. hammer

7. LETTER is related to MESSAGE as PACKAGE is related to
   A. sender   B. merchandise
   C. insurance   D. business

8. FOOD is related to HUNGER as SLEEP is related to
   A. night   B. dream   C. weariness   D. rest

9. KEY is related to TYPEWRITER as DIAL is related to
   A. sun   B. number   C. circle   D. telephone

GRAMMAR

10. A. I think that they will promote whoever has the best record.
    B. The firm would have liked to have promoted all employees with good records.
    C. Such of them that have the best records have excellent prospects of promotion.
    D. I feel sure they will give the promotion to whomever has the best record.

11.
    A. The receptionist must answer courteously the questions of all them callers.
    B. The receptionist must answer courteously the questions what are asked by the callers.
    C. There would have been no trouble if the receptionist had have always answered courteously.
    D. The receptionist should answer courteously the questions of all callers.

11.____

SPELLING

12.
    A. collapsible
    B. colapseble
    C. collapseble
    D. none of the above

12.____

13.
    A. ambigeuous
    B. ambigeous
    C. ambiguous
    D. none of the above

13.____

14.
    A. predesessor
    B. predecesar
    C. predecesser
    D. none of the above

14.____

15.
    A. sanctioned
    B. sancktioned
    C. sanctionned
    D. none of the above

15.____

READING

16. "The secretarial profession is a very old one and has increased in importance with the passage of time. In modern times, the vast expansion of business and industry has greatly increased the need and opportunities for secretaries, and for the first time in history their number has become large."
The above quotation BEST supports the statement that the secretarial profession
    A. is older than business and industry
    B. did not exist in ancient times
    C. has greatly increased in size
    D. demands higher training than it did formerly

16.____

17. "Civilization started to move ahead more rapidly when man freed himself of the shackles that restricted his search for the truth."
The above quotation BEST supports the statement that the progress of civilization
    A. came as a result of man's dislike for obstacles
    B. did not begin until restrictions on learning were removed
    C. has been aided by man's efforts to find
    D. the truth is based on continually increasing efforts

17.____

18. *Vigilant* means MOST NEARLY
    A. sensible   B. watchful   C. suspicious   D. restless

18.____

19. *Incidental* means MOST NEARLY
    A. independent   B. needless   C. infrequent   D. casual

19.____

20. *Conciliatory* means MOST NEARLY
    A. pacific B. contentious C. obligatory D. offensive

21. *Altercation* means MOST NEARLY
    A. defeat
    B. concurrence
    C. controversy
    D. vexation

22. *Irresolute* means MOST NEARLY
    A. wavering
    B. insubordinate
    C. impudent
    D. unobservant

23. DARKNESS is related to SUNLIGHT as STILLNESS is related to
    A. quiet B. moonlight C. sound D. dark

24. DESIGNED is related to INTENTION as ACCIDENTAL is related to
    A. purpose B. caution C. damage D. chance

25. ERROR is related to PRACTICE as SOUND is related to
    A. deafness B. noise C. muffler D. horn

26. RESEARCH is related to FINDINGS as TRAINING is related to
    A. skill
    B. tests
    C. supervision
    D. teaching

27. A. If properly addressed, the letter will reach my mother and I.
    B. The letter had been addressed to myself and my mother.
    C. I believe the letter was addressed to either my mother or I.
    D. My mother's name, as well as mine, was on the letter.

28. A. The supervisor reprimanded the typist, whom she believed had made careless errors.
    B. The typist would have corrected the errors had she of known that the supervisor would see the report.
    C. The errors in the typed report were so numerous that they could hardly be overlooked.
    D. Many errors were found in the report which she typed and could not disregard them.

29. A. minieture
    B. minneature
    C. mineature
    D. none of the above

30. A. extemporaneous
    B. extempuraneus
    C. extemporraneous
    D. none of the above

31. A. problemmatical
    B. problematical
    C. problematicle
    D. none of the above

32. A. descendant
    B. decendant
    C. desendant
    D. none of the above

33. "The likelihood of America's exhausting her natural resources seems to be growing less. All kinds of waste are being reworked and new uses are constantly being found for almost everything. We are getting more use out of our goods and are making many new byproducts out of what was formerly thrown away."
The above quotation BEST supports the statement that we seem to be in less danger of exhausting our resources because
    A. economy is found to lie in the use of substitutes
    B. more service is obtained from a given amount of material
    C. we are allowing time for nature to restore them
    D. supply and demand are better controlled

33._____

34. "Memos should be clear, concise, and brief. Omit all unnecessary words. The parts of speech most often used in memos are nouns, verbs, adjectives, and adverbs. If possible, do without pronouns, prepositions, articles, and copulative verbs. Use simple sentences, rather than complex or compound ones.
The above quotation BEST supports the statement that in writing memos one should always use
    A. common and simple words
    B. only nouns, verbs, adjectives, and adverbs
    C. incomplete sentences
    D. only the word essential to the meaning

34._____

35. To *counteract* means MOST NEARLY to
    A. undermine   B. censure   C. preserve   D. neutralize

35._____

36. *Deferred* means MOST NEARLY
    A. reversed   B. delayed
    C. considered   D. forbidden

36._____

37. *Feasible* means MOST NEARLY
    A. capable   B. justifiable   C. practicable   D. beneficial

37._____

38. To *encounter* means MOST NEARLY to
    A. meet   B. recall   C. overcome   D. retreat

38._____

39. *Innate* means MOST NEARLY
    A. eternal   B. well-developed
    C. native   D. prospective

39._____

40. STUDENT is to TEACHER as DISCIPLE is related to
    A. follower   B. master   C. principal   D. pupil

40._____

41. LECTURE is related to AUDITORIUM as EXPERIMENT is related to
    A. scientist   B. chemistry   C. laboratory   D. discovery

41._____

42. BODY is related to FOOD as ENGINE is related to
    A. wheels   B. fuel   C. motion   D. smoke

42._____

43. SCHOOL is related to EDUCATION as THEATER is related to
    A. management B. stage
    C. recreation D. preparation

44. A. Most all these statements have been supported by persons who are reliable and can be depended upon.
    B. The persons which have guaranteed these statements are reliable.
    C. Reliable persons guarantee the facts with regards to the truth of these statements.
    D. These statements can be depended on, for their truth has been guaranteed by reliable persons.

45. A. The success of the book pleased both his publisher and he.
    B. Both his publisher and he was pleased with the success of the book.
    C. Neither he or his publisher was disappointed with the success of the book.
    D. His publisher was as pleased as he with the success of the book.

46. A. extercate B. extracate
    C. extricate D. none of the above

47. A. hereditory B. hereditary
    C. hereditairy D. none of the above

48. A. auspiceous B. auspiseous
    C. auspicious D. none of the above

49. A. sequance B. sequence
    C. sequense D. none of the above

50. "The prevention of accidents makes it necessary not only that safety devices be used to guard exposed machinery but also that mechanics be instructed in safety rules which they must follow for their own protection, and that the lighting in the plant be adequate."
    The above quotation BEST supports the statement that industrial accidents
    A. may be due to ignorance
    B. are always avoidable
    C. usually result from inadequate machinery
    D. cannot be entirely overcome

51. "The English language is peculiarly rich in synonyms, and there is scarcely a language spoken among men that has not some representative in English speech. The spirit of the Anglo-Saxon race has subjugate these various elements to one idiom, making not a patchwork, but a composite language."
    The above quotation BEST supports the statement that the English language
    A. has few idiomatic expressions
    B. is difficult to translate
    C. is used universally
    D. has absorbed words from other languages

52. To *acquiesce* means MOST NEARLY to
    A. assent   B. acquire   C. complete   D. participate

53. *Unanimity* means MOST NEARLY
    A. emphasis
    B. namelessness
    C. harmony
    D. impartiality

54. *Precedent* means MOST NEARLY
    A. example   B. theory   C. law   D. conformity

55. *Versatile* means MOST NEARLY
    A. broad-minded
    B. well-known
    C. up-to-date
    D. many-sided

56. *Authentic* means MOST NEARLY
    A. detailed   B. reliable   C. valuable   D. practical

57. BIOGRAPHY is related to FACT as NOVEL is related to
    A. fiction   B. literature   C. narration   D. book

58. COPY is related to CARBON PAPER as MOTION PICTURE is related to
    A. theater   B. film   C. duplicate   D. television

59. EFFICIENCY is related to REWARD as CARELESSNESS is related to
    A. improvement
    B. disobedience
    C. reprimand
    D. repetition

60. ABUNDANT is related to CHEAP as SCARCE is related to
    A. ample
    B. costly
    C. inexpensive
    D. unobtainable

61. A. Brown's & Company employees have recently received increases in salary.
    B. Brown & Company recently increased the salaries of all its employees.
    C. Recently, Brown & Company has increased their employees' salaries.
    D. Brown & Company have recently increased the salaries of all its employees.

62. A. In reviewing the typists' work reports, the job analyst found records of unusual typing speeds.
    B. It says in the job analyst's report that some employees type with great speed.
    C. The job analyst found that, in reviewing the typists' work reports, that some unusual typing speeds had been made.
    D. In the reports of typists' speeds, the job analyst found some records that are kind of unusual.

63. A. obliterate
    B. oblitterat
    C. obbliterate
    D. none of the above

64. A. diagnoesis   B. diagnossis
    C. diagnosis   D. none of the above

65. A. contenance   B. countenance
    C. knowledge   D. none of the above

66. A. conceivably B. concieveably
    C. conceiveably D. none of the above

67. "Through advertising, manufacturers exercise a high degree of control over consumers' desires. However, the manufacturer assumes enormous risks in attempting to predict what consumers will want and in producing goods in quantity and distributing them in advance of final selection by the consumers."
    The above quotation BEST supports the statement that manufacturers
    A. can eliminate the risk of overproduction by advertising
    B. distribute goods directly to the consumers
    C. must depend upon the final consumers for the success of their undertakings
    D. can predict with great accuracy the success of any product they put on the market

68. "In the relations of man to nature, the procuring of food and shelter is fundamental. With the migration of man to various climates, ever new adjustments to the food supply and to the climate became necessary."
    The above quotation BEST supports the statement that the means by which man supplies his material needs are
    A. accidental   B. varied   C. limited   D. inadequate

69. *Strident* means MOST NEARLY
    A. swaggering   B. domineering
    C. angry   D. harsh

70. To *confine* means MOST NEARLY to
    A. hide   B. restrict   C. eliminate   D. punish

71. To *accentuate* means MOST NEARLY to
    A. modify   B. hasten   C. sustain   D. intensify

72. *Banal* means MOST NEARLY
    A. commonplace   B. forceful
    C. tranquil   D. indifferent

73. *Incorrigible* means MOST NEARLY
    A. intolerable   B. retarded
    C. irreformable   D. brazen

74. POLICEMAN is related to ORDER as DOCTOR is related to
    A. physician   B. hospital   C. sickness   D. health

75. ARTIST is related to EASEL as WEAVER is related to
    A. loom   B. cloth   C. threads   D. spinner

76. CROWD is related to PERSONS as FLEET is related to
    A. expedition   B. officers   C. navy   D. ships

77. CALENDAR is related to DATE as MAP is related to
    A. geography   B. trip   C. mileage   D. vacation

78. A. Since the report lacked the needed information, it was of no use to him.
    B. This report was useless to him because there were no needed information in it.
    C. Since the report did not contain the needed information, it was not real useful to him.
    D. Being that the report lacked the needed information, he could not use it.

79. A. The company had hardly declared the dividend till the notices were prepared for mailing.
    B. They had no sooner declared the dividend when they sent the notices to the stockholders.
    C. No sooner had the dividend been declared than the notices were prepared for mailing.
    D. Scarcely had the dividend been declared than the notices were sent out.

80. A. compitition   B. competition
    C. competetion   D. none of the above

81. A. occassion   B. ocassion
    C. occasion   D. none of the above

82. A. knowlege   B. knowledge
    C. knolledge   D. none of the above

83. A. deliborate   B. deliberate
    C. deliberate   D. none of the above

84. "What constitutes skill in any line of work is not always easy to determine; economy of time must be carefully distinguished from economy of energy, as the quickest method may require the greatest expenditure of muscular effort, and may not be essential or at all desirable."
    The above quotation BEST supports the statement that
    A. the most efficiently executed task is not always the one done in the shortest time
    B. energy and time cannot both be conserved in performing a single task
    C. a task is well done when it is performed in the shortest time
    D. skill in performing a task should not be acquired at the expense of time

85. "It is difficult to distinguish between bookkeeping and accounting. In attempts to do so, bookkeeping is called the art, and accounting the science, of recording business transactions. Bookkeeping gives the history of the business in a systematic manner; and accounting classifies, analyzes, and interpret the facts thus recorded."

The above quotation BEST supports the statement that
  A. accounting is less systematic than bookkeeping
  B. accounting and bookkeeping are closely related
  C. bookkeeping and accounting cannot be distinguished from one another
  D. bookkeeping has been superseded by accounting

85.____

KEY (CORRECT ANSWERS)

1.	C	16.	C	31.	B	46.	C	61.	B	76.	D
2.	B	17.	C	32.	A	47.	B	62.	A	77.	C
3.	C	18.	B	33.	B	48.	C	63.	A	78.	A
4.	D	19.	D	34.	D	49.	B	64.	C	79.	C
5.	B	20.	A	35.	D	50.	A	65.	B	80.	B
6.	A	21.	C	36.	B	51.	D	66.	A	81.	B
7.	B	22.	A	37.	C	52.	A	67.	C	82.	C
8.	C	23.	C	38.	A	53.	C	68.	B	83.	B
9.	D	24.	D	39.	C	54.	A	69.	D	84.	A
10.	A	25.	C	40.	B	55.	D	70.	B	85.	B
11.	D	26.	A	41.	C	56.	B	71.	D		
12.	A	27.	D	42.	B	57.	A	72.	A		
13.	C	28.	C	43.	C	58.	B	73.	C		
14.	D	29.	D	44.	D	59.	C	74.	D		
15.	A	30.	A	45.	D	60.	B	75.	A		

TEST 2

DIRECTIONS: Each question or incomplete statement is followed by several suggested answers or completions. Select the one that BEST answers the question or completes the statement. *PRINT THE LETTER OF THE CORRECT ANSWER IN THE SPACE AT THE RIGHT.*

1. *Option* means MOST NEARLY
   - A. use
   - B. choice
   - C. value
   - D. blame
   - E. mistake

2. *Irresolute* means MOST NEARLY
   - A. wavering
   - B. insubordinate
   - C. impudent
   - D. determined
   - E. unobservant

3. *Flexible* means MOST NEARLY
   - A. breakable
   - B. inflammable
   - C. pliable
   - D. weak
   - E. impervious

4. To *counteract* means MOST NEARLY to
   - A. undermine
   - B. censure
   - C. preserve
   - D. sustain
   - E. neutralize

5. To *verify* means MOST NEARLY to
   - A. justify
   - B. explain
   - C. confirm
   - D. guarantee
   - E. examine

6. *Indolent* means MOST NEARLY
   - A. moderate
   - B. relentless
   - C. selfish
   - D. lazy
   - E. hopeless

7. To say that an action is *deferred* means MOST NEARLY that it is
   - A. delayed
   - B. reversed
   - C. considered
   - D. forbidden
   - E. followed

8. To *encounter* means MOST NEARLY to
   - A. meet
   - B. recall
   - C. overcome
   - D. weaken
   - E. retreat

9. *Feasible* means MOST NEARLY
   - A. capable
   - B. practicable
   - C. justifiable
   - D. beneficial
   - E. reliable

10. *Respiration* means MOST NEARLY
    - A. dehydration
    - B. breathing
    - C. pulsation
    - D. sweating
    - E. recovery

11. *Vigilant* means MOST NEARLY
    A. sensible   B. ambitious   C. watchful
    D. suspicious   E. restless

12. To say that an action is taken *before the proper time* means MOST NEARLY that it is taken
    A. prematurely   B. furtively   C. temporarily
    D. punctually   E. presently

13. *Innate* means MOST NEARLY
    A. eternal   B. learned   C. native
    D. prospective   E. well-developed

14. *Precedent* means MOST NEARLY
    A. duplicate   B. theory   C. law
    D. conformity   E. example

15. To say that the flow of work into an office is *incessant* means MOST NEARLY that it is
    A. more than can be handled   B. uninterrupted
    C. scanty   D. decreasing in volume
    E. orderly

16. *Unanimity* means MOST NEARLY
    A. emphasis   B. namelessness C. disagreement
    D. harmony   E. impartiality

17. *Incidental* means MOST NEARLY
    A. independent   B. needless   C. infrequent
    D. necessary   E. casual

18. *Versatile* means MOST NEARLY
    A. broad-minded B. well-known   C. old-fashioned
    D. many-sided   E. up-to-date

19. *Conciliatory* means MOST NEARLY
    A. pacific   B. contentious   C. disorderly
    D. obligatory   E. offensive

20. *Altercation* means MOST NEARLY
    A. defeat   B. concurrence   C. controversy
    D. consensus   E. vexation

21. "The secretarial profession is a very old one and has increased in importance with the passage of time. In modern times, the vast expansion of business and industry has greatly increased the need and opportunities for secretaries, and for the first time in history their number as become large."

The above quotation BEST supports the statement that the secretarial profession
- A. is older than business and industry
- B. did not exist in ancient times
- C. has greatly increased in size
- D. demands higher training than it did formerly
- E. has always had many members

22. "The modern system of production unites various kinds of workers into a well-organized body in which each has a definite place."
The above quotation BEST supports the statement that the modern system of production
- A. increases production
- B. trains workers
- C. simplifies tasks
- D. combines and places workers
- E. combines the various plants

22.____

23. "The prevention of accidents makes it necessary not only that safety devices be used to guard exposed machinery but also that mechanics be instructed in safety rules which they must follow for their own protection, and that the lighting in the plant be adequate.
The above quotation BEST supports the statement that industrial accidents
- A. may be due to ignorance
- B. are always avoidable
- C. usually result from inadequate machinery
- D. cannot be entirely overcome
- E. result in damage to machinery

23.____

24. "It is wise to choose a duplicating machine that will do the work required with the greatest efficiency and at the least cost. Users with a large volume of business need speedy machines that cost little to operate and are well made."
The above quotation BEST supports the statement that
- A. most users of duplicating machines prefer low operating cost to efficiency
- B. a well-built machine will outlast a cheap one
- C. a duplicating machine is not efficient unless it is sturdy
- D. a duplicating machine should be both efficient and economical
- E. in duplicating machines speed is more usual than low operating cost

24.____

25. "The likelihood of America's exhausting her natural resources seems to be growing less. All kinds of waste are being reworked and new uses are constantly being found for almost everything. We are getting more use out of our goods and are making many new byproducts out of what was formerly thrown away."
The above quotation BEST supports the statement that we seem to be in less danger of exhausting our resources because
- A. economy is found to lie in the use of substitutes
- B. more service is obtained from a given amount of material
- C. more raw materials are being produced
- D. supply and demand are better controlled
- E. we are allowing time for nature to restore them

25.____

26. "Probably few people realize, as they drive on a concrete road, that steel is used to keep the surface flat and even, in spite of the weight of busses and trucks. Steel bars, deeply imbedded in the concrete, provide sinews to take the stresses so that they cannot crack the slab or make it wavy."
The above quotation BEST supports the statement that a concrete road
    A. is expensive to build
    B. usually cracks under heavy weights
    C. looks like any other road
    D. is used exclusively for heavy traffic
    E. is reinforced with other material

27. "Through advertising, manufacturers exercise a high degree of control over consumers' desires. However, the manufacturer assumes enormous risks in attempting to predict what consumers will want and in producing goods in quantity and distributing them in advance of final selection by the consumers."
The above quotation BEST supports the statement that manufacturers
    A. can eliminate the risk of overproduction by advertising
    B. completely control buyers' needs and desires
    C. must depend upon the final consumers for the success of their undertakings
    D. distribute goods directly to the consumers
    E. can predict with great accuracy the success of any product they put on the market

28. "Success in shorthand, like success in any other study, depends upon the interest the student takes in it. In writing shorthand, it is not sufficient to know how to write a word correctly; one must also be able to write it quickly."
The above quotation BEST supports the statement that
    A. one must be able to read shorthand as well as to write it
    B. shorthand requires much study
    C. if a student can write correctly, he can also write quickly
    D. proficiency in shorthand requires both speed and accuracy
    E. interest in shorthand makes study unnecessary

29. "The countries in the Western Hemisphere were settled by people who were ready each day for new adventure. The peoples of North and South America have retained, in addition to expectant and forward-looking attitudes, the ability and the willingness that they have often shown in the past to adapt themselves to new conditions.
The above quotation BEST supports the statement that the peoples in the Western Hemisphere
    A. no longer have fresh adventures daily
    B. are capable of making changes as new situations arise
    C. are no more forward-looking than the peoples of other regions
    D. tend to resist regulations
    E. differ considerably among themselves

30. "Civilization started to move ahead more rapidly when man freed himself of the shackles that restricted his search for the truth."
The above quotation BEST supports the statement that the progress of civilization
   A. came as a result of man's dislike for obstacles
   B. did not begin until restrictions on learning were removed
   C. has been aided by man's efforts to find the truth
   D. is based on continually increasing efforts
   E. continues at a constantly increasing rate

30.____

31. "It is difficult to distinguish between bookkeeping and accounting. In attempts to do so, bookkeeping is called the art, and accounting the science, of recording business transactions. Bookkeeping gives the history of the business in a systematic manner, and accounting classifies, analyzes, and interprets the facts thus recorded."
The above quotation BEST supports the statement that
   A. accounting is less systematic than bookkeeping
   B. accounting and bookkeeping are closely related
   C. bookkeeping and accounting cannot be distinguish from one another
   D. bookkeeping has been superseded by accounting
   E. the facts recorded by bookkeeping may be interpreted in many ways

31.____

32. "Some specialists are willing to give their services to the Government entirely free of charge; some feel that a nominal salary, such as will cover traveling expenses, is sufficient for a position that is recognized as being somewhat honorary in nature; many other specialists value their time so highly that they will not devote any of it to public service that does not repay them at a rate commensurate with the fees that they can obtain from a good private clientele."
The above quotation BEST supports the statement that the use of specialists by the Government
   A. is rare because of the high cost of securing such persons
   B. may be influenced by the willingness of specialists to serve
   C. enables them to secure higher salaries in private fields
   D. has become increasingly common during the past few years
   E. always conflicts with private demands for their services

32.____

33. "The leader of an industrial enterprise has two principal functions. He must manufacture and distribute a product at a profit, and he must keep individuals and groups of individuals working effectively together."
The above quotation BEST supports the statement that an industrial leader should be able to
   A. increase the distribution of his plant's product
   B. introduce large-scale production methods
   C. coordinate the activities of his employees
   D. profit by the experience of other leaders
   E. expand the business rapidly

33.____

34. "The coloration of textile fabrics composed of cotton and wool generally requires two processes, as the process used in dyeing wool is seldom capable of fixing the color upon cotton. The usual method is to immerse the fabric in the requisite baths to dye the wool and then to treat the partially dyed material in the manner found suitable for cotton."
The above quotation BEST supports the statement that the dyeing of textile fabrics composed of cotton and wool
    A. is less complicated than the dyeing of wool alone
    B. is more successful when the material contains more cotton than wool
    C. is not satisfactory when solid colors are desired
    D. is restricted to two colors for any one fabric
    E. is usually based upon the methods required for dyeing the different materials

35. "The fact must not be overlooked that only about one-half of the international trade of the world crosses the oceans. The other half is merely exchanges of merchandise between countries lying alongside each other or at least within the same continent."
The above quotation BEST supports the statement that
    A. the most important part of any country's trade is transoceanic
    B. domestic trade is insignificant when compared with foreign trade
    C. the exchange of goods between neighboring countries is not considered international trade
    D. foreign commerce is not necessarily carried on by water
    E. about one-half of the trade of the world is international

36. "In the relations of man to nature, the procuring of food and shelter is fundamental. With the migration of man to various climate, ever new adjustments to the food supply and to the climate became necessary."
The above quotation BEST supports the statement that the means by which man supplies his material needs are
    A. accidental   B. varied   C. limited
    D. uniform   E. inadequate

37. "Every language has its peculiar word associations that have no basis in logic and cannot therefore be reasoned about. These idiomatic expressions are ordinarily acquired only by much reading and conversation although questions about such matters may sometimes be answered by the dictionary. Dictionaries large enough to include quotations from standard authors are especially serviceable in determining questions of idiom."
The above quotation BEST supports the statement that idiomatic expressions
    A. give rise to meaningless arguments because they have no logical basis
    B. are widely used by recognized authors
    C. are explained in most dictionaries
    D. are more common in some languages than in others
    E. are best learned by observation of the language as actually used

38. "Individual differences in mental traits assume importance in fitting workers to jobs because such personal characteristics are persistent and are relatively little influenced by training and experience."
The above quotation BEST supports the statement that training and experience
   A. are limited in their effectiveness in fitting workers to jobs
   B. do not increase a worker's fitness for a job
   C. have no effect upon a person's mental traits
   D. have relatively little effect upon the individual's chances for success
   E. should be based on the mental traits of an individual

39. "The telegraph networks of the country now constitute wonderfully operated institutions, affording for ordinary use of modern, business an important means of communication. The transmission of message by electricity has reached the goal for which the postal service has long been striving, namely, the elimination of distance as an effective barrier of communication."
The above quotation BEST supports the statement that
   A. a new standard of communication has been attained
   B. in the telegraph service, messages seldom go astray
   C. it is the distance between the parties which creates the need for communication
   D. modern business relies more upon the telegraph than upon the mails
   E. the telegraph is a form of postal service

40. "The competition of buyers tends to keep prices up, the competition of sellers to send them down. Normally, the pressure of competition among sellers is stronger than that amount by buyers since the seller has his article to sell and must get rid of it, whereas the buyer is not committed to anything."
The above quotation BEST supports the statement that low prices are caused by
   A. buyer competition
   B. competition of buyers with sellers fluctuations in demand
   C. greater competition among sellers than among buyers
   D. more sellers than buyers

Questions 41-60.

DIRECTIONS: In answering Questions 41 through 60, find the CORRECT spelling of the word. Sometimes there is no correct spelling; if none of the suggested spellings is correct, indicate the letter D in the space at the right.

41. A. compitition   B. competition
    C. competetion   D. none of the above

42. A. diagnoesis   B. diagnossis
    C. diagnosis   D. none of the above

43. A. contenance   B. countenance
    C. countinance   D. none of the above

44. A. deliborate   B. deliberate   44.____
    C. delibrate   D. none of the above

45. A. knowlege   B. knolledge   45.____
    C. knowledge   D. none of the above

46. A. occassion   B. occasion   46.____
    C. ocassion   D. none of the above

47. A. sanctioned   B. sancktioned   47.____
    C. sanctionned   D. none of the above

48. A. predesessor   B. predecesar   48.____
    C. predecessor   D. none of the above

49. A. problemmatical   B. problematical   49.____
    C. problematicle   D. none of the above

50. A. descendant   B. decendant   50.____
    C. desendant   D. none of the above

51. A. collapsible   B. collapseable   51.____
    C. collapseble   D. none of the above

52. A. sequance   B. sequence   52.____
    C. sequense   D. none of the above

53. A. oblitorate   B. obbliterat   53.____
    C. obbliterate   D. none of the above

54. A. ambigeuous   B. ambigeous   54.____
    C. ambiguous   D. none of the above

55. A. minieture   B. minneature   55.____
    C. mineature   D. none of the above

56. A. extemporaneous   B. extempuraneus   56.____
    C. extemperaneous   D. none of the above

57. A. hereditory   B. hereditary   57.____
    C. hereditairy   D. none of the above

58. A. conceivably   B. concieveably   58.____
    C. conceiveably   D. none of the above

59. A. extercate   B. extracate   59.____
    C. extricate   D. none of the above

60. A. auspiceous B. auspiseous
 C. auspicious D. none of the above 60.____

Questions 61-80.

DIRECTIONS: In answering Questions 61 through 80, select the sentence that is preferable with respect to grammar and usage such as would be suitable in a formal letter or report.

61. A. The receptionist must answer courteously the questions of all them callers.
 B. The questions of all callers had ought to be answered courteously.
 C. The receptionist must answer courteously the questions what are asked by the callers.
 D. There would have been no trouble if the receptionist had have always answered courteously.
 E. The receptionist should answer courteously the questions of all callers. 61.____

62. A. I had to learn a great number of rules, causing me to dislike the course.
 B. I disliked that study because it required the learning of numerous rules.
 C. I disliked that course very much, caused by the numerous rules I had to memorize.
 D. The cause of my dislike was on account of the numerous rules I had to learn in that course.
 E. The reason I disliked this study was because there were numerous rules that had to be learned. 62.____

63. A. If properly addressed, the letter will reach my mother and I.
 B. The letter had been addressed to myself and mother.
 C. I believe the letter was addressed to either my mother or I.
 D. My mother's name, as well as mine, was on the letter.
 E. If properly addressed, the letter it will reach either my mother or me. 63.____

64. A. A knowledge of commercial subjects and a mastery of English are essential if one wishes to be a good secretary.
 B. Two things necessary to a good secretary are the she should speak good English and too know commercial subjects.
 C. One cannot be a good secretary without she knows commercial subjects and English grammar.
 D. Having had god training in commercial subjects, the rules of English grammar should also be followed.
 E. A secretary seldom or ever succeeds without training in English as well as in commercial subjects. 64.____

65.
- A. He suspicions that the service is not so satisfactory as it should be.
- B. He believes that we should try and find whether the service is satisfactory.
- C. He raises the objection that the way which the service is given is not satisfactory.
- D. He believes that the quality of our services are poor.
- E. He believes that the service that we are giving is unsatisfactory.

65._____

66.
- A. Most all these statements have been supported by persons who are reliable and can be depended upon.
- B. The persons which have guaranteed these statements are reliable.
- C. Reliable persons guarantee the facts with regard to the truth of these statements.
- D. These statements can be depended on, for their truth has been guaranteed by reliable persons.
- E. Persons as reliable as what these are can be depended upon to make accurate statements.

66._____

67.
- A. Brown's & Company's employees have all been given increases in salary.
- B. Brown & Company recently increased the salaries of all its employees.
- C. Recently Brown & Company has increased their employees' salaries.
- D. Brown's & Company employees have recently received increases in salary.
- E. Brown & Company have recently increased the salaries of all its employees.

67._____

68.
- A. The personnel office has charge of employment, dismissals, and employee's welfare.
- B. Employment, together with dismissals and employees' welfare, are handled by the personnel department.
- C. The personnel office takes charge of employment, dismissals, and etc.
- D. The personnel office hires and dismisses employees, and their welfare is also its responsibility.
- E. The personnel office is responsible for the employment, dismissal, and welfare of employees.

68._____

69.
- A. This kind of pen is some better than that kind.
- B. I prefer having these pens than any other.
- C. This kind of pen is the most satisfactory for my use.
- D. In comparison with that kind of pen, this kind is more preferable.
- E. If I were to select between them all, I should pick this pen.

69._____

70.
- A. He could not make use of the report, as it was lacking of the needed information.
- B. This report was useless to him because there were no needed information in it.
- C. Since the report lacked the needed information, it was of no use to him.
- D. Being that the report lacked the needed information, he could not use it.
- E. Since the report did not contain the needed information, t was not real useful to him.

70._____

71.
   A. The paper we use for this purpose must be light, glossy, and stand hard usage as well.
   B. Only a light and a glossy, but durable, paper must be used for this purpose.
   C. For this purpose, we want a paper that is light, glossy, but that will stand hard wear.
   D. For this purpose, paper that is light, glossy, and durable is essential.
   E. Light and glossy paper, as well as standing hard usage, is necessary for this purpose.

71.____

72.
   A. The company had hardly declared the dividend till the notices were prepared for mailing.
   B. They had no sooner declared the dividend when they sent the notices to the stockholders.
   C. No sooner had the dividend been declared than the notices were prepared for mailing.
   D. Scarcely had the dividend been declared than the notices were sent out.
   E. The dividend had not scarcely been declared when the notices were ready for mailing.

72.____

73.
   A. Of all the employees, he spends the most time at the office.
   B. He spends more time at the office than that of his employees.
   C. His working hours are longer or at least equal to those of the other employees.
   D. He devotes as much, if not more, time to his work than the rest of the employees.
   E. He works the longest of any other employee in the office.

73.____

74.
   A. In the reports of typists' speeds, the job analyst found some records that are kind of unusual.
   B. It says in the job analyst's report that some employees type with great speed.
   C. The job analyst found that, in reviewing the typists' work Reports, that some unusual typing speeds had been made.
   D. Work reports showing typing speeds include some typists who are unusual.
   E. In reviewing the typists' work reports, the job analyst found records of unusual typing speeds.

74.____

75.
   A. It is quite possible that we shall reemploy anyone whose training fits them to do the work.
   B. It is probable that we shall reemploy those who have been trained to do the work.
   C. Such of our personnel that have been trained to do the work will be again employed.
   D. We expect to reemploy the ones who have had training enough that they can do the work.
   E. Some of these people have been trained.

75.____

76. A. He as well as his publisher were pleased with the success of the book. 76.____
    B. The success of the book pleased both his publisher and he.
    C. Both his publisher and he was pleased with the success of the book.
    D. Neither he or his publisher was disappointed with the success of the book.
    E. His publisher was as pleased as he with the success of the book.

77. A. You have got to get rid of some of these people if you expect to have the quality of the work improve 77.____
    B. The quality of the work would improve if they would leave fewer people do it.
    C. I believe it would be desirable to have fewer persons during this work.
    D. If you had planned on employing fewer people than this to do the work, this situation would not have arose.
    E. Seeing how you have all those people on that work, it is not surprising that you have a great deal of confusion.

78. A. She made lots of errors in her typed report, and which caused her to be reprimanded. 78.____
    B. The supervisor reprimanded the typist, whom she believed had made careless errors.
    C. Many errors were found in the report which she typed and could not disregard them.
    D. The typist would have corrected the errors, had she of known that the supervisor would see the report.
    E. The errors in the typed report were so numerous that they could hardly be overlooked.

79. A. This kind of a worker achieves success through patience. 79.____
    B. Success does not often come to men of this type except they who are patient.
    C. Because they are patient, these sort of workers usually achieve success.
    D. This worker has more patience than any man in his office.
    E. This kind of worker achieves success through patience.

80. A. I think that they will promote whoever has the best record. 80.____
    B. The firm would have liked to have promoted all employees with good records.
    C. Such of them that have the best records have excellent prospects of promotion.
    D. I feel sure they will give the promotion to whomever has the best record.
    E. Whoever they find to have the best record will, I think, be promoted.

KEY (CORRECT ANSWERS)

1.	B	21.	C	41.	B	61.	E
2.	A	22.	D	42.	C	62.	B
3.	C	23.	A	43.	B	63.	D
4.	E	24.	D	44.	B	64.	A
5.	C	25.	B	45.	C	65.	E
6.	D	26.	E	46.	B	66.	D
7.	A	27.	C	47.	A	67.	B
8.	A	28.	D	48.	D	68.	E
9.	B	29.	B	49.	B	69.	C
10.	B	30.	C	50.	A	70.	C
11.	C	31.	B	51.	A	71.	D
12.	A	32.	B	52.	B	72.	C
13.	C	33.	C	53.	D	73.	A
14.	E	34.	E	54.	C	74.	E
15.	B	35.	D	55.	D	75.	B
16.	D	36.	B	56.	A	76.	E
17.	E	37.	E	57.	B	77.	C
18.	D	38.	A	58.	A	78.	E
19.	A	39.	A	59.	C	79.	E
20.	C	40.	D	60.	C	80.	A

CLERICAL ABILITIES TEST
EXAMINATION SECTION
TEST 1

DIRECTIONS: Each question or incomplete statement is followed by several suggested answers or completions. Select the one that BEST answers the question or completes the statement. *PRINT THE LETTER OF THE CORRECT ANSWER IN THE SPACE AT THE RIGHT.*

Questions 1-10.

DIRECTIONS: Questions 1 through 10 consist of lines of names, dates and numbers. For each question, you are to choose the option (A, B, C, or D) in Column II which EXACTLY matches the information in Column I. *PRINT THE LETTER OF THE CORRECT ANSWER IN THE SPACE AT THE RIGHT.*

SAMPLE QUESTION

Column I
Schneider 11/16/75 581932

Column II
A. Schneider 11/16/75 518932
B. Schneider 11/16/75 581932
C. Schnieder 11/16/75 581932
D. Shnieder 11/16/75 518932

The correct answer is B. Only Option B shows the name, date, and number exactly as they are in Column I. Option A has a mistake in the number. Option C has a mistake in the name. Option D has a mistake in the name and in the number. Now answer Questions 1 through 10 in the same manner.

Column I
1. Johnston 12/26/74 659251

Column II
A. Johnson 12/23/74 659251
B. Johston 12/26/74 659251
C. Johnston 12/26/74 695251
D. Johnston 12/26/74 659251

1._____

2. Allison 1/26/75 9939256

A. Allison 1/26/75 9939256
B. Alisson 1/26/75 9939256
C. Allison 1/26/76 9399256
D. Allison 1/26/75 9993356

2._____

3. Farrell 2/12/75 361251

A. Farell 2/21/75 361251
B. Farrell 2/12/75 361251
C. Farrell 2/21/75 361251
D. Farrell 2/12/75 361151

3._____

4. Guerrero 4/28/72 105689
   A. Guererro 4/28/72 105689
   B. Guererro 4/28/72 105986
   C. Guererro 4/28/72 105869
   D. Guerrero 4/28/72 105689

4.____

5. McDonnell 6/05/73 478215
   A. McDonnell 6/15/73 478215
   B. McDonnell 6/05/73 478215
   C. McDonnell 6/05/73 472815
   D. MacDonell 6/05/73 478215

5.____

6. Shepard 3/31/71 075421
   A. Sheperd 3/31/71 075421
   B. Shepard 3/13/71 075421
   C. Shepard 3/31/71 075421
   D. Shepard 3/13/71 075241

6.____

7. Russell 4/01/69 031429
   A. Russell 4/01/69 031429
   B. Russell 4/10/69 034129
   C. Russell 4/10/69 031429
   D. Russell 4/01/69 034129

7.____

8. Phillips 10/16/68 961042
   A. Philipps 10/16/68 961042
   B. Phillips 10/16/68 960142
   C. Phillips 10/16/68 961042
   D. Philipps 10/16/68 916042

8.____

9. Campbell 11/21/72 624856
   A. Campbell 11/21/72 624856
   B. Campbell 11/21/72 624586
   C. Campbell 11/21/72 624686
   D. Campbel 11/21/72 624856

9.____

10. Patterson 9/18/71 76199176
   A. Patterson 9/18/72 76191976
   B. Patterson 9/18/71 76199176
   C. Patterson 9/18/72 76199176
   D. Patterson 9/18/71 76919176

10.____

Questions 11-15.

DIRECTIONS: Questions 11 through 15 consist of groups of numbers and letters which you are to compare. For each question, you are to choose the option (A, B, C, or D) in Column I which EXACTLY matches the group of numbers and letters given in Column I.

SAMPLE QUESTION

Column I
B92466

Column II
A. B92644
B. B94266
C. A92466
D. B92466

The correct answer is D. Only Option D in Column II shows the group of numbers and letters EXACTLY as it appears in Column I. Now answer Questions 11 through 15 in the same manner.

	Column I	Column II	
11.	925AC5	A. 952CA5 B. 925AC5 C. 952AC5 D. 925CA6	11.____
12.	Y006925	A. Y060925 B. Y006295 C. Y006529 D. Y006925	12.____
13.	J236956	A. J236956 B. J326965 C. J239656 D. J932656	13.____
14.	AB6952	A. AB6952 B. AB9625 C. AB9652 D. AB6925	14.____
15.	X259361	A. X529361 B. X259631 C. X523961 D. X259361	15.____

Questions 16-25.

DIRECTIONS: Each of questions 16 through 25 consists of three lines of code letters and three lines of numbers. The numbers on each line should correspond with the code letters on the same line in accordance with the table below.

Code Letter	S	V	W	A	Q	M	X	E	G	K
Corresponding Number	0	1	2	3	4	5	5	7	8	9

On some of the lines, an error exists in the coding. Compare the letters and numbers in each question carefully. If you find an error or errors on:
  only one of the lines in the question, mark your answer A;
  any two lines in the question, mark your answer B;
  all three lines in the question, mark your answer C;
  none of the lines in the question, mark your answer D.

SAMPLE QUESTION

WQGKSXG	2489068
XEKVQMA	6591453
KMAESXV	9527061

In the above sample, the first line is correct since each code letter listed has the correct corresponding number. On the second line, an error exists because code letter E should have the number 7 instead of the number 5. On the third line, an error exists because the code letter A should have the number 3 instead of the number 2. Since there are errors in two of the three lines, the correct answer is B. Now answer Questions 16 through 25 in the same manner.

16. SWQEKGA   0247983   16.____
     KEAVSXM   9731065
     SSAXGKQ   0036894

17. QAMKMVS   4259510   17.____
     MGGEASX   5897306
     KSWMKWS   9125920

18. WKXQWVE   2964217   18.____
     QKXXQVA   4966413
     AWMXGVS   3253810

19. GMMKASE   8559307   19.____
     AWVSKSW   3210902
     QAVSVGK   4310189

20. XGKQSMK   6894049   20.____
     QSVKEAS   4019730
     GSMXKMV   8057951

21. AEKMWSG   3195208   21.____
     MKQSVQK   5940149
     XGQAEVW   6843712

22. XGMKAVS   6858310   22.____
     SKMAWEQ   0953174
     GVMEQSA   8167403

23. VQSKAVE   1489317   23.____
     WQGKAEM   2489375
     MEGKAWQ   5689324

24. XMQVSKG   6541098   24.____
     QMEKEWS   4579720
     KMEVGKG   9571983

25. GKVAMEW   88912572   25.____
     AXMVKAE   3651937
     KWAGMAV   9238531

Questions 26-35.

DIRECTIONS: Each of Questions 26 through 35 consists of a column of figures. For each question, add the column of figures and choose the correct answer from the four choices given.

26. 5,665.43   26.____
     2,356.69
     6,447.24
     7,239.65

     A. 20,698.01   B. 21,709.01
     C. 21,718.01   D. 22,609.01

27. 817,209.55   27.____
     264,354.29
      82,368.76
     849,964.89

     A. 1,893.977.49   B. 1,989,988.39
     C. 2,009,077.39   D. 2,013,897.49

28. 156,366.89   28.____
     249,973.23
     823,229.49
      56,869.45

     A. 1,286,439.06   B. 1,287,521.06
     C. 1,297,539.06   D. 1,296,421.06

29.   23,422.15   29.____
     149,696.24
     238,377.53
      86,289.79
     505,533.63

     A. 989,229.34   B. 999,879.34
     C. 1,003,330.34   D. 1,023,329.34

30. 2,468,926.70
     656,842.28
     49,723.15
     832,369.59

     A. 3,218,062.72   B. 3,808,092.72
     C. 4,007,861.72   D. 4,818,192.72

31. 524,201.52
     7,775,678.51
     8,345,299.63
     40,628,898.08
     31,374,670.07

     A. 88,646,647.81   B. 88,646,747.91
     C. 88,648,647.91   D. 88,648,747.81

32. 6,824,829.40
     682,482.94
     5,542,015.27
     775,678.51
     7,732,507.25

     A. 21,557,513.37   B. 21,567,513.37
     C. 22,567,503.37   D. 22,567,513.37

33. 22,109,405.58
     6,097,093.43
     5,050,073.99
     8,118,050.05
     4,313,980.82

     A. 45,688,593.87   B. 45,688,603.87
     C. 45,689,593.87   D. 45,689,603.87

34. 79,324,114.19
     99,848,129.74
     43,331,653.31
     41,610,207.14

     A. 264,114,104.38   B. 264,114,114.38
     C. 265,114,114.38   D. 265,214,104.38

35. 33,729,653.94
    5,959,342.58
    26,052,715.47
    4,452,669.52
    7,079,953.59

    A. 76,374,334.10   B. 76,375,334.10
    C. 77,274,335.10   D. 77,275,335.10

35.____

Questions 36-40.

DIRECTIONS: Each of Questions 36 through 40 consists of a single number in Column I and four options in Column II. For each question, you are to choose the option (A, B, C, or D) in Column II which EXACTLY matches the number in Column I.

SAMPLE QUESTION

Column I
5965121

Column II
A. 5956121
B. 5965121
C. 5966121
D. 5965211

The correct answer is B. Only Option B shows the number EXACTLY as it appears in Column I. Now answer Questions 36 through 40 in the same manner.

Column I
36. 9643242

Column II
A. 9643242
B. 9462342
C. 9642442
D. 9463242

36.____

37. 3572477

A. 3752477
B. 3725477
C. 3572477
D. 3574277

37.____

38. 5276101

A. 5267101
B. 5726011
C. 5271601
D. 5276101

38.____

39. 4469329

A. 4496329
B. 4469329
C. 4496239
D. 4469239

39.____

40. 2326308   A. 2236308   40._____
                 B. 2233608
                 C. 2326308
                 D. 2323608

KEY (CORRECT ANSWERS)

1.	D	11.	B	21.	A	31.	D
2.	A	12.	D	22.	C	32.	A
3.	B	13.	A	23.	B	33.	B
4.	D	14.	A	24.	D	34.	A
5.	B	15.	D	25.	A	35.	C
6.	C	16.	D	26.	B	36.	A
7.	A	17.	C	27.	D	37.	C
8.	C	18.	A	28.	A	38.	D
9.	A	19.	D	29.	C	39.	B
10.	B	20.	B	30.	C	40.	C

TEST 2

DIRECTIONS: Each question or incomplete statement is followed by several suggested answers or completions. Select the one that BEST answers the question or completes the statement. *PRINT THE LETTER OF THE CORRECT ANSWER IN THE SPACE AT THE RIGHT.*

Questions 1-5.

DIRECTIONS: Each of Questions 1 through 5 consists of a name and a dollar amount. In each question, the name and dollar amount in Column II should be an EXACT copy of the name and dollar amount in Column I. If there is:
    a mistake only in the name, mark your answer A;
    a mistake only in the dollar amount, mark your answer B;
    a mistake in both the name and the dollar amount, mark your answer C;
    no mistake in either the name or the dollar amount, mark your answer D.

SAMPLE QUESTION

Column I	Column II
George Peterson	George Petersson
$125.50	$125.50

Compare the name and dollar amount in Column II with the name and dollar amount in Column I. The name *Petersson* in Column II is spelled *Peterson* in Column I. The amount is the same in both columns. Since there is a mistake only in the name, the answer to the sample question is A. Now answer Questions 1 through 5 in the same manner.

	Column I	Column II	
1.	Susanne Shultz $3440	Susanne Schultz $3440	1.____
2.	Anibal P. Contrucci $2121.61	Anibel P. Contrucci $2112.61	2.____
3.	Eugenio Mendoza $12.45	Eugenio Mendozza $12.45	3.____
4.	Maurice Gluckstadt $4297	Maurice Gluckstadt $4297	4.____
5.	John Pampellonne $4656.94	John Pammpellonne $4566.94	5.____

Questions 6-11.

DIRECTIONS: Each of Questions 6 through 11 consist of a set of names and addresses, which you are to compare. In each question, the name and addresses in Column II should be an EXACT copy of the name and address in Column I. If there is:
- a mistake only in the name, mark your answer A;
- a mistake only in the address, mark your answer B;
- a mistake in both the name and address, mark your answer C;
- no mistake in either the name or address, mark your answer D.

SAMPLE QUESTION

Column I	Column II
Michael Filbert	Michael Filbert
456 Reade Street	645 Reade Street
New York, N.Y. 10013	New York, N.Y. 10013

Since there is a mistake only in the address (the street number should be 456 instead of 645), the answer to the sample question is B. Now answer Questions 6 through 11 in the same manner.

	Column I	Column II	
6.	Hilda Goettelmann 55 Lenox Rd. Brooklyn, N.Y. 11226	Hilda Goettelman 55 Lenox Ave. Brooklyn, N.Y. 11226	6.____
7.	Arthur Sherman 2522 Batchelder St. Brooklyn, N.Y. 11235	Arthur Sharman 2522 Batcheder St. Brooklyn, N.Y. 11253	7.____
8.	Ralph Barnett 300 West 28 Street New York, New York 10001	Ralph Barnett 300 West 28 Street New York, New York 10001	8.____
9.	George Goodwin 135 Palmer Avenue Staten Island, New York 10302	George Godwin 135 Palmer Avenue Staten Island, New York 10302	9.____
10.	Alonso Ramirez 232 West 79 Street New York, N.Y. 10024	Alonso Ramirez 223 West 79 Street New York, N.Y. 10024	10.____
11.	Cynthia Graham 149-34 83 Street Howard Beach, N.Y. 11414	Cynthia Graham 149-35 83 Street Howard Beach, N.Y. 11414	11.____

3 (#2)

Questions 12-20.

DIRECTIONS: Questions 12 through 20 are problems in subtraction. For each question do the subtraction and select your answer from the four choices given.

12. 232,921.85
    -179,587.68

    A. 52,433.17
    C. 53,334.17
    B. 52,434.17
    D. 53,343,17

    12._____

13. 5,531,876.29
    -3,897,158.36

    A. 1,634,717.93
    C. 1,734,717.93
    B. 1,644,718.93
    D. 1,7234,718.93

    13._____

14. 1,482,658.22
    -937,925.76

    A. 544,633.46
    C. 545,632.46
    B. 544,732.46
    D. 545,732.46

    14._____

15. 937,828.17
    -259,673.88

    A. 678,154.29
    C. 688,155.39
    B. 679,154.29
    D. 699,155.39

    15._____

16. 760,412.38
    -263,465.95

    A. 496,046.43
    C. 496,956.43
    B. 496,946.43
    D. 497,046.43

    16._____

17. 3,203,902.26
    -2,933,087.96

    A. 260,814.30
    C. 270,814.30
    B. 269,824.30
    D. 270,824.30

    17._____

18. 1,023,468.71
    -934,678.88

    A. 88,780.83
    C. 88,880.83
    B. 88,789.83
    D. 88,889.83

    18._____

19. 831,549.47
    -772,814.78

    A. 58,734.69   B. 58,834.69
    C. 59,735.69   D. 59,834.69

19.____

20. 6,306,181.74
    -3,617,376.99

    A. 2,687,904.99   B. 2,688,904.99
    C. 2,689,804.99   D. 2,799,905.99

20.____

Questions 21-30.

DIRECTIONS: Each of Questions 21 through 30 consists of three lines of code letters and three lines of numbers. The numbers on each line should correspond with the code letters on the same line in accordance with the table below.

Code Letter	J	U	B	T	Y	D	K	R	L	P
Corresponding Number	0	1	2	3	4	5	5	7	8	9

On some of the lines, an error exists in the coding. Compare the letters and numbers in each question carefully. If you find an error or errors on:
   only *one* of the lines in the question, mark your answer A;
   any *two* lines in the question, mark your answer B;
   all *three* lines in the question, mark your answer C;
   none of the lines in the question, mark your answer D.

SAMPLE QUESTION

BJRPYUR   2079417
DTBPYKJ   5328460
YKLDBLT   4685283

In the above sample, the first line is correct since each code letter listed has the correct corresponding number. On the second line, an error exists because code letter P should have the number 9 instead of the number 8. The third line is correct since each code letter listed has the correct corresponding number. Since there is an error in *one* of the three lines, the correct answer is A. Now answer Questions 21 through 30 in the same manner.

21. BYPDTJL   2495308
    PLRDTJU   9815301
    DTJRYLK   5207486

21.____

22. RPBYRJK   7934706
    PKTYLBU   9624821
    KDLPJYR   6489047

22.____

23.	TPYBUJR	3942107	23._____
	BYRKPTU	2476931	
	DUKPYDL	5169458	
24.	KBYDLPL	6345898	24._____
	BLRKBRU	2876261	
	JTULDYB	0318542	
25.	LDPYDKR	8594567	25._____
	BDKDRJL	2565708	
	BDRPLUJ	2679810	
26.	PLRLBPU	9858291	26._____
	LPYKRDJ	88936750	
	TDKPDTR	3569527	
27.	RKURPBY	7617924	27._____
	RYUKPTJ	7426930	
	RTKPTJD	7369305	
28.	DYKPBJT	5469203	28._____
	KLPJBTL	6890238	
	TKPLBJP	3698209	
29.	BTPRJYL	2397148	29._____
	LDKUTYR	8561347	
	YDBLRPJ	4528190	
30.	ULPBKYT	1892643	30._____
	KPDTRBJ	6953720	
	YLKJPTB	4860932	

KEY (CORRECT ANSWERS)

1.	A	11.	D	21.	B
2.	C	12.	C	22.	C
3.	A	13.	A	23.	D
4.	D	14.	B	24.	B
5.	C	15.	A	25.	A
6.	C	16.	B	26.	C
7.	C	17.	C	27.	A
8.	D	18.	B	28.	D
9.	A	19.	A	29.	B
10.	B	20.	B	30.	D

GENERAL INFORMATION AND BACKGROUND
EXAMINATION SECTION
TEST 1

DIRECTIONS: Each question or incomplete statement is followed by several suggested answers or completions. Select the one that *BEST* answers the question or completes the statement. *PRINT THE LETTER OF THE CORRECT ANSWER IN THE SPACE AT THE RIGHT.*

1. Written by one who is often called the greatest storyteller of all literature, this masterpiece deserves praise for its narrative interest and its vivid and realistic pictures of life and people. It contains a wide diversity of types of story, including romances, adventure stories, stories of illicit love, satiric stories directed against the clergy, and comic anecdotes. The stories are told during a period of 10 successive days by a group of people gathered in the country to escape the Great Plague.
The work referred to in this passage was written by

   A. Marco Polo   B. Rabelais   C. Castiglione
   D. Boccaccio   E. Cervantes

   1._____

2. In the United States, in the 1920's, the trend toward uniformity was hastened by *which* of the following?
   I. An increase in the number of independent newspapers
   II. The development of national advertising media
   III. The radio
   IV. The movies

   The *CORRECT* combination is:

   A. I and II   B. III and IV   C. I, II, and IV
   D. II, III, and IV   E. I, II, III, and IV

   2._____

3. Which of the following is the *MOST IMPORTANT* argument for laws stringently controlling the use of DDT?

   A. It is responsible for the near extinction of the whooping crane.
   B. Its use has resulted in the extermination of some insect species.
   C. It becomes concentrated in certain body tissues of organisms high in food chains.
   D. It has resulted in the starvation of the songbirds that commonly winter in the northern states.
   E. Chemically it has a long half-life.

   3._____

4. The figures in the graph on the following page pertain to the United States. They are figures for the number of

   A. cities   B. counties   C. towns
   D. school districts E. townships

   4._____

39

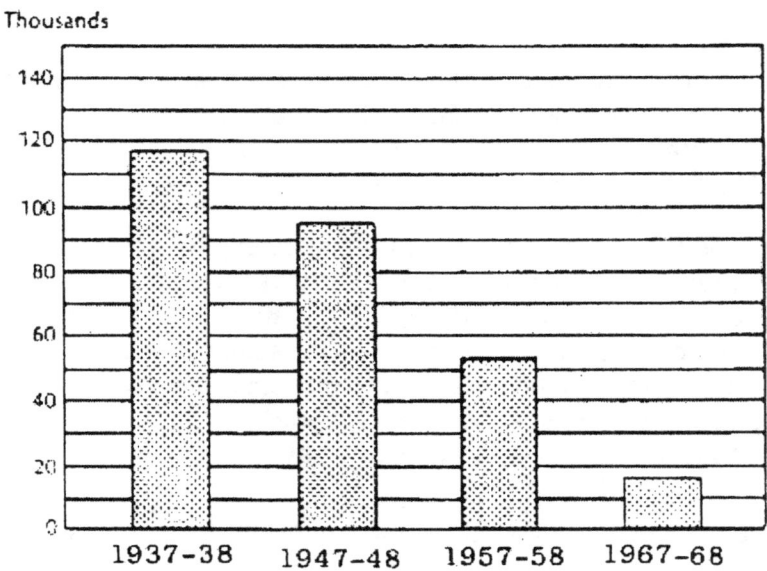

5. An increase in which of the following was a NECESSARY condition for the development of the earliest urban areas?

   A. Agricultural productivity
   B. Immigration
   C. Contact with other cultures
   D. Birth rate
   E. Mechanization

6. A classicist in literature, royalist in politics, and Anglo-Catholic in religion is the description of *himself* given by

   A. T. S. Eliot
   B. Stephen Spender
   C. W. H. Auden
   D. Archibald MacLeish
   E. John Masefield

7. Which of the following has had the GREATEST effect on the rate of population change in the less developed of the developing nations?

   A. Increases in the average age at marriage
   B. Modern medicine and pesticides
   C. Rises in the net reproduction rate
   D. Improvements in birth-control techniques
   E. Sterilization and abortion programs

8. Which of the following BEST characterizes the situation of the European powers during the 10 years before the First World War?

A. Relations were fluid, with few indications of final alignments.
B. Major alignments were maintained without change as crises decreased in number and intensity.
C. The status quo was maintained in a period of relative calm.
D. The absence of serious clashes facilitated the formulation of new alignments.
E. Major alignments were completed while crises accelerated.

9. He sees the drama in functional terms as a social instrument to help organize and motivate black communities. He wants the black theatre not only to be entertaining and artful, but also to reflect, inerpret, teach, chronicle, take part in, and, in a sense, lead a black revolution.
The dramatist described above is

A. Marc Connelly B. LeRoi Jones C. Edward Albee
D. Arthur Miller E. Tennessee Williams

10. The explanation for the red appearance of the setting sun *also* explains why

A. a red barn looks redder at sunset than at noon
B. red is a better color than blue for the navigation lights on top of radio transmission towers
C. a blue object looks black in red light
D. the flame from burning calcium is red
E. blood looks red under white light

11.

The *structural system* used in this building is

A. load-bearing masonry   B. prestressed concrete
C. cast-iron panels   D. steel frame
E. thin-shell concrete

12. Cities often grow up in locations near bulky raw materials, if power and markets are fairly accessible.
The factors above influenced the development of *all* of the following cities EXCEPT

- A. Birmingham, Alabama
- B. Wilmington, Delaware
- C. Duluth, Minnesota
- D. Des Moines, Iowa
- E. Oklahoma City, Oklahoma

13. Which of the following has had the effect of *STRENGTHENING* the system of checks and balances in the national government?

    A. National political parties
    B. The power of judicial review
    C. The popular election of United States senators
    D. Federal grants-in-aid
    E. The trend toward bipartisanship in foreign affairs

14. A musical program devoted solely to major compositions by Mahler, Beethoven, and Shostakovich would, *most likely,* be a(n)

    - A. piano recital
    - B. symphony orchestra concert
    - C. string quartet recital
    - D. organ recital
    - E. song recital

15. Which of the following is the *BEST* criterion for objectively determining an individual's social class in the United States?

    - A. Income
    - B. Ancestry
    - C. Religious belief
    - D. Political belief
    - E. Interests

16. If Country I can produce Commodity A with 1 unit of input and Commodity B with 3 units of input and if Country II can produce Commodity A with 5 units of input and Commodity B with 10 units of input, it would be *most likely* that

    A. Country I would produce both commodities and that Country II would produce neither
    B. no trade would take place between the two countries
    C. Country II would gain from trade but that Country I would not
    D. Country I would gain from trade but that Country II would not
    E. each country would gain by trading with the other

17. Which of the following statements concerning executives in the Federal Government of the United States is *CORRECT?*

    A. Political executives, appointed by the President or by heads of agencies, tend to have a common background and work experience.
    B. While the President has had little success in coordinating and directing the work of the executive branch, the department heads have successfully overcome the preference of their bureaus and divisions for operating autonomy,
    C. Salaries of executives compare favorably with salaries of business executives.
    D. Normally, Congress has clearly defined the objectives of various administrative programs and so has reduced the range and degree of discretion exercised by executives.
    E. Heads of agencies and their political assistants rarely have complete control over their programs partly because other agencies with related and perhaps conflicting interests must be consulted.

18. The artist *most closely* associated with works such as the one following is   18.____

    A. Picasso   B. Calder
    C. Braque   D. Dali
    E. Brancusi

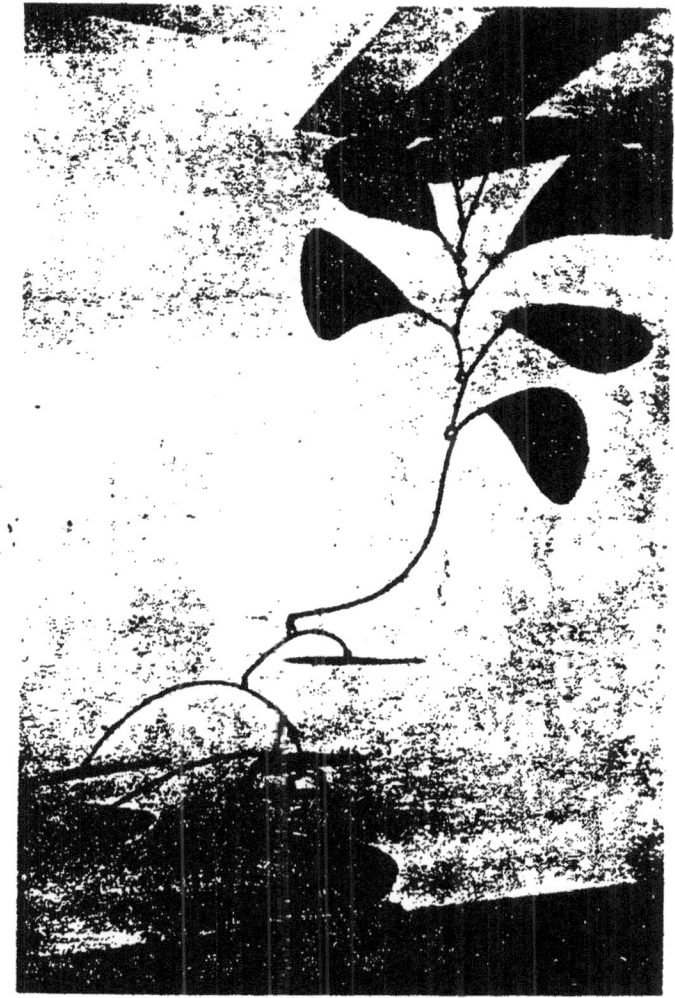

19. The Emancipation Proclamation, January 1, 1863, granted freedom *to*   19.____

    A. all slaves
    B. slaves in the border states
    C. slaves in the North
    D. slaves in areas occupied by the Union Army
    E. slaves in areas still in rebellion

20. What was thy pity's recompense?   20.____
    A silent suffering, and intense;
    The rock, the vulture, and the chain.
    All that the proud can feel of pain.
    These lines *probably* refer to the fate of

    A. Laocoön   B. Cassandra   C. Tantalus
    D. Prometheus   E. Atlas

21. The number of voters participating in the 1920 United States presidential election increased relatively more than the total population increased from 1916-1920 PRIMARILY because

    A. the increase in the urban population made it relatively easy for a larger percent to vote
    B. improvements in educational methods increased popular interest, in politics
    C. the Nineteenth Amendment was ratified in 1920
    D. voters turned out in large numbers to vote against the League of Nations
    E. Harding waged a vigorous campaign for the presidency

22. Which of the following statements is *typically* associated with Hobbes?

    A. Men require government for civil peace.
    B. Government should be limited by certain constitutional safeguards.
    C. The best protection for individual liberty is freedom of private associations.
    D. Government is a trust that may be revoked by the governed whenever those who govern violate it.
    E. Political conflict results from competition among economic forces in society.

23. Political boundaries in Africa at the mid-twentieth century were determined PRIMARILY by

    A. geographic realities
    B. economic factors
    C. tribal organization
    D. nineteenth-century European power politics
    E. nationalist sentiments

24. During the 1930's, an *important* reason for friction between the United States and Mexico was Mexico's

    A. alignment with Germany
    B. support for neutralism
    C. expropriation of foreign mineral concessions
    D. trade expansion in South America
    E. opposition to reciprocal trade agreements

25. Which of the following has contributed MOST to the increase in real wages in the United States since 1900?

    A. Rising prices
    B. Increasing productivity
    C. Increasing strength of labor unions
    D. Increasing use of the corporate form of business organization
    E. Increasing legislation favorable to labor

KEY (CORRECT ANSWERS)

1. D
2. D
3. C
4. D
5. A

6. A
7. B
8. E
9. B
10. B

11. D
12. B
13. B
14. B
15. A

16. E
17. E
18. B
19. E
20. D

21. C
22. A
23. D
24. C
25. B

TEST 2

DIRECTIONS: Each question or incomplete statement is followed by several suggested answers or completions. Select the one that *BEST* answers the question or completes the statement. *PRINT THE LETTER OF THE CORRECT ANSWER IN THE SPACE AT THE RIGHT.*

1. The present international political system is MOST ACCURATELY characterized as a 1.____

   A. loose concert of power tending toward a world empire
   B. unit-veto system tending toward a balance of power
   C. tight bipolar system tending toward a universal system
   D. balance of power system tending toward a loose bipolar system
   E. loose bipolar system tending toward a multi-polar or unit-veto system

2. W. E. B. Du Bois led the early twentieth-century reaction against the doctrines of Booker T. Washington on the ground that blacks should 2.____

   A. repatriate themselves to Africa
   B. demand their full constitutional rights
   C. work through the Republican party rather than the Colored Farmers' Alliance
   D. seek to win a place in American society through vocational training
   E. remain in rural areas rather than be encouraged to migrate to cities

3. *Which* of the following are *CHANGES* in the pattern of economic behavior in the United States that have occurred during the past 50 years? A(n) 3.____
   I. decrease in the proportion of farm workers
   II. decrease in the hours worked per week
   III. decrease in the proportion of service workers
   IV. increase in productivity per hours worked
   The *CORRECT* combination is:

   A. I and II   B. III and IV   C. I, II, and III
   D. I, II, and IV   E. II, III, and IV

4. With two films, Z and STATE OF SEIGE, he has emerged as the contemporary director who has best mastered the technique of transforming odious political situations into tension-filled feature films, and he has moved the political film from a genre with sectarian appeal to one with a mass audience. 4.____
   The film director described above is

   A. Costa Gavras   B. Jean-Luc Godard
   C. Michelangelo Antonioni D. Luis Bunuel
   E. Ingmar Bergman

5. An *essential* feature of French economic planning is 5.____

   A. close regulation of foreign trade
   B. close collaboration of business in the planning process
   C. close collaboration of labor in the planning process
   D. the wide use of formal mathematical planning models
   E. the close coordination of short-term stabilization policies with medium-term plans

6. Which of the following are TRUE of the *majority* of immigrants who came to the United States between 1880 and 1920? They
    I. came under contract and worked primarily as domestics
    II. arrived able to speak and write the English language
    III. were from Southern and Eastern Europe
    IV. settled in small cities
    V. settled in large cities
The *CORRECT* combination is:

A. I and II
B. I and V
C. II and IV
D. III and IV
E. III and V

7. The painting reproduced above is characteristic of the work of

A. Andrew Wyeth
B. Gilbert Stuart
C. Norman Rockwell
D. William Harnett
E. Grant Wood

8. Although their objectives are frequently similar, business and public administration differ *MOST* in which of the following respects?

A. Public administration is more interested in research and development than is business administration.
B. As a measure of performance, profit is often lacking in public administration.
C. Business is concerned primarily with production whereas government is concerned primarily with long-range planning activities.
D. Business furnishes goods to the public whereas government furnishes services.
E. Unlike the situation in business administration, there are no measurable units of output in the provision of public goods and services.

9. Which of the following contributed *MOST* to increasing the yield of rice in Asian countries in the 1960's?

A. Use of fertilizers
B. Use of insecticides
C. Increased use of irrigation
D. Rotation of crops
E. Development of new strains

10.

Which of the following statements about the building shown above is CORRECT?

A. The use of flying buttresses to support the roof indicates that it is a Gothic cathedral.
B. Although the structure of the nave and transept is basically Romanesque, eclectic additions have been made to the cathedral.
C. The minarets interspersed among the domes indicate a Chinese influence.
D. The several domes indicate that it was originally a Roman temple, later converted into a Christian church.
E. Although at first glance the building seems to be High Renaissance, the rose window in the facade identifies it as Gothic.

11. In recent decades the composition of the population of Japan has been changed PRIMARILY by which of the following?

A. Emigration planned and directed by the government
B. The accelerated rate of industrialization since the Second World War
C. An increase in life expectancy
D. The restriction of immigration
E. The drastic reduction of the birthrate

12. The reply was to the effect that the *Creative Power*, when he made the earth, made no marks, no lines of division or separation upon it, and that it should be allowed to remain as then made. The earth was his mother. He was made of the earth and grew up on its bosom. The earth, as his mother and nurse, was sacred to his affections, too sacred to be valued by or sold for silver and gold. He could not consent to sever his affections from the land that bore him. He was content to live upon such fruits as the *Creative Power* placed within and upon it, and unwilling to barter these and his free habits away for the new modes of life proposed by us.

This reply was *most likely* made by a(n)

A. Massachusetts Puritan to the English Privy Council
B. American Indian to a United States Government commission
C. Mormon leader to the governor of the Utah Territory
D. Mexican official to American settlers in Texas
E. New England transcendentalist to a local tax assessor

13.

PERCENT OF FEMALE-HEADED FAMILIES
IN THE UNITED STATES IN 1960
BY INCOME, RACE, AND PLACE OF RESIDENCE

	Rural	Urban	Total
	Percent	Percent	Percent
Black			
Under $3,000	18	47	36
$3,000 and over	5	8	7
Total	14	23	21
White			
Under $3,000	12	18	22
$3,000 and over	2	4	3
Total	4	7	6

The data in the table above indicate that in the United States in 1960 female-headed families were *more common*

- A. in rural areas than in urban areas
- B. among whites than among blacks at the same income level
- C. among poor whites than among nonpoor blacks
- D. among the poor than the nonpoor only in urban areas
- E. among blacks than whites in urban areas but not in rural areas

14. If each of the following groups of artists could collaborate on a work, *which group* would *most probably* create an American folk opera based upon themes drawn from the early history of the nation?

- A. Leonard Bernstein, Jack Kerouac, and Pearl Primus
- B. Aaron Copland, Carl Sandburg, and Agnes de Mille
- C. Lukas Foss, Ernest Hemingway, and George Balanchine
- D. Paul Hindemith, Henry Miller, and Anthony Tudor
- E. Gian-Carlo Menotti, Tennessee Williams, and Martha Graham

15. Assume that in a United States presidential election, salient campaign issues favored the Republican party and the Republican presidential nominee was very popular but not highly partisan. In these circumstances, a postelection analysis would be *most likely* to show that

- A. voters who considered themselves strong Democrats supported the Democratic candidate almost without defection
- B. the independent vote split giving a slight advantage to the Republican party
- C. voters who considered themselves Democrats defected in large numbers and voted for the Republican nominee
- D. voters who classified themselves as strong Republicans tended not to vote if they thought the Republican nominee was too liberal
- E. the independent vote split in roughly the same proportions as party affiliations in the United States

16. The Nazi-Soviet Nonaggression Pact in 1939 was followed *almost immediately* by

- A. Germany's attack on Poland
- B. Germany's attack on the Soviet Union

C. United States entry into the Second World War
D. the Munich Agreement the Atlantic Charter

17. Studies of social class in the United States show that the *overwhelming majority* of Americans

   A. conceptualize themselves as middle-class
   B. refer to themselves as working-class people
   C. believe that there are no social classes in the United States
   D. resent the dominance of middle-class values
   E. believe that education is no longer essential for social mobility

18. Easy access to raw materials, the availability of a large and efficient labor supply, well established railway facilities, proximity to a large steel market, and a stimulating climate due to the moderating influence of the lake were factors in the establishment of major iron and steel manufacturing plants in this area.
    Which of the following areas is described in the passage above?

   A. Pittsburgh
   B. Birmingham
   C. Duluth
   D. Chicago-Gary
   E. Los Angeles-Fontana

19. *All* of the following statements express policies of the United States government during the Cold War *EXCEPT:*

   A. Our policy with regard to Europe was not to interfere with her internal concerns but to consider each European government de facto as the legitimate government and to cultivate friendly relations with it.
   B. Even though Soviet leaders professed to believe that the conflict between capitalism and communism was irreconcilable and must eventually be resolved by the triumph of the latter, was our hope that a fair and equitable . settlement would be reached when they realize that we were too strong to be beaten and too determined to be frightened.
   C. If we find it impossible to enlist Soviet cooperation in the solution of world problems, we should be prepared to join with the British and other Western countries in an attempt to build up a world of our own.
   D. The role of this country should consist of friendly aid in the drafting of a European economic program to get Europe on its feet and to provide financial support for such a program so far as it may be practical for us to do so.
   E. The United States seeks no territorial expansion or selfish advantage and has no plans for aggression against any other state, large or small, but is committed to the mutual security of non-Communist nations in Europe.

20. A high level of industrialization has *generally* been accompanied by

   A. greater interdependence of various sectors of the society
   B. a rigidity in the class structure
   C. lessening of competition for scarce commodities and resources
   D. increased demands for animate sources of power
   E. increased importance of the family as an agency of socializat ion

21. Which of the following has the GREATEST proportion of its foreign trade with the United States?

    A. Australia B. West Germany C. Japan
    D. Great Britain E. Canada

22. The question of the rights of neutrals on the high seas was a major issue in the involvement of the United States in which of the following wars?
    I. The War of 1812
    II. The Spanish-American War
    III. The First World War
    IV. The Second World War
    The CORRECT answer is:

    A. I only B. IV only C. I and III
    D. III and IV E. I, II, III, and IV

23. Which of the following is the MAJOR significance of the Wagner Act? It

    A. provided federal recognition for labor organization and collective bargaining
    B. established procedures for compulsory arbitration of labor-management disputes
    C. defined unfair labor practices on the part of unions
    D. established a cooperative federal-state system of unemployment compensation
    E. marked the beginning of government regulation of labor unions

24. The MOST EFFECTIVE power of the United States Congress in influencing executive action in foreign policy making is its

    A. role in the treaty-making process
    B. exclusive authority to declare war
    C. control over the appropriations process
    D. role in confirming presidential appointments
    E. authority to regulate the nation's armed forces

25. Prior to the nineteenth century, state formation in the interior of East Africa was stimulated by all of the following EXCEPT

    A. the growth of long-distance trade
    B. increases in population
    C. the development of an economy based on fixed cultivation
    D. a need to control conquered territory
    E. introduction of European forms of political organization

KEY (CORRECT ANSWERS)

1.	E	11.	E
2.	B	12.	B
3.	D	13.	C
4.	A	14.	B
5.	B	15.	C
6.	E	16.	A
7.	E	17.	A
8.	B	18.	D
9.	E	19.	A
10.	B	20.	A

21. E
22. C
23. A
24. C
25. E

EXAMINATION SECTION
TEST 1

DIRECTIONS: Each question or incomplete statement is followed by several suggested answers or completions. Select the one that BEST answers the question or completes the statement. *PRINT THE LETTER OF THE CORRECT ANSWER IN THE SPACE AT THE RIGHT.*

1. If a gasoline engine cylinder is excessively worn, it will be found that the wear is practically always GREATEST
   A. at the top of the ring travel
   B. at the middle of the ring travel
   C. at the lowest ring travel
   D. where the cylinder is coolest

2. After boring or honing a worn gasoline engine cylinder, it is good practice to clean the grit out of the pores of the cast iron block.
   In the absence of continuous cleaning facilities, this is done BEST by cleaning the cylinder with
   A. gasoline
   B. hot water and soap
   C. benzene
   D. kerosene and waste

3. One of the BEST ways to check the concentricity of the valve guide and valve seat is by the use of a(n)
   A. expanding reamer
   B. dial indicator
   C. inside micrometer
   D. bevel protractor

4. The thimble of a micrometer is slightly before the .475" graduation on the barrel.
   If the thimble reading is between .018" and .019", and the reading on the Vernier is .006", then the full opening is
   A. .4946"   B. .4696"   C. .4686"   D. .4936"

5. The sum of 9/16", 11/32", 15/64", and 1 3/32" is MOST NEARLY
   A. 2.234"   B. 2.134"   C. 2.334"   D. 2.214"

6. The diameter of a circle whose circumference is 14.5" is MOST NEARLY
   A. 4.62"   B. 4.81"   C. 4.72"   D. 4.51"

7. A *literate* worker is one who is MOST NEARLY
   A. unlearned   B. sinuous   C. educated   D. impervious

8. If a mechanic is told that a certain repair job is *feasible*, this means it is MOST NEARLY
   A. laborious   B. moderate   C. practicable   D. easy

9. A mechanic who is *dexterous* at his job is one who is MOST NEARLY
   A. proficient   B. devious   C. devoted   D. impartial

10. To obtain a certain type of fit, an intentional difference in the dimensions of the mating parts is usually specified on the blueprints.
This intentional difference is called
A. allowance   B. tolerance   C. clearance   D. nominal

11. A micro-inch is
A. an inch measured on a micrometer
B. an inch measured with a microscope
C. a ten-thousandth of an inch
D. one-millionth of an inch

12. Assuming the bore of a gasoline engine cylinder measures 3 inches and the piston for this cylinder has a stroke of 4 inches, the piston displacement, in cubic inches per stroke of piston, will be MOST NEARLY
A. 36   B. 48   C. 32   D. 28

13. If an engine cylinder should be worn in such a way that there is a taper of 0.008" from top to bottom, the piston ring and gap, when traveling up and down over this surface, will be opening and closing MOST NEARLY
A. 0.008"   B. 0.016"   C. 0.020"   D. 0.024"

14. In freezing weather, a lead-acid storage battery should NOT have a specific gravity reading
A. above 1.250
B. above 1.235
C. below 1.250
D. of 1.285

15. In servicing a worn and badly tapered gasoline engine cylinder that has quite a *step* at the bottom of the ring travel, it is BEST to
A. start the honing in the unworn area below the ring travel
B. start the honing in the center of the ring travel
C. start the honing in the unworn area above the ring travel
D. just fit an oversized piston for the top part of the cylinder

16. In a gasoline engine, if the distributor breaker points are replaced twice as often as the generator brushes, but the generator brushes are replaced one-quarter as often as the spark plugs, then it is CORRECT to say that the spark plugs are replaced _____ as often as the distributor breaker points.
A. twice   B. four times   C. one-half   D. one-quarter

17. In the four stroke cycle gasoline engine, the sequence of the steps in each cylinder to complete a cycle is which one of the following?
A. power stroke, compression stroke, exhaust stroke
B. compression stroke, exhaust stroke, power stroke
C. exhaust stroke, compression stroke, power stroke
D. compression stroke, power stroke, exhaust stroke

18. The cutting edge of a cold chisel should be tempered at a temperature corresponding to a color of
A. blue   B. pale blue   C. light straw   D. purple

19. To properly service a clutch, the type that is commonly used on gasoline engines, it is important that the face or frictional surface of the flywheel should run true blue within a tolerance of MOST NEARLY
    A. .006" B. .012" C. .018" D. .025"

20. The BEST way to check a warped cylinder head is by means of a
    A. straight edge
    B. surface gauge
    C. feeler gauge
    D. dial indicator

21. Upon inspecting a cam ground piston skirt, while cold, it will be found that the skirt is USUALLY
    A. circular in cross-section
    B. smaller in diameter than the piston head
    C. widest at wrist pin bosses
    D. oval in cross-section

22. If a transmission main drive gear, having 20 teeth, rotates at 450 RPM. and drives a countershaft drive gear at 300 RPM, the TOTAL number of teeth on the countershaft drive gear will be
    A. 30 B. 15 C. 25 D. 45

23. In reference to the piston, wrist pin, and connecting rod assembly of a gasoline engine, it is NOT common practice to ever
    A. fix the pin to the piston by a set screw
    B. allow the pin to rotate in both the connecting rod and piston bosses
    C. anchor the pin to connecting rod
    D. use precision type split bearings at the wrist pin end of connecting rod

24. Upon dismantling a gasoline engine, it was found that the piston rings were stuck in the grooves, not being free to rotate.
    This was MOST LIKELY caused by
    A. operating the engine with spark setting in advanced position
    B. the thermostat maintaining too low an engine temperature
    C. dirty or contaminated lubricating oil
    D. using the wrong type of spark plugs in the engine

25. Many gasoline engines today are being built with cylinder heads of cast aluminum alloy.
    The reason for using aluminum is MAINLY because it
    A. is a better conductor of heat
    B. will not rust
    C. has less expansion per degree F. than cast iron
    D. is lighter in weight

26. A gasoline engine that utilizes a rocker arm for operating intake and exhaust valves is COMMONLY classified as a(n) _____ engine.
    A. T-head B. I-head C. L-head D. 2 cam haft

27. Assuming that a sliding gear transmission is so built that there is a gear ratio between the transmission main drive gear and the countershaft drive gear of 1.5 to 1, and, with gears shifted to low speed, there is an additional gear ratio between the countershaft low-speed gear and the low-and-reverse mainshaft gear of 1.5 to 1, then, for the propeller shaft to rotate 200 RPM, the crankshaft will have to rotate MOST NEARLY _____ RPM.
   A. 450   B. 600   C. 500   D. 300

28. Which one of the following statements concerning shop safety precautions would you select as being CORRECT?
   A. Starting a machine while it is being adjusted or repaired is a good practice.
   B. Guards may be removed by the operator to expedite the work.
   C. Gears, pulleys, and belts should be guarded to a height of 6 feet above the floor.
   D. Knowledge and care will not prevent most accidents.

29. The breaker point on a six lobe cam distributor are USUALLY brought and held together by means of a
   A. cam   B. spring   C. worm gear   D. timer

30. Pitted or burned distributor breaker points may BEST be refaced by using
   A. emery cloth   B. sandpaper
   C. an oil stone   D. a steel file

31. The piece of equipment commonly used on many gasoline engines that is composed of such parts as yokes, struts, release levers, pressure springs, and pilot bearing is MOST LIKELY a
   A. clutch   B. transmission
   C. torque converter   D. differential

32. Upon installing a reconditioned clutch in a gasoline engine that uses a clutch foot pedal, the proper adjustment to make on the clutch pedal *free play* on most cars is MOST NEARLY
   A. 2"   B. 1"   C. 0.25"   D. none

33. A gasoline engine cylinder that is worn and has been found to have a taper of .012" can BEST be reconditioned before being placed into operation again by
   A. replacing the oil ring backed with an expander
   B. replacing the original oil ring with a very active one
   C. reboring or honing the cylinder and using an oversized piston
   D. reboring or honing the cylinder and using an undersized piston

34. In the S.A.E. Standard Series of Screw Threads, a screw size 7/16"-20 would be classified as
   A. NC   B. NF   C. EF   D. NS

35. In the 90° V-type eight cylinder gasoline engine, the number of *throws* or *cranks* the crankshaft is USUALLY
    A. eight   B. six   C. four   D. two

36. Grinding and refinishing exhaust valves and seats on most gasoline engines should be done so that the seat angle (relative to the centerline passing through the valve guide is USUALLY
    A. 60°   B. 25°   C. 35°   D. 45°

37. An automotive gasoline engine is being completely reconditioned, including the fitting of the valve stem in its guide.
    In the absence of specific information from the manufacturer, the proper exhaust valve stem to guide clearance for MOST engines should be
    A. .003"   B. .010"   C. .018"   D. .030"

38. An instrument which can be used generally to measure inside and outside measurements without making any calculations to called a _____ caliper.
    A. Gear tooth   B. Vernier
    C. Telescoping   D. Micrometer

Questions 39-40.

DIRECTIONS: Questions 39 and 40 are based upon the following paragraph. Use only the information contained in this paragraph in answering these questions.

With the engine running at normal idling speed, and the engine hood open, attach the vacuum gauge to the intake manifold. The vacuum gauge should read about 18 to 21 inches, and the pointer should be steady. A needle fluctuating between 10 and 15 inches may indicate a defective cylinder-head, gasket, or valve. An extremely low reading indicates a leak in the intake manifold or gaskets. Accelerate the engine with full throttle momentarily. Notice if the gauge indicator fails to drop to approximately 2 inches as the throttle is opened, and recoil to at least 24 inches as the throttle is closed. If so, this may be an indication of diluted oil, poor piston ring sealing, or an abnormal restriction in the exhaust, carburetor, or air cleaner. The above readings apply to sea level. There will be approximately 1 inch drop for each 1,000 feet of altitude.

39. If a vacuum test is made on a properly operating engine at an altitude of 3,000 feet, the vacuum gauge should read MOST NEARLY
    A. 12"   B. 15"   C. 13"   D. 24"

40. If a vacuum test is made on an engine which has an abnormal restriction in the exhaust, this will be evidenced by
    A. a leak in the intake manifold
    B. the gauge indicator failing to drop to approximately 3 inches on opening the throttle
    C. the gauge fluctuating around 12 inches
    D. a steady high gauge reading

41. The PROPER thing to do in checking the fuel pump of a gasoline engine which will NOT start because of insufficient gas is to
    A. remove the pump from the engine in order to check
    B. disconnect the fuel line from the tank to the pump and run the pump
    C. disconnect the pump to the carburetor line and run the pump
    D. make sure that the external plugs over the pump valve are loosened before running the pump

42. It is a good policy to occasionally change the brake fluid in a hydraulic brake system.
    However, before refilling with fresh brake fluid, it is advisable to flush out the system with
    A. alcohol   B. kerosene   C. gasoline   D. a light oil

43. Battery hydrometers are calibrated to give the correct specific gravity readings of lead-acid storage batteries at a temperature of
    A. 70°F.   B. 80°F.   C. 32°F.   D. 60°F.

44. In a gasoline engine, if grease should leak into the cooling system by way of the water pump and, in addition, combustion gases should leak into the coolant, a test of the coolant will be found MOST LIKELY to be
    A. slightly alkaline
    B. slightly acid
    C. strongly alkaline
    D. free of foreign deposits

45. Reverse flushing of a clogged gasoline engine block and radiator cooling system is done PROPERLY by
    A. not removing the thermostat out of the engine block
    B. connecting the flushing gun at the bottom of the engine block
    C. using air and water
    D. using low pressure steam

46. In an automotive gasoline engine water cooling system, the water distributing tube is USUALLY found
    A. at the top of the radiator
    B. at the bottom of the radiator
    C. on top of the cylinder head
    D. in the engine block

47. When reference is made to the *compression ratio* of an automotive gasoline engine, this is BEST described to be the
    A. volume above the piston at top dead center
    B. displacement volume as the piston moves down to bottom dead center
    C. total volume of a cylinder divided by its clearance volume
    D. displacement volume of a cylinder divided by its clearance volume

48. When the piston of a gasoline engine is said to be in *rock* position, it is meant that the
    A. piston has reached rock bottom of its stroke
    B. crankshaft cannot move without causing the piston to move

C. crankshaft can move about 20° without causing the valves to open or close
D. crankshaft can move about 15° without causing the piston to move up or down

49. Regarding the automatic transmission which today is very popular with most automobile engines, the features that are found on MOST of the various transmission units are
    A. hydraulic controls
    B. full power automatic shifting planetaries
    C. double pinion planetary full torque shifts
    D. split torque fluid drives

49.____

50. An air leak between the intake manifold and the engine block can BEST be checked by
    A. applying a soapy solution to each joint on the block
    B. applying a little gasoline at each manifold and block joint
    C. using a heavy oil at each joint in the block
    D. listening for the sucking sound of air entering the joint

50.____

KEY (CORRECT ANSWERS)

1. A	11. D	21. D	31. A	41. C
2. B	12. D	22. A	32. B	42. A
3. B	13. D	23. D	33. C	43. B
4. C	14. C	24. C	34. B	44. B
5. A	15. A	25. A	35. C	45. C
6. A	16. A	26. B	36. D	46. D
7. C	17. D	27. A	37. A	47. C
8. C	18. C	28. C	38. B	48. D
9. A	19. A	29. B	39. B	49. A
10. A	20. A	30. C	40. B	50. B

TEST 2

DIRECTIONS: Each question or incomplete statement is followed by several suggested answers or completions. Select the one that BEST answers the question or completes the statement. *PRINT THE LETTER OF THE CORRECT ANSWER IN THE SPACE AT THE RIGHT.*

1. The LEAST likely reason for a shunt generator to lose most of its residual magnetism is due to
   A. alternating current fed to the field winding
   B. too much vibration of generator
   C. excessive operating temperature
   D. the generator delivering too much current

   1._____

2. In today's modern high compression engines, hard starting, rough running, and poor gas economy are LEAST likely to be due to the electrical system having
   A. high resistor plugs   B. cracked distributor cap
   C. worn insulation   D. fouled plugs

   2._____

3. The method that is NOT used for detecting cracks that may exist in a gasoline engine block or head is by
   A. dye penetrants   B. pressure testing
   C. the sheradizing method   D. the magnetic method

   3._____

4. Before making any front wheel alignment checks on a car, such as toe-in and camber, it is ADVISABLE to
   A. first make sure that the vehicle has no load in it
   B. jack up the front wheels so that they are free to turn
   C. inflate the tire to recommended pressure
   D. first check the wheel brakes

   4._____

5. When replacing a new cylinder head gasket on a gasoline engine, it is good practice to tighten the cylinder head nuts with a torque wrench to a gauge reading, in foot pounds, of MOST NEARLY
   a. 60   B. 40   C. 90   D. 25

   5._____

6. Assume that a carburetor has been reconditioned and the mechanic replaced the metering rod with one of a larger diameter than the original one.
   On operating the carburetor, it is MOST LIKELY that
   A. at idling, the engine would run at a higher speed
   B. the engine will receive a leaner mixture
   C. the carburetor would easily flood
   D. there will be very little noticeable difference in engine operation

   6._____

7. A mechanic, running a test on a gasoline engine, has noted on the job sheet that the cam angle is 32 degrees.
   From this information, it is evident that the mechanic is running a test on the
   A. camshaft   B. ignition system
   C. front wheel   D. valve timing

   7._____

8. An idler gear that is often found in a sliding gear transmission is used MAINLY
   A. when more power is desired
   B. when engine is idling and car is not in motion
   C. to reverse the direction of rotation
   D. to obtain a reduced gear speed

9. Assume that a compression test is made of a six-cylinder gasoline engine having a compression ratio of 6.5 to 1. A reading of 95 lbs. was obtained for cylinders #1, #2, #4, and #6, 52 lbs. for cylinder #3, and 71 lbs. for cylinder #5. Upon squirting engine oil into the cylinder and rechecking pressures again, it was found that cylinder #5 read 93 lbs., and cylinder #3 read 52 lbs.
   From the above results, it is MOST probable that the
   A. exhaust valve on cylinder #5 does not seat properly
   B. cylinder #5 piston rings or cylinder are worn
   C. cylinder #5 piston rings are worn
   D. oil leaks past the cylinder #5 valve guides

10. In operating a gasoline engine using a manual gear shift, if it becomes difficult to shift, especially into low gear, the trouble is MOST LIKELY due to the
    A. clutch plate not burning
    B. clutch shaft spines tapering toward the end
    C. clutch facing being too dry
    D. clearance between the pressure plate and the flywheel being too great

11. In reference to the internal combustion engine, the term *mechanical efficiency* is frequently used.
    The meaning of this term is BEST defined as the
    A. thermal efficiency divided by the volumetric efficiency
    B. thermal efficiency multiplied by the volumetric efficiency
    C. indicated horsepower divided by the brake horsepower
    D. brake horsepower divided by the indicated horsepower

12. In calculating the *indicated* horsepower of a gasoline engine by means of a formula, the item that is NOT considered in the calculations is USUALLY the
    A. number of power strokes per cycle
    B. pressure exerted on the piston during the power stroke
    C. diameter of the piston
    D. length of the piston

13. The type of gear drive that will operate MORE quietly under similar conditions in a differential unit is one consisting of a _____ gear.
    A. worm and
    B. drive pinion and spur bevel
    C. drive pinion and hypoid
    D. drive pinion and spiral-bevel

14. The differential of many trucks is very often made up of a worm and gear drive. In reference to this type of drive, which one of the following statements is TRUE?
    A. The worm is usually made of bronze and the worm gear of steel
    B. The rear worm bearing need not be very rugged since it takes very little thrust.

C. This type of drive allows a large speed reduction.
D. This type of drive is not recommended because the worm must be mounted on top of the worm gear.

15. It is common practice today for some manufacturers to make the outside surface of aluminum alloy pistons highly resistant to wear by
    A. spheroidizing
    B. case hardening
    C. anodizing
    D. annealing

16. The ease with which the front wheels of a car return to the straight-ahead position after having completed a turn is due to the
    A. toe-in
    B. side thrust
    C. camber
    D. caster

17. If you should be driving a truck downhill on a slippery road and the rear end of the truck begins to skid to the right, it would be BEST for you to
    A. apply the brakes slowly and disengage the clutch
    B. let up on the gas pedal slowly and turn the wheels to the right
    C. turn the wheels to the right and disengage the clutch
    D. apply the brakes hard and turn the wheels to the left

18. If a *no load test* is made on the electric starting motor used on most passenger cars today, it will be found that the number of amperes the motor would draw, at its rated speed, is MOST NEARLY
    A. 70
    B. 105
    C. 210
    D. 20

19. By the correct valve timing of a gasoline engine is meant the proper opening and closing of valves with reference to the
    A. carburetor mixing jets
    B. distributor setting
    C. position of piston
    D. cylinder compression ratio

20. The *primary* ignition circuit of an automotive gasoline engine is composed of the battery,
    A. starting motor, generator, ignition coil, spark plugs
    B. ammeter, ignition coil, ignition switch, distributor rotor
    C. ammeter, ignition switch, ignition coil, secondary winding
    D. ammeter, ignition switch, coil primary winding, breaker points

21. To increase the ampere-hour capacity of a lead-acid storage battery, it is necessary to increase the
    A. number of cells
    B. amount of the electrolyte
    C. number of plates per cell
    D. voltage of the cells

22. Intake and exhaust manifolds, used on the present day gasoline engine, are designed and built so that their walls come in contact with each other in order to
    A. prevent condensation of fuel vapor
    B. save space
    C. get better valve action
    D. reduce vaporization

23. By referring to the *torque* of a gasoline engine crankshaft is meant the
    A. ratio of crankshaft to rear axle
    B. horsepower developed at axles
    C. turning moment of the crankshaft
    D. permissible bend of flexibility in the crankshaft

24. Upon making a running test of the braking system of a car, it was found that the brake drum on one of the wheels ran abnormally cool.
    From this result, the auto mechanic will find that this is MOST LIKELY due to
    A. worn brake lining
    B. a broken return spring
    C. the brake drum surface worn too smooth
    D. an inoperative brake

25. The factor that has no relation upon the determination of proper wheel alignment is
    A. pivot inclination   B. toe-out
    C. caster   D. drop-center rim

26. If a gasoline engine is continued in operation with the contact points of a reverse current relay or *cut-out* being fused together, the result would MOST LIKELY be to
    A. *run down* the battery
    B. reverse the current through the voltage coils
    C. demagnetize the relay iron core
    D. overcharge the battery

27. Starting motors that mesh directly with the flywheel gears and are used on most modern cars today are designed to give an engine cranking speed, in RMP, of MOST NEARLY
    A. 150   B. 250   C. 350   D. 400

28. The type of electric starting motor used on most cars today, because of its high starting torque, is USUALLY the _____ type.
    A. shunt wound   B. series wound
    C. compound wound   D. capacitor

29. If an engine, while running, has a noticeable piston slap, it is LIKELY that this is caused by
    A. worn cylinder walls
    B. excessively advanced ignition timing
    C. worn main bearings
    D. worn end-thrust bearings

30. Vapor-lock in a gasoline engine is MOST LIKELY due to
    A. an over-rich gas-air mixture
    B. fuel forming bubbles in the gas line
    C. a tear in the fuel pump diaphragm
    D. the carburetor being clogged with dirt

31. In starting on a cold day, the choke is pulled out.
    The PRIMARY reason for this is that it
    A. allows more fuel to enter the carburetor enriching the mixture
    B. increases the amount of air in the carburetor
    C. reduces the amount of fuel entering the carburetor
    D. speeds up the supply of air and fuel to the motor

31._____

32. When driving at night toward another car, the CORRECT procedure as to lights is to put on
    A. your high beams
    B. your low beams
    C. whatever lights the other driver uses
    D. your parking lights

32._____

33. The liquid in a battery in good condition is
    A. an acid solution   B. a caustic solution
    C. a salt water solution   D. water only

33._____

34. The ammeter of an automobile indicates the flow of electric current
    A. from the battery to the starting motor
    B. outside of the starting circuit
    C. to the lights
    D. to and from the storage battery

34._____

35. Manifolds are used to conduct
    A. gases out of an engine only   B. gases into an engine only
    C. gases into or out of an engine D. heat into the piston

35._____

36. Of the following, the one NOT concerned with transmitting the driving power from the engine to the driving wheels is the
    A. clutch   B. drive shaft   C. flywheel   D. front axle

36._____

37. To prevent short circuits in the electrical system of a car, we use
    A. a layer of rust   B. insulation   C. oil   D. water

37._____

38. An alert auto mechanic knows that if the center tread of the tires of a car show little wear while the outer edges show considerable wear, it is a sign of driving
    A. on over-inflated tires   B. on properly inflated tires
    C. on under-inflated tires   D. too fast for proper braking

38._____

39. The working parts of an engine are lubricated by
    A. grease in the transmission   B. oil in the transmission
    C. oil from the carburetor   D. oil in the crankcase

39._____

40. The water in the cooling system of a car should be
    A. acid   B. alkaline   C. neutral   D. salty

40._____

41. Of the following, the type of service that a mechanic should be personally concerned with is
    A. adjustment of small parts such as spark plugs
    B. daily inspection of vehicles for gas, oil, and water
    C. general overhauls of large unit assemblies
    D. replacement of unit assemblies such as fuel pumps

42. The part of a car which allows one wheel to go faster than the other in going around a corner is the
    A. brake
    B. differential
    C. slip joint
    D. universal joint

43. If the temperature gauge indicates the engine is getting overheated,
    A. allow it to cool down
    B. pour cold water in immediately
    C. pour hot water in immediately
    D. pour in a cooling antifreeze at one

44. The clutch pedal is being used properly when you
    A. press it down in order to change gears
    B. push it down to the floor going down hill
    C. rest your left foot on it
    D. use it only for emergencies

45. The part of an engine in which the gasoline and air burns is the
    A. camshaft   B. carburetor   C. cylinder   D. piston

46. The part of an engine which mixes the gasoline with the air is the
    A. camshaft   B. carburetor   C. cylinder   D. piston

47. The function of a generator in a car is to supply the
    A. ignition system with current
    B. lights with current
    C. battery with current to recharge t
    D. starting motor with current

48. The accelerator pedal is used for controlling the
    A. carburetor throttle
    B. ignition system
    C. oil pressure
    D. spark plug

49. Alcohol is put into the radiator of an automobile in cold weather because it _____ the _____ point of the mixture.
    A. lowers; boiling
    B. lowers; freezing
    C. raises; boiling
    D. raises; freezing

50. A good rule to follow when driving in winter when roads may be icy is to   50.____
    A. be prepared to come to a quick stop when the car starts to skid
    B. be sure of your brakes so you can come down hard on them
    C. keep your speed down and turn the wheels in the direction of any skid that may occur
    D. put the car in neutral and gently pat the brakes into position

---

KEY (CORRECT ANSWERS)

1.	D	11.	D	21.	C	31.	A	41.	B
2.	A	12.	D	22.	A	32.	B	42.	B
3.	C	13.	C	23.	C	33.	A	43.	A
4.	C	14.	C	24.	D	34.	D	44.	A
5.	A	15.	C	25.	D	35.	C	45.	C
6.	B	16.	D	26.	D	36.	D	46.	B
7.	B	17.	B	27.	A	37.	B	47.	C
8.	C	18.	A	28.	B	38.	C	48.	A
9.	C	19.	C	29.	A	39.	D	49.	B
10.	B	20.	D	30.	B	40.	C	50.	C

TEST 3

DIRECTIONS: Each question or incomplete statement is followed by several suggested answers or completions. Select the one that BEST answers the question or completes the statement. *PRINT THE LETTER OF THE CORRECT ANSWER IN THE SPACE AT THE RIGHT.*

1. A sudden falling back of about 5 points on a vacuum gauge with the engine running under 15 m.p.h. indicates
   A. a leaky manifold gasket
   B. loose or worn valve guides
   C. points are pitted
   D. a burned valve in one cylinder

   1.____

2. When the vacuum gauge needle drifts regularly between 5 and 19, it means that
   A. the carburetor is poorly adjusted
   B. there is a compression leak between cylinders
   C. the exhaust system is clogged
   D. the ignition advance is incorrect

   2.____

3. A bent steering arm will affect
   A. caster
   B. toe-out
   C. camber
   D. king pin inclination

   3.____

4. When the accelerator is depressed quickly, the
   A. vacuum in the intake manifold increases
   B. vacuum in the intake manifold remains the same
   C. pressure in the float chamber increases
   D. pressure in the intake manifold increases

   4.____

5. When an air cleaner has collected an excessive amount of road dust, the
   A. mixture becomes leaner
   B. compression pressure is increased
   C. volumetric efficiency increases
   D. mixture becomes richer

   5.____

6. The full weight of the rear of a vehicle is carried by the axle shaft of a
   A. semi-floating axle
   B. full floating axle
   C. three-quarter floating axle
   D. jack shaft

   6.____

7. Certain engines are designed with the spark plug port over the exhaust valve because
   A. this keeps spark plugs at proper temperature
   B. this design reduces detonation
   C. spark plugs last longer
   D. this prevents loss of power

   7.____

8. The MAIN advantage of valve seat inserts is to
   A. reduce wear on the valve face
   B. reduce frequency of valve grinding
   C. keep clearance on valve more nearly constant
   D. increase the life of the valves

   8.____

9. The harmonic balancer on a crankshaft is used
   A. as a flywheel
   B. to neutralize torsional crankshaft vibration
   C. to offset the weight of the flywheel
   D. to offset the weight of the connecting rods

   9.____

10. Sealed clutch release bearings require
    A. cup grease
    B. spicer grease
    C. engine oil
    D. no grease

    10.____

11. The pressure which forces the gas from the fuel pump to the carburetor is produced by
    A. the expanding action of the diaphragm spring
    B. the upstroke of the pump arm
    C. the vacuum created in the pump
    D. decreased pressure in the fuel bowl

    11.____

12. A low reading on the oil gauge is a PROBABLE indication of
    A. high engine temperature
    B. bearings too tight
    C. oil dilution
    D. too heavy a grade of oil

    12.____

13. Pressure plate springs are checked for
    A. number of coils
    B. thickness of coils
    C. weight
    D. height and pressure

    13.____

14. Of the following, the CHIEF advantage of *over-drive* in modern transmissions is that it
    A. allows the engine to run slower at high car speeds
    B. allows the car to coast on hills
    C. requires less shifting
    D. provides greater power at high speeds

    14.____

15. The oil circuit through a gear type oil pump is
    A. between the gear teeth
    B. over the gear teeth
    C. under the gear teeth
    D. between the gear teeth and pump housing

    15.____

16. Good compression in an engine depends upon
    A. ignition timing
    B. carburetor adjustment
    C. type of gasoline used
    D. condition of rings and valves

    16.____

17. The differential pinion gear meshes with the ring gear below the horizontal center line of the ring gear on a _____ gear.
    A. spiral bevel
    B. hypoid
    C. spur
    D. straight bevel

    17.____

18. Heavy flank contact on teeth between drive pinion gear and ring gear will result in
    A. excessive play between gear teeth
    B. noisy gear operation
    C. broken drive pinion bearings
    D. excessive end play in differential case bearings

    18.____

19. Back firing in the carburetor is caused by
    A. too rich a mixture
    B. excess oil in combustion chamber
    C. faulty fuel pump
    D. too lean a mixture

    19.____

20. A worn metering pin will cause
    A. fast idle speed
    B. rich mixture under load
    C. leaner mixture under load
    D. engine stalling

    20.____

21. Broken gear teeth on differential side gears will cause a
    A. squeak when the car is traveling in a straight ahead direction
    B. broken axle
    C. knock in rear end when car is making a turn
    D. loss of power

    21.____

22. Excessive accumulation of soft carbon deposit on intake valve stems and under intake valve head is an indication that the
    A. intake valve guides are worn
    B. carburetor is set too rich
    C. gasoline is stale
    D. spark is weak, causing poor compression

    22.____

23. The MOST popular type of clutch used today in modern vehicle is the _____ clutch.
    A. wet
    B. 3-plate
    C. multiple-disc
    D. single plate

    23.____

24. When a Timken bearing is used in a transmission, it is readily identified by
    A. its tapered rollers
    B. the concave races
    C. the barrel-shaped rollers
    D. an exclusive retainer design

    24.____

25. The MOST common type of cooling system in use today is
    A. pump or pressure
    B. splash and gravity
    C. radiator and fan
    D. thermosyphon

    25.____

26. Scoring of pistons and cylinder walls is caused by
    A. pistons fitting too loose
    B. infrequent oil changes
    C. high piston temperatures
    D. insufficient piston clearances

    26.____

27. Regardless of the number of cylinders, the distributor of the magneto MUST always be driven at _____ speed.
    A. engine
    B. one-half engine
    C. twice engine
    D. constant

    27.____

28. The capacity of a battery is determined by the
    A. rate at which a battery can be charged
    B. quantity of electrolyte the case can hold
    C. rate at which it can be discharged
    D. voltage of the battery

29. While driving along the road, all lights suddenly flare up and burn out because
    A. a fuse blew out
    B. a short circuit occurred in a lighting wire
    C. a wire became loose on the ground switch
    D. the battery cable broke off

30. A solenoid is often used to operate the
    A. generator   B. starter   C. battery   D. ignition

31. In a storage battery, the H_2SO_4 after reacting with the active material in the plates forms H_2O^4 in the electrolyte when
    A. a battery is discharging   B. it is being charged
    C. it is gassing   D. it is sulphated

32. Voltage and current regulators prevent
    A. overload of starter   B. static in radio
    C. spark plug failure   D. overcharging of battery

33. Batteries not in service will become discharged because of
    A. drop in specific gravity   B. open circuit
    C. lack of agitation   D. local action

34. Throwing of solder from generator commutator is caused USUALLY by
    A. poor insulation   B. overload
    C. underload   D. high tension current

35. A low generator output with a fully charged battery indicates
    A. worn or pitted vibrator points
    B. eroded battery terminals
    C. correct generator control
    D. the vibrator armature spring is too weak

36. Generator output control or regulation is based on controlling the
    A. armature magnetism   B. field current
    C. third brush   D. polarity

37. When an armature is revolved between the pole pieces of a growler, a heavy vibration is caused by a _____ voltage current induced in a(n) _____ coil.
    A. low; open   B. high; open
    C. high; short-circuited   D. low; short-circuited

38. In shunt wound generators, full control of the generator output is obtained through the use of
    A. third brush
    B. current regulator
    C. voltage regulator
    D. current and voltage regulator

39. The function of the cut-out relay in the battery generator circuit is to
    A. regulate the generator voltage
    B. regulate the generator amperage
    C. prevent the loss of battery current
    D. prevent the battery from being overcharged

40. A cracked distributor cap usually would cause misfiring because of
    A. poor contact
    B. short circuit
    C. high resistance
    D. overloading

41. In a sealed beam headlight, the
    A. lamp is sealed in the car fender
    B. light rays are sealed within the lamp
    C. lens and reflector are sealed together
    D. light beam is sealed in one direction on the road

42. The capacity of a storage battery is determined by the
    A. number of cells
    B. composition of the case
    C. number of plates
    D. shape of the battery

43. Armature *neutral point* is obtained by
    A. adjusting position of brushes
    B. neutralizing residual magnetism
    C. aligning the ignition contacts
    D. unmeshing the starter pinion gear

44. Cam angle is increased by
    A. increasing the point gap
    B. decreasing the point gap
    C. centrifugal advance
    D. greater advance

45. A shorted armature coil
    A. must be shellacked
    B. may be corrected by undercutting the commutator
    C. must have commutator refaced
    D. must be baked

46. A steady miss at all speeds is USUALLY caused by
    A. clogged low speed jet
    B. low float level
    C. defective spark plug
    D. poor condenser

47. When testing an armature, if the sawblade vibrates, it indicates that the armature is
    A. grounded
    B. correct
    C. short-circuited
    D. open-circuited

48. If an electric gasoline gauge registers full at all times, trouble is in the
    A. wire to the tank
    B. line to the switch
    C. gasoline line
    D. battery terminal

49. The Dyer Starter Drive
    A. is an over-running clutch drive
    B. works like the Bendix Drive
    C. rotates the starter pinion while it is moved towards the flywheel
    D. has a special gear reduction

50. The MOST accurate method used to time the ignition of an engine is by
    A. locating the piston position with a wire
    B. use of neon timing light
    C. watching for contact point opening
    D. watching valve position

KEY (CORRECT ANSWERS)

1. D	11. A	21. C	31. A	41. C
2. B	12. C	22. A	32. D	42. C
3. B	13. D	23. D	33. D	43. A
4. D	14. A	24. A	34. B	44. B
5. D	15. D	25. A	35. C	45. B
6. A	16. D	26. D	36. B	46. C
7. B	17. B	27. B	37. C	47. C
8. B	18. B	28. C	38. D	48. A
9. B	19. D	29. D	39. C	49. C
10. D	20. B	30. B	40. B	50. B

EXAMINATION SECTION
TEST 1

DIRECTIONS: Each question or incomplete statement is followed by several suggested answers or completions. Select the one that BEST answers the question or completes the statement. *PRINT THE LETTER OF THE CORRECT ANSWER IN THE SPACE AT THE RIGHT.*

1. The vibration damper on an auto engine is fastened to the

   A. camshaft
   B. flywheel
   C. crankshaft
   D. driveshaft

    1.____

2. MOST small gas engines use a(n) _____ ignition system.

   A. magneto
   B. transistorized
   C. battery
   D. induction

    2.____

3. Carburetor icing occurs MOST often

   A. on humid, hot days
   B. when an engine is overheated
   C. on cool, damp days
   D. when an engine is run for long periods at idle speed

    3.____

4. The function of the float in a carburetor is to

   A. close the needle valve
   B. control flow of gas into pump circuit
   C. operate choke circuit when engine is cold
   D. bleed off gasoline from primary tubes

    4.____

5. To improve stability when cornering, manufacturers add a device to cars called a

   A. control arm
   B. stabilizer bar
   C. constant velocity joint
   D. Pitman arm

    5.____

6. Adjustment of the tie rods on a car will affect

   A. camber
   B. king pin inclination
   C. caster
   D. toe-in

    6.____

7. A restriction in the exhaust system is indicated on a vacuum gauge by a

   A. steady needle
   B. low reading
   C. gradual decrease in reading
   D. fast fluctuating needle

    7.____

8. Disc brakes on a car have a distinct advantage over conventional drum brakes in that they

   A. fade less when hot
   B. are cheaper to manufacture
   C. are easier to service
   D. require less pedal pressure to apply

    8.____

9. In a diesel engine, the fuel is ignited by the

   A. spark plug B. injector plug
   C. heat of compression D. magneto

10. Engine timing is GENERALLY set by using a

    A. torque wrench B. dividing head
    C. strobe light D. centrifugal mechanism

11. If an engine is operated for long periods of time at part throttle opening, the

    A. spark plugs will become covered with carbon
    B. carburetor will become clogged
    C. fuel filter will accumulate more water
    D. points will blacken

12. Leaking intake valve guides will cause

    A. excessive oil consumption
    B. overheating
    C. valves to act sluggishly
    D. valve seats to burn

13. Flooding of a carburetor is GENERALLY caused by

    A. loose bolts holding carburetor to manifold
    B. air leaks in float bowl
    C. loose jets in carburetor body
    D. stuck float needle valve

14. On many cars, the fuel pump is combined with the

    A. vacuum pump B. power steering pump
    C. generator D. power brake booster

15. Carbon fouling of a spark plug is an indication of

    A. excessive oil burning B. too rich a mixture
    C. poor grade of gasoline D. plug misfiring

16. If tests show that generator output is excessive even after the F terminal has been disconnected, the trouble may be traced to

    A. the regulator B. the generator
    C. poor ground D. discharged battery

17. An automobile alternator converts alternating current to direct current by means of

    A. silicon diodes B. a current regulator
    C. a solenoid coil D. a magnetic shunt circuit

18. Hard starting is very often caused by

    A. a faulty condenser B. poor grade of gasoline
    C. improper grade of oil D. improper choke operation

19. A car with a history of *burned-points* would PROBABLY indicate 19._____
    A. improper gap setting
    B. improper condenser
    C. too high a setting of the voltage regulator
    D. incorrect dwell angle

20. When it is necessary to recondition brake drums, the MAXIMUM allowable amount of oversize is _____ inches. 20._____
    A. .025   B. .030   C. .040   D. .060

KEY (CORRECT ANSWERS)

1.	C	11.	A
2.	A	12.	A
3.	C	13.	D
4.	A	14.	A
5.	B	15.	B
6.	D	16.	B
7.	C	17.	A
8.	A	18.	D
9.	C	19.	C
10.	C	20.	D

TEST 2

DIRECTIONS: Each question or incomplete statement is followed by several suggested answers or completions. Select the one that BEST answers the question or completes the statement. *PRINT THE LETTER OF THE CORRECT ANSWER IN THE SPACE AT THE RIGHT.*

1. The amount of air-fuel mixture taken into the cylinder on the intake stroke is a measure of the engine's

    A. thermal efficiency
    B. volumetric efficiency
    C. rated horsepower
    D. mechanical efficiency

2. Welch plugs are installed on engines to provide

    A. a means of removing the sand after the engine is cast
    B. inspection of the water jackets
    C. a means of cleaning the cooling system more effectively
    D. a means of draining the cooling system more quickly

3. The two-cycle engine produces a power stroke with every _____ of the crankshaft.

    A. one-half revolution
    B. revolution
    C. two revolutions
    D. four revolutions

4. Pre-ignition may be caused by

    A. carbon deposits
    B. a stuck valve
    C. an inoperative choke
    D. a broken ignition wire

5. The size of an outboard motor propeller is ALWAYS given in

    A. degrees of thrust
    B. diameter and pitch
    C. circumference and number of blades
    D. diametral pitch

6. Closed crankcase ventilation systems are used to

    A. get more power out of the engine
    B. reduce oil consumption
    C. increase the efficiency of the engine
    D. aid in prevention of air contamination

7. The angular motion about the vertical axis of an aircraft or space craft is known as

    A. yaw   B. pitch   C. roll   D. bank

8. The carburetor circuit that maintains a constant level of fuel in the float bowl is the _____ circuit.

    A. fuel
    B. accelerating pump
    C. float
    D. choke

9. A jet engine combustion chamber liner is cooled by

    A. liquid coolants
    B. air streams
    C. heat exchangers
    D. convectors

10. Regenerative gas turbine engines have been successfully developed for use on   10._____

   A. automobiles   B. motorcycles
   C. helicopters   D. tractors

11. Power impulses from the engine are *smoothed out* by the   11._____

   A. camshaft   B. clutch
   C. crankshaft   D. flywheel

12. The service ratings M S, S E, and S G refers to   12._____

   A. automotive fuels   B. automotive sealers
   C. motor oils   D. automotive greases

13. The intake and exhaust openings on a two-stroke cycle engine are known as   13._____

   A. vents   B. manifolds   C. scoops   D. ports

14. Ball-joint type front suspension eliminates   14._____

   A. the conventional kingpin
   B. the need for front-end alignment
   C. caster and camber adjustments
   D. the need for the usual tie-rods

15. Gasoline CANNOT be used in a diesel because the   15._____

   A. viscosity of gasoline is too low
   B. gasoline would start to burn long before the piston reached the top of the stroke
   C. injectors could not force gasoline into the cylinders
   D. injection pumps would *seize up* due to lack of lubrication

16. On the compression stroke, the diesel engine compresses   16._____

   A. air   B. air fuel mixture
   C. diesel fuel   D. heated engine oil

17. The idle and low speed circuit in a carburetor is inoperative   17._____

   A. at speeds under 20 mph
   B. at speeds over 20 mph
   C. when the choke is closed
   D. when the choke is open

18. A generator should be polarized to prevent damage whenever   18._____

   A. an adjustment is made to the regulator
   B. a low charging condition exists
   C. a high charging condition exists
   D. the generator or regulator wires have been disconnected

19. Turbo-prop engines are more efficient than turbo-jet engines for aircraft flying   19._____

   A. short trips   B. long trips
   C. over 500 mph   D. at high altitudes

20. A blower or pump which forces air into cylinders at higher than atmospheric pressures is known as a   20._____

    A. dynamometer   B. tachometer
    C. supercharger   D. stroboscope

KEY (CORRECT ANSWERS)

1.	B	11.	D
2.	A	12.	C
3.	B	13.	D
4.	A	14.	A
5.	B	15.	B
6.	D	16.	A
7.	A	17.	B
8.	C	18.	D
9.	B	19.	A
10.	A	20.	C

TEST 3

DIRECTIONS: Each question or incomplete statement is followed by several suggested answers or completions. Select the one that BEST answers the question or completes the statement. *PRINT THE LETTER OF THE CORRECT ANSWER IN THE SPACE AT THE RIGHT.*

1. The fuel pump is actuated by the   1.____
   - A. camshaft
   - B. crankshaft
   - C. fan belt
   - D. engine vacuum

2. A storage battery becomes sulfated when the   2.____
   - A. battery is charged
   - B. battery is discharged
   - C. acid content in the electrolyte is high
   - D. battery is overcharged

3. The MOST common cause for excess tire wear on edges is   3.____
   - A. poor braking habits
   - B. overinflation
   - C. underinflation
   - D. excessive speed

4. The CORRECT order of piston rings above the piston pin is   4.____
   - A. compression - oil - compression - oil
   - B. oil - oil - compression - compression
   - C. oil - compression - oil - compression
   - D. compression - compression - oil - oil

5. The voltage in the secondary of the ignition coil may reach _____ volts.   5.____
   - A. 5000
   - B. 10,000
   - C. 20,000
   - D. 30,000

6. Burnt ignition points are GENERALLY the result of   6.____
   - A. faulty condenser
   - B. points open too far
   - C. reverse battery polarity
   - D. defective ignition coil

7. The MOST reliable method of testing a storage battery is by using a   7.____
   - A. 6-volt test lamp
   - B. voltmeter
   - C. hydrometer
   - D. high rate discharge cell tester

8. In a normal operating engine, the vacuum gauge will read   8.____
   - A.
   - B. 8-11
   - C. B,
   - D. 17-21
   - E.

9. All of the following have moving parts EXCEPT the _____ jet engine.   9.____
   - A. pulse
   - B. turbo-
   - C. ram
   - D. astro-

79

10. The speed necessary to escape the gravitational pull of the earth is _____ miles per hour.

    A. 8,000   B. 40,000   C. 16,000   D. 25,000

11. The rocket designed to carry a man into space is the

    A. Titan   B. Jupiter   C. Saturn   D. Thor

12. Of the following statements about the flywheel, the one that is NOT true is: It is

    A. joined to the camshaft
    B. joined with the clutch driver plate
    C. a storer of energy
    D. joined with the crankshaft

13. A radiator fan is MOST essential

    A. in warm weather   B. at low speeds
    C. at high speeds   D. when idling

14. Rockets differ MAINLY from jet engines in that they

    A. are more powerful
    B. carry their own oxygen with them
    C. rely on gases thrusting out of the rear of the engine
    D. are heavier

15. For MAXIMUM power, the spark plug is timed to fire when the piston reaches

    A. top dead center   B. after top dead center
    C. before top dead center   D. a neutral position

16. Engine timing may be set MOST accurately with a

    A. dwell meter   B. vacuum gauge
    C. neon timing light   D. multimeter

17. The color around the electrodes of spark plugs which indicates normal wear is

    A. black   B. white to yellow
    C. brown   D. blue

18. On some late models of distributors, the cam angle is set with

    A. the cap left on
    B. the cap taken off
    C. a rotation of the rotor
    D. the removal of the distributor to a test bench

19. A soft brake is GENERALLY the result of

    A. grease on the brake lining
    B. air in the lines
    C. insufficient fluid
    D. poor brake adjustment

20. Toe-in is controlled by adjusting the

    A. tie rod
    B. spindle downward
    C. king pin angle
    D. steering knuckle

KEY (CORRECT ANSWERS)

1.	A	11.	C
2.	B	12.	A
3.	C	13.	D
4.	B	14.	B
5.	C	15.	C
6.	A	16.	A
7.	D	17.	B
8.	B	18.	A
9.	C	19.	B
10.	D	20.	A

TEST 4

DIRECTIONS: Each question or incomplete statement is followed by several suggested answers or completions. Select the one that BEST answers the question or completes the statement. *PRINT THE LETTER OF THE CORRECT ANSWER IN THE SPACE AT THE RIGHT.*

1. The MAIN reason car manufacturers use a pressurized cooling system is that it   1._____

    A. simplifies the cooling system
    B. permits any type of anti-freeze to be used
    C. permits the engine to run at high temperatures without evaporation of the coolant
    D. permits less maintenance

2. Testing an outboard motor in a test barrel requires   2._____

    A. reduced speed
    B. a test wheel
    C. an external fuel supply
    D. a constant source of cool water

3. On two-cycle engines, oil changes are NOT necessary because   3._____

    A. the sealed bearings they are equipped With require no lubrication
    B. the oil is generally mixed with the fuel
    C. the non-leaded gas which they require has lubricating qualities of its own
    D. modern detergent oils retain their lubricating qualities indefinitely .

4. The governor that many small one-cylinder gasoline engines use to maintain a constant speed under varying loads is *generally* connected to the   4._____

    A. throttle   B. flywheel
    C. choke   D. intake valve or reed

5. Fuel is supplied to the carburetor on power lawn mowers by means of   5._____

    A. a fuel pump   B. vacuum
    C. intake reeds   D. gravity

6. Some jet engines are equipped with an afterburner; the purpose of this device is to   6._____

    A. provide extra power in emergencies
    B. reduce air pollution
    C. reduce the speed of the turbine itself
    D. reduce the overall size of the engine

7. Magneto Armature Air Gap refers to the space between the   7._____

    A. points and the magneto
    B. magneto coil and its armature
    C. points
    D. rotating flywheel and the coil-armature pole shoes

8. In a magneto ignition system, the primary current is supplied by means of

   A. a 6-volt battery supply
   B. a 1 1/2-volts battery supply
   C. a primary coil and a permanent magnet
   D. any D.C. source

9. In a standard hydraulic brake system, the brake pedal leverage is in the ratio of

   A. 10 to 1   B. 8 to 1   C. 5 to 1   D. 1 to 1

10. A quick test to determine the condition of a storage battery is to

    A. use a cadmium test
    B. inspect the level of the electrolyte
    C. observe its charging rate in the car
    D. use a high discharge tester

11. Cavitation is a condition which causes

    A. air to enter the cooling system
    B. a boat propeller to lose its *grip* on the water
    C. bubbles to form around a boat hull, thus preventing ice from forming
    D. spark plug fouling

12. If, during a tune-up, a vacuum gauge reading shows a slowly floating needle over a range of 4 or 5 points, it is an indication of

    A. a defective heat value
    B. a normal operating condition
    C. a faulty carburetor adjustment
    D. leaking cylinder rings

13. Dwell angle is an IMPORTANT factor to consider during a tune-up because it refers to

    A. degrees of rotation of the distributor cam during which the points remain open
    B. degrees of rotation of the distributor cam during which time the points remain closed
    C. the gap between the points
    D. the angle formed by the cam and the points

14. Pistons are cam-ground so as to produce

    A. a perfectly symmetrical cylinder
    B. a smooth surface
    C. pistons whose diameter is less at the pin bosses
    D. pistons whose diameter is greater at the pin bosses

15. Advertised horsepower ratings of automotive engines are almost always assumed to be *indicated horsepower*.
    These ratings are obtained by

    A. adding the brake horsepower to the friction horsepower
    B. using the SAE horsepower formula
    C. using a brake test
    D. formula only

16. During a tune-up, an electrical tachometer should be hooked up as follows: one lead to the ground, the other lead to the

    A. distributor side of the coil
    B. engine side of the coil
    C. number one spark plug
    D. ignition switch

17. When testing diodes from an alternator with a diode tester, a reading of two amperes *generally* indicates a(n) _____ diode.

    A. faulty   B. good   C. open   D. shorted

18. One of the MAIN disadvantages of the PCV system is that it causes

    A. corrosion on the precisely fitted engine parts
    B. excessive gasoline consumption
    C. some degree of engine overheating
    D. increased oil consumption

19. The average operating pressure of a conventional mechanical-type fuel pump is _____ pounds.

    A. 5   B. 8   C. 10   D. 12

20. Casing-head gasoline is an extremely volatile liquid obtained from

    A. low grade petroleum
    C. selective cracking
    B. natural gas
    D. Pennsylvania crude oil

KEY (CORRECT ANSWERS)

1.	C	11.	B
2.	B	12.	C
3.	B	13.	B
4.	A	14.	C
5.	D	15.	A
6.	A	16.	A
7.	D	17.	B
8.	C	18.	A
9.	B	19.	A
10.	D	20.	B

EXAMINATION SECTION
TEST 1

DIRECTIONS: Each question or incomplete statement is followed by several suggested answers or completions. Select the one that BEST answers the question or completes the statement. *PRINT THE LETTER OF THE CORRECT ANSWER IN THE SPACE AT THE RIGHT.*

1. The length of a Marconi-type antenna is _____ wavelength.
   A. ¼   B. ½   C. ¾   D. 1

2. A whip antenna of less than ¼ wavelength will present an electrical impedance that is
   A. resistive
   B. capacitive
   C. inductive
   D. 180° out-of-phase

3. Frequency multiplication is achieved in transmitter stages by operating them as Class _____ amplifiers.
   A. A   B. AB   C. B   D. C

4. The power factor of a resonant circuit is
   A. lagging   B. leading   C. unity   D. zero

5. The power factor of a *parallel* circuit consisting of a 51-ohm resistor and a 51-ohm capacitive reactance is
   A. .500   B. .667   C. .707   D. .887

6. A tunable *series* RLC circuit will have MINIMUM impedance when the
   A. capacitive reactance equals the inductive reactance
   B. inductive reactance or capacitive reactance equals zero
   C. capacitive reactance equals the resistance
   D. inductive reactance equals the resistance

7. At resonance, a tunable *parallel* RLC circuit will be characterized by
   A. broadest bandwidth
   B. lowest "Q"
   C. maximum impedance
   D. equal currents through the resistance, inductance, and capacitance

8. If the number of turns of an inductor is halved, the value of the inductance is
   A. doubled
   B. unchanged
   C. reduced to one-half
   D. reduced to one-quarter

9. The resistivity of copper is GREATER than that of the element
   A. silicon   B. germanium   C. silver   D. gold

10. The MINIMUM number of 10-microfarad, 25-volt capacitors that can be connected up to yield an equivalent capacitance of 5 microfarads, usable on 150 volts, is
    A. 2   B. 6   C. 18   D. 24

11. The number of DB's (decibels) corresponding to a power ratio of 200 is MOST NEARLY _____ DB's.
    A. 20   B. 23   C. 26   D. 40

12. The MAXIMUM current carrying capacity, in amperes, of a resistor marked "5,000 ohms, 200 watts" is
    A. 1/25   B. 1/5   C. 5   D. 25

13. The combined equivalent resistance of a 12-ohm resistor, a 6-ohm resistor, and a 4-ohm resistor connected in *parallel* is
    A. ½ ohm B. 1 ohm C. 2 ohms D. 3 ohms

14. The percentage regulation of a power supply with a no-load voltage output of +25.3 volts and a full-load voltage output of +23.0 volts is
    A. 1.9%   B. 2.1%   C. 9%   D. 10%

15. A capacitance of .0015 microfarads is equal to
    A. 150 picofarads   B. 1500 picofarads
    C. 150 nanofarads   D. 1500 nanofarads

16. A diode is color coded with a purple, a green, and a red ring in that order (the purple ring is at the end of the diode). It should be concluded from the coding that the diode is a
    A. IN752 B. IN7500 C. IN75B D. IN7511

17. The time constant of a resistance and an inductance in *series* can be increased by
    A. *increasing* either the resistance or the inductance
    B. *increasing* the resistance or decreasing the inductance
    C. *decreasing* the resistance or increasing the inductance
    D. *decreasing* either the resistance or the inductance

18. The combined equivalent impedance of a 50-ohm inductive reactance connected in *parallel* with a 25-ohm capacitive reactance is
    A. 75 ohms inductive reactance   B. 75 ohms capacitive reactance
    C. 50 ohms inductive reactance   D. 50 ohms capacitive reactance

19. The tree connections of an SCR are the
    A. collector, emitter, and gate   B. base 1, base 2, and emitter
    C. anode, cathode, and gate   D. emitter 1, emitter 2, and base

20. FET is the abbreviation for a _____ transistor.
    A. fast epitaxial   B. field effect
    C. frequency extended   D. forward emitting

21. The resonant frequency of a .1 henry inductance and a .001 microfarad capacitance "tank" circuit is MOST NEARLY
    A. 160 Hz   B. 1600 Hz   C. 16 KHz   D. 16 MHz

22. At 300 MHz, electromagnetic energy in air has a wavelength of
    A. 1 centimeter   B. 10 centimeters
    C. 100 centimeters   D. 1000 centimeters

23. The frequency range from 300 MHz to 3000 MHz is designated by RETMA and ASA as the _____ range.
    A. HF   B. VHF   C. UHF   D. SHF

24. A modulated carrier wave has a maximum magnitude of 150 volts and 50% modulation.
    If the modulation is removed, the carrier will have a magnitude of _____ volts.
    A. 50   B. 75   C. 100   D. 150

25. If 50 microamperes produces a full-scale deflection on a DC voltmeter, the sensitivity of the instrument is _____ ohms/volt.
    A. 5,000   B. 10,000   C. 20,000   D. 50,000

26. A "beat-frequency meter" is also called a
    A. frequency synthesizer   B. distortion meter
    C. wave analyzer   D. heterodyne-frequency meter

27. Assume that a voltmeter uses the same scale for three ranges, 0-300 volts, 0-75 volts, and 0-15 volts.
    If the scale is marked only for the 0-300 volt range, then a scale reading of 120 when the 0-75 volt range is being used will correspond to an ACTUAL voltage of _____ volts.
    A. 10   B. 12   C. 24   D. 30

28. Variations in the signals introduced in the "Z" axis input of an oscilloscope produce corresponding changes in the
    A. positioning of the time-delayed sweep
    B. intensity of the trace
    C. "Y" axis frequency response
    D. "X" axis sawtooth repetition rate

29. When using an ohmmeter to measure resistance, the GREATEST accuracy is obtained when the range selected results in a deflection that is APPROXIMATELY
    A. ¼ full-scale   B. ½ full-scale
    C. ¾ full-scale   D. full-scale

30. A grid-dip meter is GENERALLY used to measure
    A. Q   B. modulation   C. RF current   D. frequency

4 (#1)

31. A 0-150 volt voltmeter has an accuracy of 2% F.S.
When the pointer shows 75 volts, the MAXIMUM error is plus or minus
 A. .5 volt   B. 1.5 volts   C. 2.0 volts   D. 3.0 volts

32. Certain attenuation probes used with oscilloscopes provide for an adjustment to be made in each probe, prior to its use. The adjustment is required in order to _____ on which it is used.
 A. match the probe to the circuitry
 B. match the probe to the input of the scope
 C. adjust the DC volts/division sensitivity of the input to the scope
 D. adjust the DC balance of the input to the scope

33. When an oscilloscope is set up to display a lissajous pattern, the feature that is inhibited and NOT available is the
 A. "Y" axis manual positioning control
 B. "X" axis manual positioning control
 C. automatic retrace blanking
 D. trace intensity manual control

34. In order to minimize multiple reflections in a coaxial line, the MOST effective steps that should be taken are to drive the sending end with a
 A. low impedance source and terminate the receiving end with a resistance equal to the coaxial characteristic impedance
 B. source with output impedance equal to the coaxial characteristic impedance and terminate the receiving end with a resistance equal to the coaxial characteristic impedance
 C. low impedance source and terminate the receiving end with a high impedance
 D. source with output impedance to the coaxial characteristic impedance and terminate the receiving end with a high impedance

35. Of the following statements concerning a dual-trace oscilloscope, the one which is CORRECT is that it
 A. requires a two-gun cathode-ray tube
 B. has two "Y" axis inputs that are chopped and displayed as a single trace
 C. uses a single time base when used in the "chopped" mode
 D. uses dual-time bases when used in the "chopped" mode

36. The type of display usually produced on oscilloscopes, where signal amplitude is convert4ed to a "Y" axis displacement and a time base is introduced on the "X" axis, is CLOSEST in appearance to the radar indicator that is called a(n) _____ scan.
 A. A   B. B   C. J   D. PPI

37. Of the following, the BEST instrument for measuring very low resistances is the _____ bridge.
 A. Wien   B. Kelvin   C. Hay   D. Maxwell

38. Of the following, the instrument that should be used in measuring radiation patterns produced by antennas is the
    A. spectrum analyzer
    B. field-strength meter
    C. curve tracer
    D. distortion meter

    38.____

39. Taut-band suspension is a feature which is incorporated in
    A. the internal supporting of hermetic-sealed units
    B. low-friction meter movements
    C. dial cord assemblies
    D. vibration mounts for electronic packages

    39.____

40. A "bolometer" is a device that can be used for measuring
    A. microwave power
    B. static charge
    C. magnetic-field strength
    D. vibration frequencies

    40.____

KEY (CORRECT ANSWERS)

1.	A	11.	B	21.	C	31.	D
2.	B	12.	B	22.	C	32.	B
3.	D	13.	C	23.	C	33.	C
4.	C	14.	D	24.	C	34.	B
5.	C	15.	B	25.	C	35.	C
6.	A	16.	A	26.	D	36.	A
7.	C	17.	C	27.	D	37.	B
8.	D	18.	D	28.	B	38.	B
9.	C	19.	C	29.	B	39.	B
10.	C	20.	B	30.	D	40.	A

TEST 2

DIRECTIONS: Each question or incomplete statement is followed by several suggested answers or completions. Select the one that BEST answers the question or completes the statement. *PRINT THE LETTER OF THE CORRECT ANSWER IN THE SPACE AT THE RIGHT.*

1. One of the reasons why radiotelephones are operated in the 30 MHz to 3000 MHz range is that
   A. skip transmission is very effective
   B. antenna orientation is not important
   C. the number of voice channels is great
   D. AM operation is less noisy than FM

   1.____

2. The transmission of a distress message by a radiotelephone station not itself in distress should include calling out three times the expression
   A. SOS   B. SOS relay   C. Mayday   D. Mayday relay

   2.____

3. In specifying the characteristics of an oscillator crystal, the information that should be given, together with the frequency tolerance, is the crystal
   A. age
   B. operating temperature range
   C. manufacturer
   D. power supply voltages

   3.____

4. Records indicate that a component in a certain unit has been replaced repeatedly, and no such history exists in other similar units with the same type of service and total operation time.
   Based on this information, it should be concluded that
   A. the replacement components were defective
   B. the component was replaced at times when it had not failed
   C. the replacement components were connected into the circuit improperly
   D. there is something else wrong in the unit causing the component to fail

   4.____

5. When trouble-shooting a large electronic unit, such as a console, first, power should be removed and the NEXT step should be that
   A. internal capacitors be discharged by using a shorting connection to chassis
   B. ohmmeter checks be made according to the instruction manual
   C. the operating personnel be notified that the unit is out of operation
   D. the door and panel interlocks be by-passed

   5.____

6. Metal enclosures and panels of electronic or electrical equipment should be well grounded in order to
   A. protect operating personnel from getting electric shocks
   B. insure that the contained equipment has a good reference ground
   C. prevent static charges from building up on the frame
   D. provide a solid mounting for the equipment and keep it firmly in place

   6.____

2 (#2)

7. The main reason for NOT using carbon tetrachloride as a cleaning agent on electrical equipment is that it
   A. is an electrical conductor
   B. is too expensive
   C. generates toxic fumes
   D. coats equipment with an acid deposit

   7.____

8. The MOST likely cause of damage occurring in transistorized circuitry during the process of soldering is due to the application of too much
   A. pressure   B. heat   C. solder   D. rosin flux

   8.____

9. A 2-inch diameter hole can be made quickly and cleanly in a 16-gauge aluminum plate by the use of a
   A. rat-tail file   B. nibbler
   C. chassis punch   D. jig saw

   9.____

10. A reason for using teflon insulation rather than vinyl on electrical wiring is that teflon is
    A. better for bonding   B. more flexible
    C. less expensive   D. more resistant to heat

    10.____

11. Of the following statements concerning epoxy glue, the one which is CORRECT is that it
    A. dissolves quickly upon contact with water
    B. is prepared from two components that are mixed together shortly before use
    C. is a long-time favorite for making temporary bonds
    D. generally does not require clamps, nails or presses on surfaces to be joined

    11.____

12. Of the following chemicals, the one which will burn on contact with a lighted match is
    A. carbon tetrachloride   B. acetone
    C. methylene chloride   D. sodium bicarbonate

    12.____

13. Of the following, the BEST method of disposing of spray cans that contain aerosol paints or solvents is
    A. puncturing the cans and then throwing them into an incinerator
    B. puncturing the cans and then having them picked up by the sanitation men
    C. throwing them into an incinerator
    D. having them picked up by the sanitation men

    13.____

14. An ohmmeter of known polarity is connected from the base to the emitter on a transistor in such manner that the positive lead is on the base. The ohmmeter registers continuity with such conditions and then registers an "open" circuit when the leads are reversed.
    Based on this information, it should be concluded that the transistor is
    A. good   B. defective   C. an NPN   D. a PNP

    14.____

15. An ohmmeter registers "open" when connected from the emitter to the collector of a transistor (base left disconnected) and also registers "open" when the leads are reversed. This information suggests that the transistor is
    A. possibly good
    B. definitely defective
    C. an NPN
    D. a PNP

15.____

16. In order to get good indications when checking a transistor by using an ohmmeter, yet not cause damage, the voltage across the test leads should _____ 1.5 volts DC and the ohmmeter scale _____ be less than R × 100.
    A. *exceed*; should
    B. *exceed*; should not
    C. *not exceed*; should
    D. *not* exceed; should not

16.____

17. If an audio amplifier requiring a 3200-ohm load is connected to the primary winding of a 20:1 step-down output transformer, the matching speaker to be connected to the secondary winding should have an impedance of _____ ohms.
    A. 4 B. 8 C. 16 D. 32

17.____

18. The converter stage in a typical heterodyne receiver combines the functions of a(n)
    A. RF stage and the local oscillator
    B. mixer stage and the local oscillator
    C. RF stage and an IF stage
    D. mixer stage and an IF stage

18.____

19. One of the reasons why RF stages improve the performance of a typical heterodyne receiver is that they
    A. increase the sensitivity and broaden the bandwidth
    B. provide regenerative action and improve selectivity
    C. increase sensitivity and improve AVC action
    D. improve AVC action and broaden bandwidth

19.____

20. Of the following statements concerning the record heads in typical magnetic-tape recorders, the one which is CORRECT is that they are
    A. self-cleaning and require occasional realignment
    B. automatically demagnetized by the signals in the tape-erase heads
    C. easily magnetized and should not be checked for continuity with an ohmmeter
    D. not self-cleaning and are demagnetized by over-driving the record amplifiers

20.____

21. Typical recording speeds on commercial magnetic-tape recorders are
    A. 3½ ips, 7 ips, 15 ips, and 30 ips
    B. 3¾ ips, 7 ½ ips, 15 ips, and 30 ips
    C. 3¾ ips, 7 ips, 15 ips, and 25 ips
    D. 3½ ips, 7½ ips, 15 ips, and 30 ips

21.____

22. According to FCC regulations, the frequency and deviation of a crystal-controlled FM transmitter must be checked BEFORE it is put into operation, and rechecked thereafter every
    A. month   B. 3 months   C. 6 months   D. year

23. According to FCC regulations, radio transmitters may be tuned or adjusted only by persons possessing a
    A. first or second class commercial radiotelephone operator's license
    B. first class commercial radiotelephone operator's license
    C. first or second class commercial radiotelephone operator's license or by personnel working under their immediate supervision
    D. first class commercial radiotelephone operator's license or by personnel working under their immediate supervision

24. According to FCC regulations, transmitters whose oscillators are not crystal controlled should have their carrier frequencies checked BEFORE they are put into operation, and rechecked thereafter every
    A. week   B. month   C. 3 months   D. 6 months

25. The FCC dictates that the power in the output stage(s) of a 5-watt transmitter, whose modulation and power setting remain unaltered, should be checked at the time it is put into operation, and rechecked thereafter every
    A. month   B. 3 months   C. 6 months   D. year

Questions 26-40.

DIRECTIONS: Questions 26 through 40 are to be answered on the basis of the schematic diagram appearing on pages 7 (#2) and 8 (#2).

26. The circuits shown on the schematic represent the stages of a(n)
    A. transmitter   B. receiver
    C. audio-intercom   D. pulse-generator

27. The types of transistors shown on the schematic are
    A. all NPN's
    B. all PNP's
    C. some NPN's and some PNP's
    D. interchangeable and usable as either NPN's or PNP's

28. The power supply shown on the schematic supplies the stages with
    A. one B+ voltage, common to all stages
    B. two B+ voltages
    C. one B+ voltage and one B- voltage
    D. two B- voltages

29. The circuit element designated as Y101, in Oscillator F1 is a
    A. remote-bias adjustment   B. compensated-crystal assembly
    C. solid-stage switching device   D. protective interlock

30. If the unmodulated frequency at the collector of Q107, of the Final Amplifier, is 135 MHz, then the input frequency to the base of transistor Q103, in the Modulator is _____ MHz.
   A. 3.75   B. 7.50   C. 15.0   D. 22.5

31. The component in the Automatic Drive Limiter that has the designation RT101,10K is a
   A. high-resistance incandescent lamp
   B. thermistor
   C. precision wire-wound resistor
   D. ballast lamp

32. The component in the power supply that has the designation of CR103 is a
   A. double-anode clipper   B. tunnel diode
   C. zener diode   D. rectifier bridge

33. The transistor-stage configuration in which transistor 0109 of the Integrator is connected is called a(n) _____ connection.
   A. emitter-follower   B. phase-splitter
   C. Darlington   D. common-base

34. The component between the Amplifier-Clipper and the Integrator that has the designation L116,0.8H is a(n)
   A. air-core choke   B. iron-core inductor
   C. ferrite inductor   D. saturable-core inductor

35. Trouble has developed in a unit whose schematic is the one accompanying this test. DC measurements are taken and indicate that the voltage on the base of Q109 in the Integrator stage has gone to -5.6 volts and the emitter voltage has gone to 0.0 volts.
   Of the following, the condition that causes such voltage levels is
   A. the R128 potentiometer slider-arm is making poor contact
   B. Q109 has developed an "open" between base and emitter
   C. C153 has become shorted
   D. Q108, in the previous stage, has gone to cut-off

36. If, in the Pre-Amplifier stage shown in the schematic pacitor C164 were to short, the result would be that
   A. Q110 would go harder into conduction
   B. Q110 would approach cut-off
   C. Q110 would become damaged
   D. C165 would break down in the reverse direction

37. In the power supply section, capacitor C156 is required in shunt with C155 because
   A. the circuit requires a capacity of slightly more than 15 microfarads; hence, C256 would supply the additional amount
   B. C155 regulates the DC voltage while C156 shunts out ripple frequencies

C. C155 is effective in filtering low frequencies, and C156 is effective in filtering high frequencies
D. C155 and C156, in parallel, form a "pi" section of the filter network

38. R113 and C124 in the collector circuit of Q104 in the second Tripler stage form what is COMMONLY called a _____ network.
    A. self-bias
    B. low-frequency peaking
    C. parasitic-suppressor
    D. decoupling

39. The Z101 sub-miniature harmonic filter, at the output of the Final Amplifier, is a _____ filter
    A. lo-pass
    B. hi-pass
    C. notch
    D. bandpass

40. The purpose of C101, in Oscillator F1, is to
    A. adjust the bias level of the stage
    B. slightly "pull" the frequency of oscillation
    C. tune out the inductance seen looking into the transistor base
    D. suppress parasitic oscillations

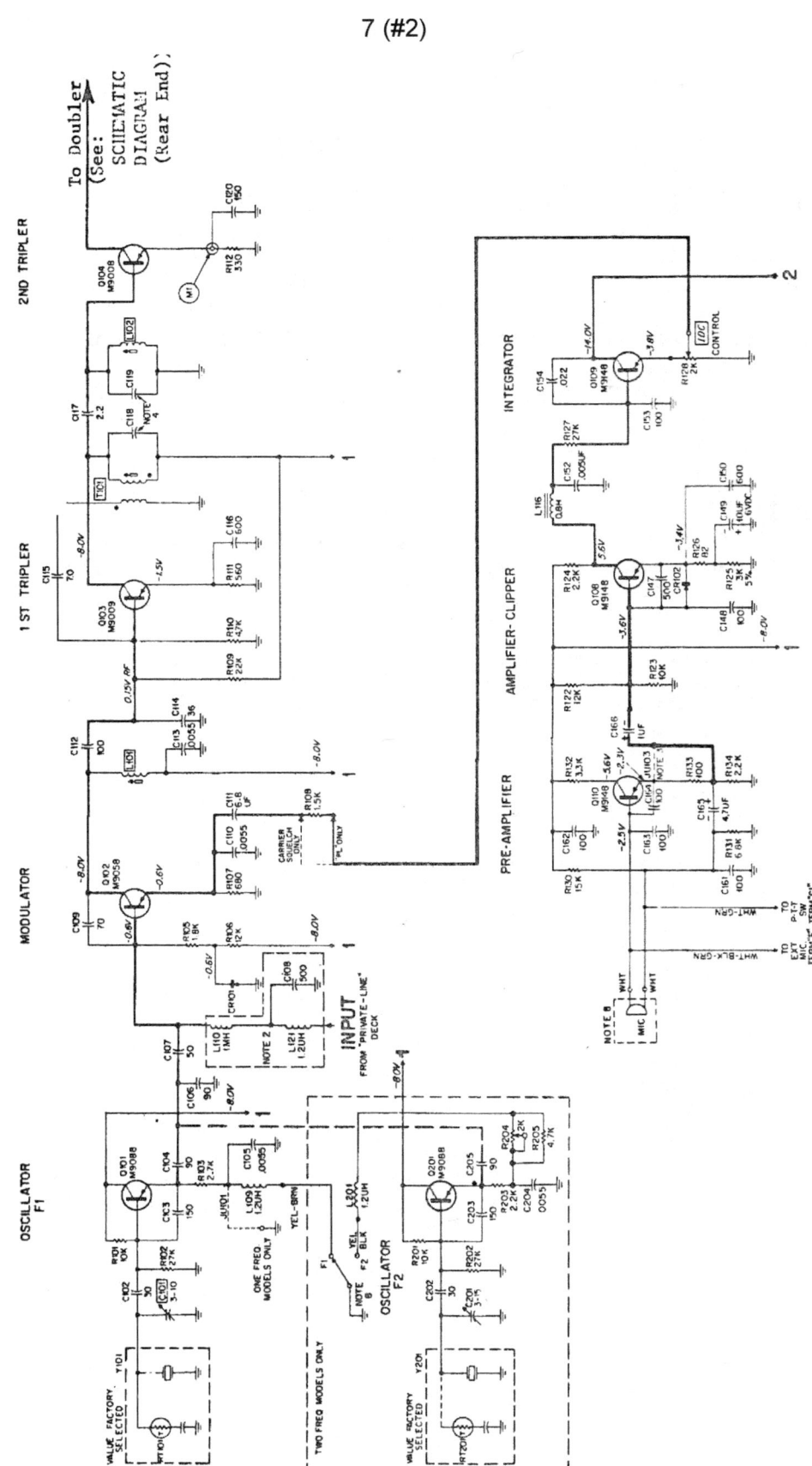

SCHEMATIC DIAGRAM (Front End)

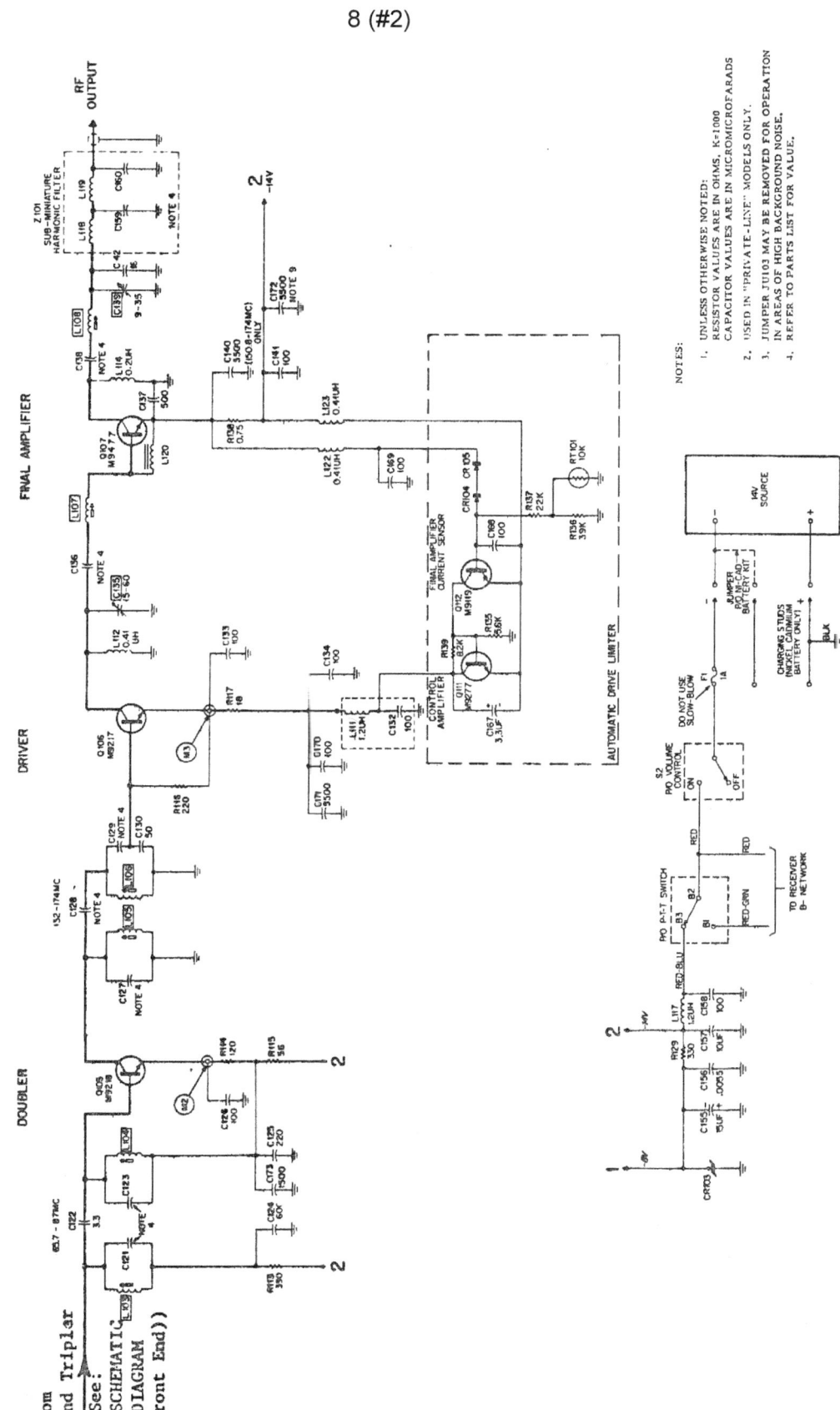

SCHEMATIC DIAGRAM (Rear End)

KEY (CORRECT ANSWERS)

1.	C	11.	B	21.	B	31.	B
2.	D	12.	B	22.	D	32.	C
3.	B	13.	D	23.	C	33.	A
4.	D	14.	C	24.	B	34.	B
5.	A	15.	A	25.	D	35.	B
6.	A	16.	D	26.	A	36.	B
7.	C	17.	B	27.	C	37.	C
8.	B	18.	B	28.	D	38.	D
9.	C	19.	C	29.	B	39.	A
10.	D	20.	C	30.	B	40.	B

TEST 3

DIRECTIONS: Each question or incomplete statement is followed by several suggested answers or completions. Select the one that BEST answers the question or completes the statement. PRINT THE LETTER OF THE CORRECT ANSWER IN THE SPACE AT THE RIGHT.

1. If an amplifier has three stages each having a gain of ten, the overall gain of the amplifier is
   A. 30 B. 300 C. 1,000 D. 1,000,000

   1.____

2. An amplitude-modulated carrier is said to be overmodulated when the
   A. carrier amplitude sometimes is zero for an appreciable time
   B. audio frequencies exceed the assigned bandwidth
   C. audio frequencies are close to the carrier frequency
   D. carrier amplitude sometimes exceeds the rated tank voltage

   2.____

3. For a radio receiver in which the tuning is done with variable air condensers, the practical ratio of highest to lowest frequency that can be tuned with a single coil for each condenser is NEAREST to
   A. 1.5:1 B. 3:1 C. 6:1 D. 12:1

   3.____

4. A 2k-ohm, a 4k-ohm, a 6k-ohm, and an 8k-ohm resistor are connected in parallel to a 100-volt power source. The resistor which must have the HIGHEST rating, in watts, is the
   A. 2k-ohm B. 4k-ohm C. 6k-ohm D. 8k-ohm

   4.____

5. A large number of 10-microfarad, 25-volt condensers are available in a particular laboratory. The MINIMUM number of these required to yield a capacitance of 5 microfarads for operation on 150 volts is
   A. 2 B. 6 C. 18 D. 24

   5.____

6. The heaters of three vacuum tubes are to be operated in series with a resistor on a 120-volt circuit.
   If the ratings of the heaters are respectively 50, 35, and 12 volts, all at 0.15 amp, the MINIMUM rating of the resistor should be
   A. 250 ohms; 5 watts B. 250 ohms, 10 watts
   C. 150 ohms, 10 watts D. 150 ohms, 5 watts

   6.____

7. An audio amplifier is stated to have a frequency response of ±3 db from 50 to 10,000 cps. If the response is down 3 db at 50 cycles, the voltage output at this frequency (50 cycles) compared to the average voltage output throughout the frequency range is ABOUT
   A. 50% B. 63% C. 67% d. 70%

   7.____

8. The MAXIMUM limits of resistance of a resistor having yellow, green, and orange color bands (reading from left to right) are
   A. 44,100 – 45,900 B. 42,750 – 47,250
   C. 41,500 – 49,500 D. 36,000 – 54,000

   8.____

9. A COMMONLY used IF for FM receivers in the 88-108 mc. range is
   A. 455 kc.   B. 456 kc.   C. 10.7 mc.   D. 22.3 mc.

10. Crystal controlled oscillator frequency stability is maintained MOST closely by
    A. feeding the output into a tuned tank circuit
    B. enclosing the crystal in a temperature controlled oven
    C. mounting the crystal in a shock-proof container
    D. obtaining the input from a tuned tank circuit

11. One COMMONLY used dual triode vacuum tube has the designation
    A. 12AU7   B. 12BE6   C. 12SA7   D. 12SQ7

12. The base radiotelephone station used for contacting surface line patrol cars in operation 24 hours per day would be meeting legal requirements if self-identification were made
    A. 24 times a day   B. every 2 hours
    C. at the end of each transmission   D. at the beginning of each day

13. The alphabet used in radiotelephone communication is
    A. Morse   B. international
    C. telephonic D. phonetic

14. A d.c. meter which gives full-scale deflection at 50 microamperes has a sensitivity of _____ ohms/volt.
    A. 1,000   B. 5,000   C. 20,000   D. 50,000

15. A certain d.c. meter which gives full-scale deflection at 50 microamperes has a resistance of 250 ohms. When used to measure current, it reads .50 of full-scale with a 2.5-ohm resistor connected across the meter terminals. The measured current, in milliamperes, is NEAREST to
    A. 1.3   B. 2.5   C. 12.5   D. 25.3

16. A certain train to wayside communication system operates at a frequency of 180 mc. This corresponds to a wavelength of
    A. 1667 meters   B. 166.7 meters
    C. 1667 centimeters   D. 166.7 centimeters

17. In an FM receiver using vacuum tubes, the tube having the lowest voltage applied to the plate is USUALLY the
    A. mixer   B. IF amplifier   C. limiter   D. AF amplifier

18. A grid-dip meter is GENERALLY used to measure
    A. frequency   B. RF current   C. AF current   D. modulation

19. To obtain a trapezoidal modulation pattern on the oscilloscope, the signal applied to the horizontal deflection plates should be a
    A. square wave
    B. saw-tooth wave
    C. sample of the final tank-circuit voltage
    D. sample of the audio modulating voltage

20. To obtain a wave-envelope modulation pattern on the oscilloscope, the signal applied to the horizontal deflection plates should be a
    A. square wave
    B. saw-tooth wave
    C. sample of the audio modulating voltage
    D. sample of the final tank-circuit voltage

21. When soldering transistorized circuitry, the transistors are MOST likely to be damaged from the use of too much
    A. solder   B. rosin flux   C. heat   D. pressure

Questions 22-28.

DIRECTIONS: Questions 22 through 28 are to be answered on the basis of the following circuit.

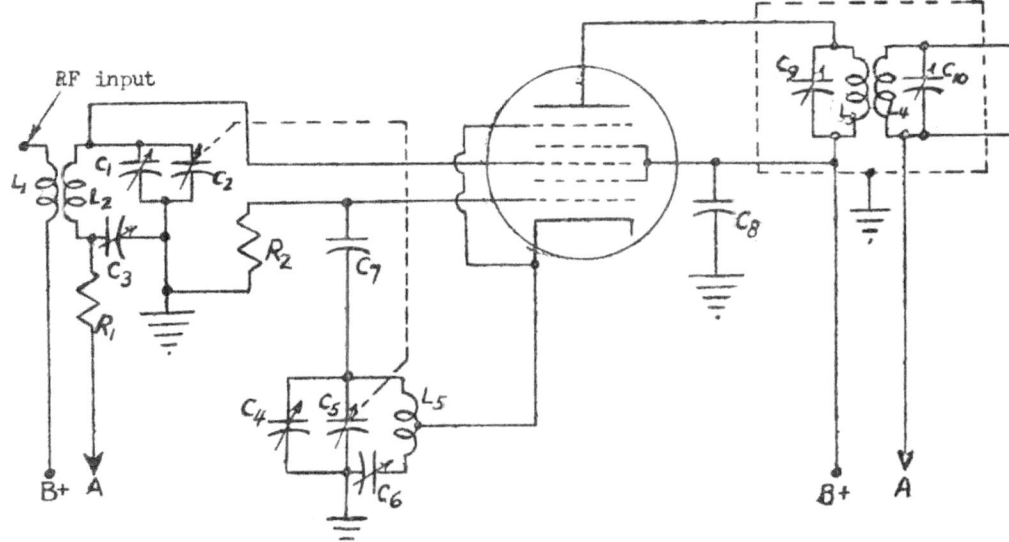

22. The name MOST commonly given to this circuit is
    A. radio-frequency amplifier   B. first detector
    C. intermediate frequency amplifier D. ratio detector

23. The vacuum tube shown is a
    A. power amplifier pentode   B. beam power pentode
    C. hexode mixer   D. pentagrid converter

24. The wires terminating in arrowheads and labeled A MOST likely connect to the
    A. chassis
    B. AVC bus
    C. cathode bias resistors
    D. power supply screen grid bias

    24._____

25. Tracking at the high-frequency end of the tuning range is synchronized by adjusting
    A. C_1 and C_4
    B. C_3 and C_6
    C. C_2 and C_5
    D. C_3 and C_4

    25._____

26. Tracking at the low-frequency end of the tuning range is synchronized by adjusting
    A. C_1 and C_4
    B. C_3 and C_6
    C. C_2 and C_5
    D. C_3 and C_4

    26._____

27. The circuit shows that there is shielding around the
    A. RF tuning stage
    B. oscillator
    C. vacuum tube
    D. IF transformer

    27._____

28. The type of oscillator shown is a
    A. tickler
    B. Colpitts
    C. Hartley
    D. TPTG

    28._____

29. A 35-ohm, 2-watt, 10% tolerance resistor should have color bands, reading from left to right, of
    A. orange, green, brown, silver
    B. orange, green, brown, gold
    C. orange, green, black, silver
    D. orange, green, black, gold

    29._____

30. The resistor of Question 29 above has a current-carrying capacity of
    A. .239 ma
    B. 2.39 ma
    C. 23.9 ma
    D. 239 ma

    30._____

31. The 20,000 ohms/volt meter having a full-scale deflection of 50 volts reads 45 volts with switch S closed in position 1, and 21 volts when the switch is in position 2 as shown. The value of R is readily calculated to be
    A. .875 megohm
    B. 1.14 megohms
    C. 87,500 ohm
    D. 114,000 ohms

    31._____

32. In the high rejection-ratio trap circuit shown, the device that must be connected between terminals 1 and 2 for proper rejection is a(n)
    A. resistor
    B. RF choke
    C. AF choke
    D. capacitor

    32._____

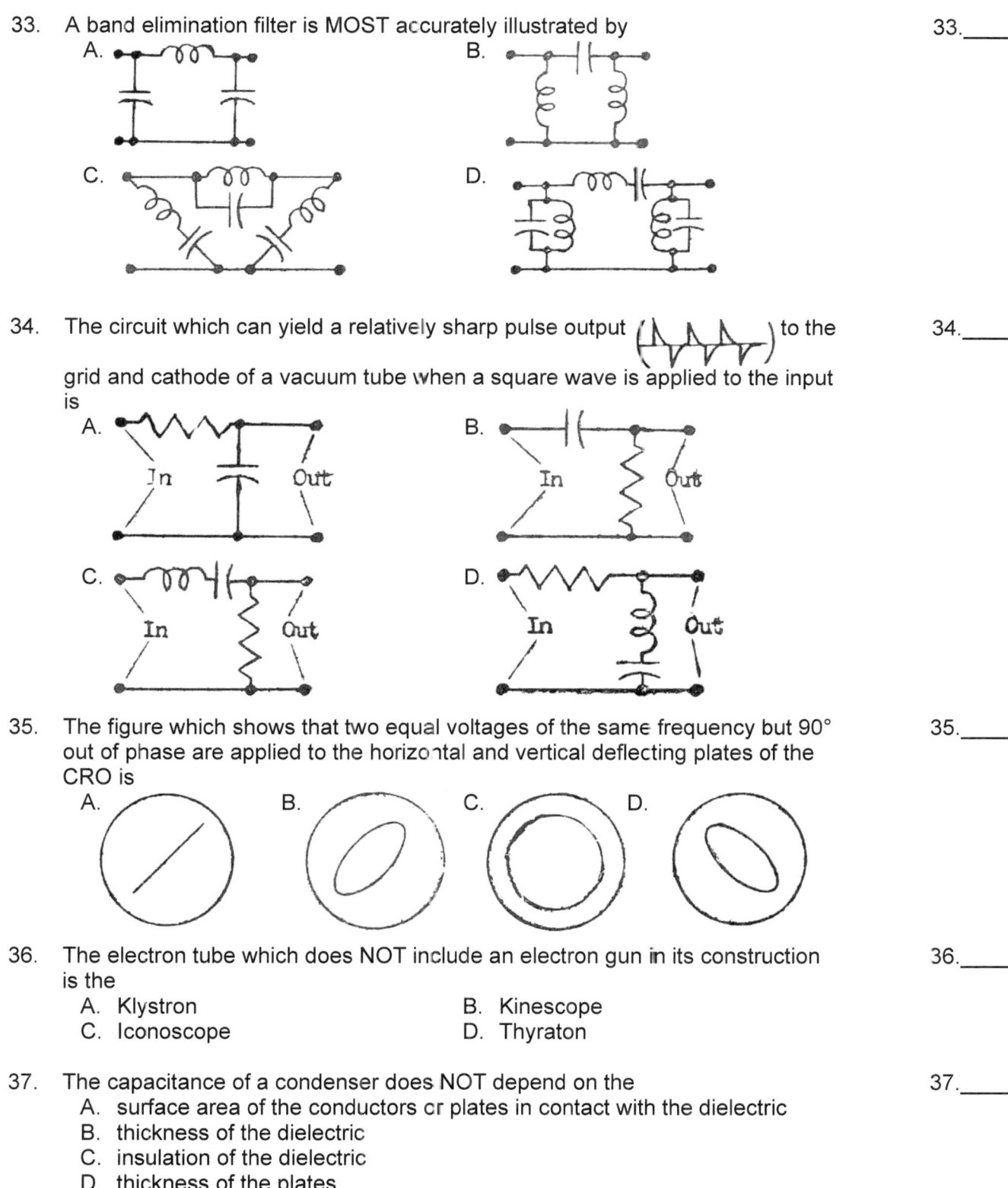

33. A band elimination filter is MOST accurately illustrated by

34. The circuit which can yield a relatively sharp pulse output to the grid and cathode of a vacuum tube when a square wave is applied to the input is

35. The figure which shows that two equal voltages of the same frequency but 90° out of phase are applied to the horizontal and vertical deflecting plates of the CRO is

36. The electron tube which does NOT include an electron gun in its construction is the
   A. Klystron
   B. Kinescope
   C. Iconoscope
   D. Thyraton

37. The capacitance of a condenser does NOT depend on the
   A. surface area of the conductors or plates in contact with the dielectric
   B. thickness of the dielectric
   C. insulation of the dielectric
   D. thickness of the plates

38. Frequency doublers and triplers are used in _____ transmitters.
   A. CW   B. pulsed   C. FM   D. keyed

39. Zener diodes are GENERALLY used for
   A. AVC rectification
   B. diode detection
   C. voltage regulation
   D. current limitation

40. An AF amplifier transistor could have the designation
   A. 2N243   B. 242N2   C. 1N105   D. 105N1

41. Carrier frequency voice transmission is used in wire telephony PRIMARILY to increase the
   A. number of voice channels
   B. clarity of tone
   C. transmission distance
   D. transmitted power

42. The circuit shown at the right is PROPERLY called a
   A. potentiometer
   B. voltage divider
   C. voltage decade
   D. current limiter

43. If R_1, R_2, and R_3 in the sketch of Question 42 above are 250k, 500k, and 50k ohms, respectively, the MAXIUM grid bias (negative) voltage available for a tube with a grounded cathode is
   A. 12.5   B. 25   C. 125   D. 250

44. Automobiles now use alternators and rectifiers instead of d.c. generators for supplying the cars' electrical demands. The rectifier that is MOST widely used is the
   A. copper oxide   B. galena   C. germanium   D. silicon

45. A circuit configuration which does NOT apply to transistors is common
   A. emitter   B. base   C. cathode   D. collector

46. The microphone that is MOST likely to require a preamplifier to operate an audio amplifier is the
   A. crystal   B. carbon   C. ceramic   D. magnetic

47. If the oscillator of a tape recorder is faulty, the MOST likely result will be
   A. incomplete erasure
   B. weak recording
   C. excessive volume
   D. variation in tape speed

48. Measurement of radiation from a radio antenna is made with a
   A. Q meter
   B. field strength meter
   C. flux meter
   D. radiometer

49. If a 0-150 volt meter is guaranteed to have an accuracy of 2% of full-scale deflection, then the MAXIMUM error of the indication when the pointer shows 25 volts is plus or minus
   A. 0.5 volt B. 1.0 volt C. 1.5 volts D. 3.0 volts

49.____

50. The contacts of relays and switches used in communication work are frequently silver plated. The purpose of the silver plating is to
   A. improve conductivity of the contacts
   B. reduce arcing at the contacts
   C. improve the flexibility of the contacts
   D. reduce the amount of copper that would otherwise be necessary

50.____

KEY (CORRECT ANSWERS)

1.	C	11.	A	21.	C	31.	B	41.	A
2.	A	12.	C	22.	B	32.	A	42.	B
3.	B	13.	D	23.	D	33.	C	43.	B
4.	A	14.	C	24.	B	34.	B	44.	D
5.	C	15.	B	25.	A	35.	C	45.	C
6.	D	16.	D	26.	B	36.	D	46.	D
7.	D	17.	C	27.	D	37.	D	47.	A
8.	D	18.	A	28.	C	38.	C	48.	B
9.	C	19.	D	29.	C	39.	C	49.	D
10.	B	20.	B	30.	D	40.	A	50.	A

TEST 4

DIRECTIONS: Each question or incomplete statement is followed by several suggested answers or completions. Select the one that BEST answers the question or completes the statement. *PRINT THE LETTER OF THE CORRECT ANSWER IN THE SPACE AT THE RIGHT.*

1. If a one microfarad condenser is connected in series with a two microfarad condenser, the capacity of the resulting combination in microfarads is
   A. three
   B. one and one-half
   C. two-thirds
   D. one-third

2. A storage battery is charged from a 112-volt d-c line through a series resistance.
   If the charging rate is 10 amperes, the electromotive force of the battery is 12 volts and its internal resistance is 0.2 ohms, the value of the series resistance is _____ ohm.
   A. 11.2   B. 10   C. 9.8   D. 1.2

3. The resistance, in ohms, of a 10 ampere 50M.V shunt is MOST NEARLY
   A. 2   B. .05   C. .005   D. .002

4. It is required to couple a 4 ohm voice coil of a loudspeaker to an output tube having a plate load of 10,000 ohms. This can best be done by using a transformer having a ratio of primary to secondary turns of APPROXIMATELY
   A. 5   B. 25   C. 50   D. 75

5. A dynamoelectric amplifier for power control having high amplification ratio is commonly called a(n)
   A. Dynatron
   B. Amplidyne
   C. Amplitherm
   D. Dynatherm

6. An amplifier has an output voltage wave form that does not exactly follow that of the input voltage. This type of distortion is called _____ distortion.
   A. amplitude   B. modular   C. resonance   D. variation

7. The frequency in cycles multiplied by 2π is COMMONLY called _____ frequency.
   A. annular   B. heaviside   C. angular   D. circular

8. An anion is a negative ion that moves toward the
   A. anode in an electrolytic cell
   B. cathode in a discharge tube
   C. positive terminal of a battery while being discharged
   D. negative terminal of a battery while being charged

9. Silicon rectifiers, as compared with selenium rectifiers of the same physical size, have
    A. greater current ratings
    B. smaller current ratings
    C. the same current ratings
    D. much greater resistance at 60 cycles

10. The germanium rectifier, as compared with other types of rectifiers, has
    A. a high forward drop
    B. a low reverse resistance
    C. no aging, and therefore has an indefinitely long life
    D. a narrow temperature range, from -5° to +40°C

11. Transistors are ideally suited for Hi-Fi amplifiers since they are inherently _____ devices.
    A. high impedance
    B. low impedance
    C. non-linear
    D. quadrature

12. An air condenser composed of two parallel flat plates of area Z, separated by a distance Y, has a capacitance which is
    A. directly proportional to the distance Y
    B. directly proportional to the area Z
    C. inversely proportional to the area Z
    D. inversely proportional to the square of the area Z

13. For audio frequency amplifiers used for Hi-Fi work, it is desirable to have a hum and noise level, at full output, of APPROXIMATELY _____ db.
    A. -80   B. -20   C. +20   D. +80

14. The maximum Q of cavity resonators is APPROXIMATELY
    A. 500   B. 5,000   C. 50,000   D. 5,000,000

15. To find out if a source of supply is D.C. or A.C., it is BEST to use a(n)
    A. iron vane voltmeter
    B. neon tester
    C. test set made up of two ordinary lamps in series
    D. dynamometer-type voltmeter

16. A vacuum tube circuit having high input impedance, low output impedance, and a gain of less than unit is MOST likely a(n) _____ circuit.
    A. anode-follower
    B. differentiating
    C. ignitron
    D. cathode-follower

17. A heart-shaped pattern obtained as the response or radiation characteristic of certain directional antennae or as the response characteristic of certain microphones is called a
    A. cardioid pattern
    B. sinusoidal pattern
    C. semicircular pattern
    D. parabolic

3 (#4)

18. A standard FM broadcast transmitter sends out a signal with a swing of ±60 kc. The percentage modulation of this signal is
    A. 60   B. 70   C. 80   D. 90

19. A standard method of securing a good signal-to-noise ratio in an FM transmitter is to
    A. keep the filament power low to reduce thermal noise
    B. use pre-emphasis
    C. use squelch circuits
    D. use thermal agitation

20. The process of determining the correct values for different positions of a meter, pointer, or settings of a control is COMMONLY called
    A. adjusting   B. measuring   C. aligning   D. calibrating

Questions 21-23.

DIRECTIONS: Questions 21 through 23, inclusive, are to be answered on the basis of the following diagram.

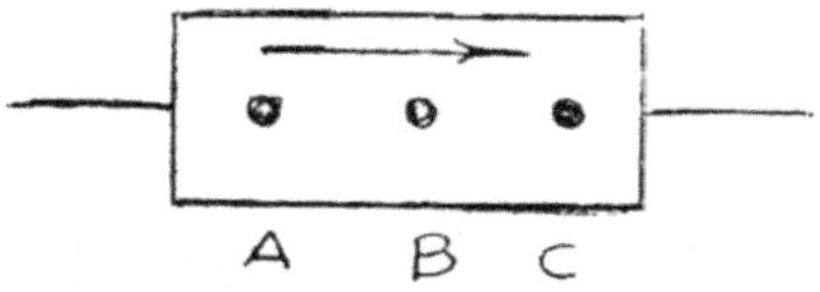

21. In the standard RMA color code for the value of fixed capacitors, when only three color dots are used, the working voltage is assumed to be
    A. 100   B. 300   C. 500   D. 600

22. In standard RMA color code for the value of fixed capacitors when only three color dots are given, the tolerance is assumed to be _____ percent.
    A. 5   B. 10   C. 15   D. 20

23. With reference to the above figure, the dot marked A represents the
    A. first significant figure   B. decimal multiplier
    C. working temperature   D. second significant figure

24. If 1000 watts of power are delivered to an antenna having a resistance of 10 ohms, the antenna current, in amperes, is MOST NEARLY
    A. 3.1   B. 5   C. 7.07   D. 10

25. A quarter-wave (90°) antenna comprised of thin wire without supporting structure and operating at a frequency of 5000 kilocycles, has a physical height of _____ feet.
    A. 24.6   B. 49.2   C. 93.8   D. 98.4

26. As compared with the series-fed antenna, the shunt-fed antenna
    A. permits the elimination of the base ground
    B. need not have an impedance match with the source for optimum operation
    C. permits the elimination of the base insulator
    D. permits the elimination of all insulators

27. The above diagram represents a(n)
    A. differentiating circuit
    B. high pass filter
    C. integrating circuit
    D. band pass filter

28. Of the following, the type of bridge used for measuring inductance is the _____ Bridge.
    A. Kelvin
    B. Wheatstone
    C. Maxwell
    D. Newton

29. A certain circuit having an input of one volt and an output of 10 volts has a power gain, in decibels, of
    A. 5
    B. 10
    C. 15
    D. 20

30. In an A.M. transmitter, if the peak value of the modulated carrier current is 2 amps and that of the unmodulated carrier current is one amp, the percentage of modulation is APPROXIMATELY
    A. 40%
    B. 60%
    C. 80%
    D. 100%

31. With reference to vacuum tubes, if the amplification factor is divided by the plate resistance, the result will be a term called
    A. efficiency
    B. transconductance
    C. emission
    D. sensitivity

32. An amplifier in which the grid bias and alternating grid are such that plate current in a specific tube flows at all times with essentially linear amplification is called a class _____ amplifier.
    A. A
    B. B
    C. C
    D. AB_2

33. Inverse feedback is used in audio amplifiers to
    A. magnify the amplification
    B. increase the power output
    C. increase the impedance of the loudspeaker
    D. reduce distortion in the output stage

34. Constant-current inverse feedback is USUALLY obtained by
    A. increasing the value of the capacitor across the cathode resistor
    B. omitting the bypass capacitor across the cathode tube
    C. increasing the gain of the output tube
    D. decreasing the plate resistance of the output tube

35. In order to make more natural the reproduction of music which has a very large volume range in a phonograph amplifier, it is BEST to use a(n)
    A. linear response amplifier
    B. volume suppressor
    C. volume expander
    D. output stage with two tubes in push-push

36. The limiter in FM receivers has the function of eliminating _____ from the input to the detector.
    A. the second harmonic
    B. the third harmonic
    C. FM-variations
    D. amplitude variations

Questions 37-39.

DIRECTIONS: Questions 37 through 39 are to be answered on the basis of the following diagram.

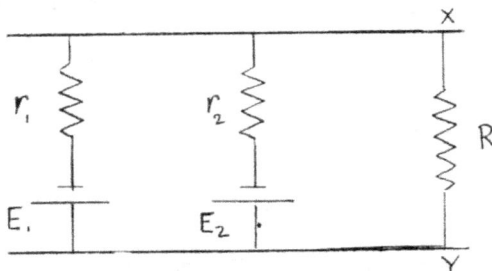

37. If $r_1 = .01$ ohm, $r_2 = .01$ ohm, $E_1 = 1$ volt, and $R = $ infinity, the voltage across xy is MOST NEARLY
    A. 2 volts
    B. 1 volt
    C. .2 volt
    D. .1 volt

38. If $r_1 = .01$ ohm, $r_2 = .01$ ohm, $E_1 = 1$ volt, $E_2 = 2$ volts, and $R = $ infinity, the voltage across xy is MOST NEARLY
    A. .5
    B. 1
    C. 1.5
    D. 2

39. If $r_1 = .01$ ohm, $r_2 = .01$ ohm, $E_1 = 1$ volt, $E_1 = 1$ volt, $E_2 = 2$ volts, and $R = 1$ ohm, the voltage across xy is MOST NEARLY
    A. .5
    B. 9
    C. 1.1
    D. 1.5

40.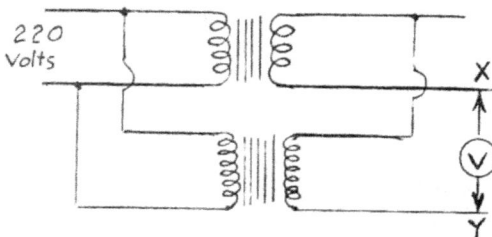

Two transformers with ratios of 2:1 are to be connected in parallel. To test for proper connections, the circuit shown above is used. The transformers may be connected in parallel by connecting Lead "X" to Lead "Y" if the voltmeter shown reads
    A. zero
    B. 120
    C. 220
    D. 340

Questions 41-42.

DIRECTIONS: Questions 41 and 42 are to be answered on the basis of the following figure.

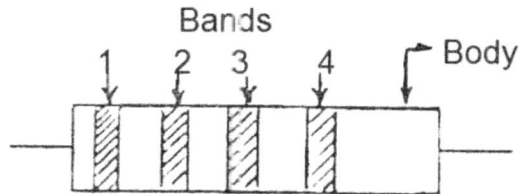

41. In the standard RMA color code chart for the value of resistors, the band numbered 1 in the above figure represents the
  A. decimal multiplier
  B. tolerance
  C. first significant figure
  D. second significant figure

41.____

42. With reference to the RMA color code chart for the value of resistors, if the 1st band is red, the 2nd band black, the 3rd band black, and the 4th band silver, the value of this resistor is
  A. 100 ohms 10%
  B. 2000 ohms 5%
  C. 100 ohms 5%
  D. q200 ohms 10%

42.____

43. A condenser having a capacitance of one microfarad is connected across a 1000-volt D-C line. The energy stored by this condenser is
  A. 10 watts B. ½ watt C. 10 joules D. ½ joule

43.____

44. If a powdered iron core is inserted into an inductance coil, the coil
  A. resistance is increased
  B. inductance is increased
  C. inductance is decreased
  D. resistance is decreased

44.____

45. If a brass core is inserted into an inductance coil, the coil
  A. resistance is increased
  B. inductance is increased
  C. inductance is decreased
  D. resistance is decreased

45.____

46. A disadvantage of the limiter commonly used in FM receivers is that it requires, for proper operation, a
  A. small signal amplitude
  B. low radio frequency amplification
  C. large signal amplitude
  D. high screen voltage

46.____

47. In the ratio detector the radio frequency is fed to the diodes in the same manner as in the FM discriminator except that the diodes in the ratio detector are connected in
  A. parallel B. push-push C. push-pull D. series

47.____

48. A general-purpose instrument that may be used for the measurement of the output frequency of an r-f oscillator within accuracies of from .25% to 2% is known as a(n)
  A. absorption wave meter
  B. Wien frequency bridge
  C. Maxwell Bridge
  D. meteorograph bridge

48.____

49. The frequency of oscillation of a multivibrator is determined by the values of the
    A. resistance and inductance
    B. inductance and capacity
    C. resistance and capacity
    D. capacity alone

50. With reference to radio-frequency measurements, a primary standard of frequency is defined as one whose frequency is determined
    A. directly in terms of time
    B. by comparison with another standard
    C. by the value of the RC constant
    D. by the values of L and C in the circuit

51. If a .75 kw transmitter produces a field intensity of 10 millivolts per meter at a distance of 5 miles and is received by an antenna having an effective height of 10 meters, the millivolts of signal induced in the antenna (neglecting losses) will be MOST NEARLY
    A. 50   B. 75   C. 100   D. 125

52. With reference to directive microwave antennae, the parabolic reflector possesses the characteristic that
    A. the intensity of the reflected rays varies as the square of the distance
    B. all rays from the radiator striking the reflecting surface are reflected as parallel rays
    C. the intensity of the reflected rays varies inversely as the square of the distance
    D. all rays striking the reflecting surface are reflected as diverging rays

53. With reference to the oscilloscope, Lissajous curves are widely used for
    A. aligning radio I.F. transformers
    B. aligning television tuners
    C. obtaining a response curve of the I.F. stages in FM receivers
    D. frequency comparison

54. The one of the following oscillators which is used to deflect periodically the electron beam of a cathode-ray tube so as to give a displacement that is a function of time is the _____ oscillator.
    A. sweep   B. beat   C. jump   D. connecting

55. The impedance in ohms measured between the terminals of a transmission line at the operating frequency is called _____ impedance.
    A. patch   B. lumped   C. surge   D. sweep

56. Decibels may be calculated by multiplying the common logarithm of the power ratio by ten. Therefore, a power ratio of 100 corresponds to MOST NEARLY
    A. 10 db   B. 20 db   C. 30 db   D. 40 db

57. Power factor is defined as the ratio of active power to apparent power, generally expressed in percent. In accordance with the definition given above, the power factor of a pure resistance is
    A. zero   B. unity   C. infinity   D. indeterminate

Questions 58-59.

DIRECTIONS: Questions 58 and 59 are to be answered on the basis of the following data.

An L resistance attenuation network is required to match, with minimum less, a 500-ohm source Z_S and a 250-ohm lead Z_L; use the design data given below.

$$R_1 = \sqrt{Z_S(Z_S - Z_L)}$$
$$R_2 = \frac{Z_S Z_L}{R_1}$$

58. Using the above data and formula, the value of resistor R_1 for this network is MOST NEARLY
    A. 353   B. 305   C. 253   D. 75

59. With reference to the above L pad and formula, the value of R_2 is MOST NEARLY
    A. 353   B. 305   C. 253   D. 75

60. In frequency modulation receivers, noise
    A. causes an amplitude disturbance only
    B. is completely eliminated by the limiter
    C. causes some variation in the frequency swing of the desired signal
    D. has no effect

61. An open quarter-wave stub may be used as a
    A. suppressor of even and odd harmonics
    B. suppressor of even harmonics only
    C. suppressor of odd harmonics only
    D. filter of odd harmonics only

62. A closed quarter-wave stub offers an infinite impedance at
    A. low frequencies   B. high frequencies
    C. the resonant frequency   D. all frequencies

63. The one of the following which is COMMONLY used as a standing wave detector operating as a current indicator is a _____ pick-up loop with the ends connected to a _____ galvanometer.
    A. one-turn; r-f thermo   B. one-turn; D'Arsonval
    C. 1000-turn; r-f thermo   D. 1000-turn; D'Arsonval

64. If a line having a characteristic impedance of 300 ohms is terminated in a resistive load of 50 ohms, the standing-wave ratio is MOST NEARLY
   A. 1 to 12   B. 12 to 1   C. 1 to 6   D. 6 to 1

64._____

65. In aligning the sound discriminator of an FM receiver with an oscilloscope, the pattern that should be obtained for proper adjustment is a(n) _____ curve.
   A. symmetrical "S"
   B. asymmetrical "S"
   C. symmetrical parabolic
   D. asymmetrical parabolic

65._____

66. In AM radio telephone transmitters, negative feedback
   A. is not used
   B. makes impractical the use of high-efficiency systems
   C. makes impractical the use of a power supply system with relatively inexpensive filtering
   D. decreases the amplitude distortion

66._____

Questions 67-70.

DIRECTIONS: Questions 67 through 70 are to be answered on the basis of the following description of a certain transmitter.

The radio transmitter is a frequency-modulated unit utilizing the phase-shift method of obtaining frequency deviations, and as such exhibits considerably different characteristics than the usual amplitude-modulated units.

Intelligence is conveyed in frequency variations of the constant-amplitude carrier wave. The use of the phase-shift method of frequency modulation allows direct crystal control of the mean carrier frequency a necessity in unattended and mobile equipment. It necessitates, however, considerable frequency multiplication after the tubes are used for this function, and a total frequency multiplication of 48 times is effected. A twin triode acts as both crystal oscillator and phase modulator. The first half of the tube operates in a resistance coupled aperiodic oscillator circuit. The output frequency range is 152-162 mc.

The second half of the twin triode acts as a phase modulator. The r-f output of the crystal oscillator is impressed on the phase-modulator grid by means of a blocking condenser. The cathode circuit is provided with a large amount of degeneration by an unbypassed cathode resistor. Because of this degeneration feedback, the transconductance of the triode is abnormally low—so low that the plate current is affected about as much by the direct grid-plate capacitance as by the transconductance. The two effects result in plate current vectors almost 180° apart, and the total plate current is the resultant of the two components. In phase it will be about 90° removed from the phase of the voltage impressed on the grid. When audio is impressed on the grid thereby periodically changing the bias, and in consequence the transconductance, the plate current undergoes a periodic change in both amplitude and phase. The amplitude modulation is unimportant, and is removed in the frequency multipliers, but the phase modulation remains and is the essential element of the transmitted signal.

67. With reference to the above information, the crystal frequency will be between
   A. 152 and 162 mc
   B. 15.2 and 16.2 mc
   C. 3166.67 and 3375.0 Kc
   D. 316.67 and 337.50 Kc

67._____

68. In the second part of the twin triode, the cathode resistor 68.____
    A. is shunted by a large condenser
    B. has no condenser
    C. is shunted by a small condenser
    D. is in series with an electrolytic condenser

69. In this transmitter, frequency multiplication occurs 69.____
    A. after modulation
    B. before modulation
    C. in the phase modulator
    D. in the oscillator circuit

70. With reference to the above information, when the audio is impressed on the grid of the second triode of the twin triode, 70.____
    A. the plate current undergoes a change in amplitude only
    B. the plate current undergoes a change in amplitude and phase
    C. any amplitude modulation is cut off by the transconductance
    D. any phase modulation is eliminated.

KEY (CORRECT ANSWERS)

1.	C	11.	B	21.	C	31.	B	41.	C	51.	C	61.	B
2.	C	12.	B	22.	D	32.	A	42.	D	52.	B	62.	C
3.	C	13.	A	23.	A	33.	D	43.	D	53.	D	63.	A
4.	C	14.	C	24.	D	34.	B	44.	B	54.	A	64.	D
5.	B	15.	B	25.	B	35.	C	45.	C	55.	C	65.	A
6.	A	16.	D	26.	C	36.	D	46.	C	56.	B	66.	D
7.	C	17.	A	27.	C	37.	B	47.	D	57.	B	67.	C
8.	A	18.	C	28.	C	38.	C	48.	A	58.	A	68.	B
9.	A	19.	B	29.	D	39.	D	49.	C	59.	A	69.	A
10.	C	20.	D	30.	D	40.	A	50.	A	60.	C	70.	B

TEST 5

DIRECTIONS: Each question or incomplete statement is followed by several suggested answers or completions. Select the one that BEST answers the question or completes the statement. *PRINT THE LETTER OF THE CORRECT ANSWER IN THE SPACE AT THE RIGHT.*

1. The unit of measure of magnetomotive force is the   1._____
   A. gilbert   B. gauss   C. henry   D. mho

2. The figure of merit of a coil or circuit is   2._____
   A. $\frac{R}{Z}$ B. $\frac{X_L}{R}$ C. $X_c X_L$ D. $Z = R$

3. The molecular friction produced by the alternating current reversals in a magnetic core material is known as   3._____
   A. retentivity   B. hysteresis
   C. eddy current   D. counter M.M.F.

4. One horsepower is equal to _____ watts.   4._____
   A. 467   B. 647   C. 1646   D. 746

5. The ability of a magnetic material to conduct magnetic lines of force is called   5._____
   A. reluctance   B. conductance
   C. permeability   D. admittance

6. A small mica condenser marked with three dots as follows—1. Red, 2. Green, 3. Brown—has a capacitance of what value?   6._____
   A. 250 mmf   B. 2500 mmf   C. 25 mmf   D. 2.5 mmf

7. If the current through the windings of an electromagnet is constantly increased, the field strength will increase in proportion to the current, up to a certain point, beyond which the field strength will increase only slightly for a further increase in current. This point is called   7._____
   A. permeability   B. saturation
   C. BH curve   D. phase point

8. Gold band on a resistor indicates a tolerance of   8._____
   A. 10%   B. 20%   C. 5%   D. 15%

9. Placing a "permeability slug" into an rf transformer will   9._____
   A. decrease the frequency of the ckt.
   B. increase the frequency of the ckt.
   C. decrease the inductance
   D. none of the above

10. What law states that the total current entering a junction in a circuit is equal to the total current leaving that junction?   10._____
    A. Lenz's   B. Coulomb's   C. Ohm's   D. Kirchhoff's

11. The MAXIMUM current carrying capacity of a resistor marked "5000 Ohms-200 Watts" is _____ amperes.
   A. 25   B. .2   C. 2   D. 2.5

12. Three condensers of 2 uF, 2 uF, and 4 uF are connected in series. The resulting capacitance of this combination will be _____ uF.
   A. 0.8   B. 8.0   C. 1.6   D. 16

13. In order to obtain the maximum short circuit current from a group of similar cells in a storage battery, they should be connected in
   A. parallel
   B. series-parallel
   C. series
   D. parallel-series

14.

   I_T equals _____ amp.
   A. .5   B. 5½   C. 2   D. 0

15. A resistor marked as follows—Body: red; Tip: Green; Band or dot: Orange—has a value of how many ohms?
   A. 1400 ohms
   B. 36,000 ohms
   C. 25,000 ohms
   D. .25 MEG

16. A 10W, 1000 ohm resistor is in parallel with a 100W, 10,000 ohm resistor and a 50W, 20,000 ohm resistor. The HIGHEST permissible line voltage for this combination without exceeding the power ratings of these resistors is
   A. 1,000 volts   B. 10 volts   C. 100 volts   D. 500 volts

17. The fully charged condition of a lead acid storage cell is indicated when a hydrometer reads
   A. 1.080   B. 1.280   C. 1.150   D. 1.500

18. You are called upon to repair, if possible, a storage battery which is discharged and in which the cells are only half full of electrolyte. You should FIRST
   A. fill with a solution of acid and water to 1200 S.G.
   B. fill with plain distilled water and charge
   C. pour out remaining electrolyte and refill with a new solution of water and acid to 1200 S.G.
   D. none of the above—the battery is beyond repair

19.

The voltmeter connected as shown above will read the voltage drop across
A. R_1 B. R_2 C. R_1 and R_2 D. R_2 and R_3

20. A radio receiver has a power transformer designed to supply 250 volts when operating from a 110-volt, 60-cycle supply line.
When the primary is connected to a 110-volt D.C. source, the
A. secondary voltage will decrease
B. secondary voltage will increase
C. primary current will decrease
D. primary current will increase

21. A coupling system that passes certain frequencies and at the same time rejects other frequencies is called
A. choke   B. phase shifter
C. filter   D. bypass condenser

22. Audio frequencies lie between
A. 200 to 200,000 cps   B. 20 to 20,000 cps
C. 60 to 120 cps   D. 5 to 4,000 cps

23. Vertical sweep circuits may be distinguished from horizontal by their
A. higher plate voltages   B. larger capacity condensers
C. greater power ratings on controls   D. lower plate voltages

24. In an inverted amplifier, output is taken from the _____ circuit.
A. plate   B. cathode   C. control grid   D. shield grid

25. Poor reception on a newly installed commercial television receiver GENERALLY indicates
A. improper adjustment of I.F. stages
B. improper adjustment of 8.25 Mc trap
C. wrong value R-C components in sweep circuits
D. poor antenna installation

26. The voltage across the output of the discriminator at resonance should
A. be a maximum
B. be a minimum
C. vary between a maximum and a minimum
D. be a value depending on the signal voltage

27. For optimum operation of an A.F. resistance coupled voltage amplifier using a triode (not considering frequency restrictions), the plate resistor should be
    A. equal to the plate resistance of the tube
    B. equal to the transconductance of the tube
    C. twice the plate resistance of the tube
    D. equal to plate voltage divided by plate current of the tube

28. Peak inverse voltage being delivered to a full wave rectifier with condenser input is equal to r.m.s. of total secondary
    A. X 1.414
    B. X .707
    C. X .636
    D. plus voltage on condenser

29. In performing a visual alignment, the voltage fed into the stages to be aligned MUST be
    A. amplitude modulated
    B. unmodulated
    C. frequency modulated
    D. demodulated

30. The discriminator in an FM receiver corresponds to the stage in an AM receiver known as the
    A. converter
    B. second detector
    C. output amplifier
    D. preselector

31. A 200 mmfd padder is connected in series with a 400 mmfd tuning condenser. The total MAXIMUM capacity will be _____ mmfd.
    A. 600
    B. 300
    C. 133
    D. 266

32. Shunting a "tank circuit" with an inducftance will make it
    A. respond to a higher frequency
    B. respond to a lower frequency
    C. destroy its oscillatory action
    D. decrease its resistive component

33. Video frequencies in modern television service range from
    A. 15-15,000 cps
    B. 30-3,500 cps
    C. 44-71 mcs
    D. 4.3-12 mcs

34. A superheterodyne is tuned to a desired signal at 1000 Kc. Its conversion oscillator is operating at 1300 Kc. A signal at _____ Kc may cause an image interference.
    A. 300
    B. 900
    C. 1600
    D. 100

35. The plate E of an RF or IF stage is above normal. The screen grid E is above normal. The cathode E is above normal. Trouble PROBABLY is (E = voltage)
    A. open screen dropping resistor
    B. shorted plate loud resistor
    C. open cathode resistor
    D. shorted screen bi-pass condenser

36. Low output voltage from AC/DC power supply may be caused by open
    A. output filter condenser
    B. condenser in power amplifier cathode circuit
    C. condenser on input side of filter
    D. coupling condenser to power amplifier

37. Adjustments in Lelcher-Wires are GENERALLY accomplished by
    A. sliding a shorting-bar along the line
    B. trimming off the ends of the line
    C. placing a variable condenser across the lines
    D. varying the spacing between the lines

38. Local oscillators in FM receivers often have a mica and a ceramic condenser in parallel across the tank. The purpose of this combination is to
    A. increase the "Q" of the circuit
    B. operate the tank at a greater C/L ratio
    C. prevent temperature co-efficient drift
    D. prevent breakdown of condensers

39. A signal reaching the grid of a grid-leak type of limiter, at a peak value greater than the bias on the tube, will PROBABLY cause
    A. lack of linearity in discriminator output
    B. second-harmonic distortion in A.F. output
    C. saturation in the discriminator "S" curve
    D. normal operation of the stage

40. Frequency adjustments in Klystron tubes are GENERALLY made by
    A. sliding a shorting-bar along the lines
    B. mechanically compressing the tube along its length
    C. tuning the pickup loop
    D. changing the grid-bias

41. The second harmonic of 200 meters is _____ meters.
    A. 400   B. 100   C. 800   D. 50

42. To reduce the natural resonant frequency of a Marconi antenna, we may
    A. place an inductance in series with the antenna
    B. place a condenser in series with the antenna
    C. operate the antenna on a harmonic
    D. reduce the physical length of the antenna

43. The length of a ¼ wave vertical radiator for 800 Kc operation should be ABOUT _____ meters.
    A. 200   B. 94   C. 400   D. 367

44. Alignment of a discriminator is BEST checked by
    A. use of an output meter   B. use of an audio analyzer
    C. use of a vacuum tube voltmeter   D. ear

45. A line may be kept non-resonant by
    A. terminating the line at its natural impedance
    B. keeping it an even number of ¼ waves long
    C. twisting or transposing the wires
    D. running one conductor inside the other

46. Placing a reflector behind a di-pole antenna makes it   46.____
    A. non-directional
    B. directional away from the reflector
    C. directional toward the side on which the reflector is placed
    D. directional toward its end

47. Klystron tubes depend for their action upon   47.____
    A. parallel-line tanks connected to the grids
    B. class "C" operation with a TPTG circuit
    C. bunching of electrons in a velocity-electron stream
    D. circular rotation of electrons under a strong magnetic influence

48. Ordinary vacuum tubes are ineffective in UHF circuits because   48.____
    A. their plate currents are too high
    B. heater voltages of 6.3V a.c. are impractical at ultra-high frequencies
    C. socket terminals will arc over at UHF
    D. inter-electrode capacities are too high for ultra-high frequencies

49. Wave-guides are NOT used at low frequencies because   49.____
    A. long waves cannot be guided
    B. power is too great at low frequencies
    C. their physical size would be impractical
    D. the wavelength of low frequencies is too short

50. The hum frequency of a full wave rectifier is _____ the frequency of the line voltage frequency.   50.____
    A. once
    B. twice
    C. three times
    D. four times

KEY (CORRECT ANSWERS)

1. A	11. B	21. C	31. C	41. B
2. B	12. A	22. B	32. A	42. A
3. B	13. A	23. B	33. B	43. B
4. D	14. B	24. B	34. C	44. C
5. C	15. C	25. D	35. C	45. A
6. A	16. C	26. B	36. C	46. B
7. B	17. B	27. C	37. A	47. C
8. C	18. B	28. A	38. C	48. D
9. A	19. D	29. C	39. D	49. C
10. D	20. D	30. B	40. B	50. B

EXAMINATION SECTION
TEST 1

DIRECTIONS: Each question or incomplete statement is followed by several suggested answers or completions. Select the one that BEST answers the question or completes the statement. *PRINT THE LETTER OF THE CORRECT ANSWER IN THE SPACE AT THE RIGHT.*

Questions 1-6.

DIRECTIONS: Questions 1 through 6 are to be answered on the basis of the circuit diagram below. All switches are initially open.

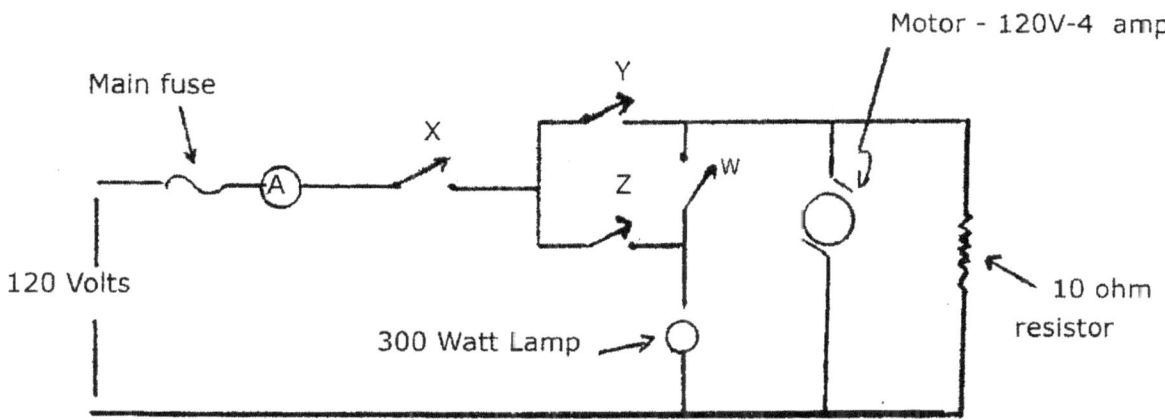

1. To light the 300 watt lamp, the following switches MUST be closed: 1.____
   A. X and Y   B. Y and Z   C. X and Z   D. X and W

2. If all of the switches W, X, Y, and Z are closed, the following will happen: 2.____
   A. The lamp will light and the motor will rotate
   B. The lamp will light and the motor will not rotate
   C. The lamp will not light and the motor will not rotate
   D. A short circuit will occur and the main fuse will blow

3. With 120 volts applied across the 10 ohm resistor, the current drawn by the resistor is _____ amp(s). 3.____
   A. 1/12   B. 1.2   C. 12   D. 1200

4. With 120 volts applied to the 10 ohm resistor, the power used by the resistor is _____ kw. 4.____
   A. 1.44   B. 1.2   C. .144   D. .12

5. The current drawn by the 300 watt lamp when lighted should be APPROXIMATELY _____ amps. 5.____
   A. 2.5   B. 3.6   C. 25   D. 36

123

6. In the circuit shown, the symbol A is used to indicate a (n)

   A. ammeter
   B. *and* circuit
   C. voltmeter
   D. wattmeter

7. Of the following materials, the BEST conductor of electricity is

   A. iron   B. copper   C. aluminum   D. glass

8. The sum of 6'6", 5'9", and 2' 1 1/2" is

   A. 13'4 1/2"   B. 13'6 1/2"   C. 14'4 1/2"   D. 14'6 1/2"

9.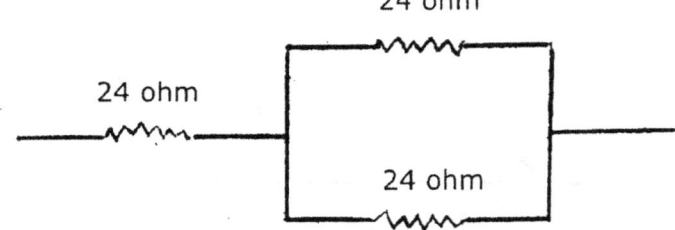

   The equivalent resistance of the three resistors shown in the sketch above is _____ ohms.

   A. 8   B. 24   C. 36   D. 72

10.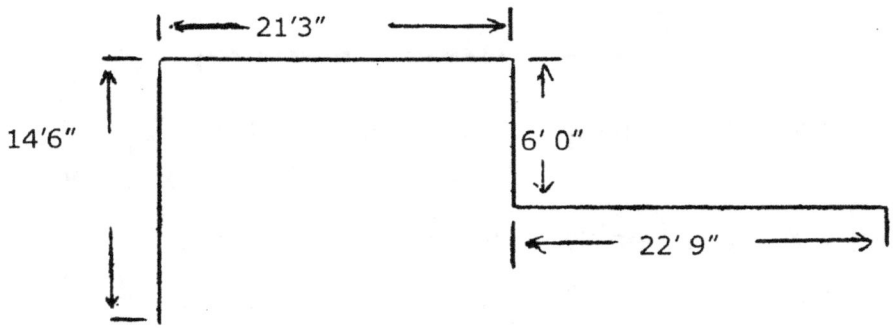

    The TOTAL length of electrical conduit that must be run along the path shown on the diagram above is

    A. 63'8"   B. 64'6"   C. 65'6"   D. 66'8"

11. Of the following electrical devices, the one that is NOT normally used in direct current electrical circuits is a (n)

    A. circuit breaker
    B. double-pole switch
    C. transformer
    D. inverter

12. The number of 120-volt light bulbs that should NORMALLY be connected in series across a 600-volt electric line is

    A. 1   B. 2   C. 3   D. 5

13. Of the following motors, the one that does NOT have any brushes is the _____ motor. 13._____

   A. d.c. shunt
   B. d.c. series
   C. squirrel cage induction
   D. compound

14. Of the following materials, the one that is COMMONLY used as an electric heating element in an electric heater is 14._____

   A. zinc
   B. brass
   C. terne plate
   D. nichrome

Questions 15-25.

DIRECTIONS: Questions 15 through 25 are to be answered on the basis of the instruments listed below. Each instrument is listed with an identifying number in front of it.

    1 - Hygrometer   9 - Vernier caliper
    2 - Ammeter   10 - Wire gage
    3 - Voltmeter   11 - 6-foot folding rule
    4 - Wattmeter   12 - Architect's scale
    5 - Megger   13 - Planimeter
    6 - Oscilloscope   14 - Engineer's scale
    7 - Frequency meter   15 - Ohmmeter
    8 - Micrometer

15. The instrument that should be used to accurately measure the resistance of a 4,700 ohm resistor is Number 15._____

   A. 3   B. 4   C. 7   D. 15

16. To measure the current in an electrical circuit, the instrument that should be used is Number 16._____

   A. 2   B. 7   C. 8   D. 15

17. To measure the insulation resistance of a rubber-covered electrical cable, the instrument that should be used is Number 17._____

   A. 4   B. 5   C. 8   D. 15

18. An AC motor is hooked up to a power distribution box.
    In order to check the voltage at the motor terminals, the instrument that should be used is Number 18._____

   A. 2   B. 3   C. 4   D. 7

19. To measure the shaft diameter of a motor accurately to one-thousandth of an inch, the instrument that should be used is Number 19._____

   A. 8   B. 10   C. 11   D. 14

20. The instrument that should be used to determine whether 25 Hz. or 60 Hz. is present in an electrical circuit is Number 20._____

   A. 4   B. 5   C. 7   D. 8

21. Of the following, the PROPER instrument to use to determine the diameter of the conductor of a piece of electrical hook-up wire is Number

    A. 10   B. 11   C. 12   D. 14

22. The amount of electrical power being used in a balanced three-phase circuit should be measured with Number

    A. 2   B. 3   C. 4   D. 5

23. The electrical wave form at a given point in an electronic circuit can be observed with Number

    A. 2   B. 3   C. 6   D. 7

24. The PROPER instrument to use for measuring the width of a door is Number

    A. 11   B. 12   C. 13   D. 14

25. A one-inch hole with a tolerance of plus or minus three-thousandths is reamed in a steel block.
    The PROPER instrument to use to accurately check the diameter of the hole is Number

    A. 8   B. 9   C. 11   D. 14

KEY (CORRECT ANSWERS)

1. C		11. C	
2. A		12. D	
3. C		13. C	
4. A		14. D	
5. A		15. D	
6. A		16. A	
7. B		17. B	
8. C		18. B	
9. C		19. A	
10. B		20. C	

21. A
22. C
23. C
24. A
25. B

TEST 2

DIRECTIONS: Each question or incomplete statement is followed by several suggested answers or completions. Select the one that BEST answers the question or completes the statement. *PRINT THE LETTER OF THE CORRECT ANSWER IN THE SPACE AT THE RIGHT.*

1. The number of conductors required to connect a 3-phase delta connected heater bank to an electric power panel board is

   A. 2 B. 3 C. 4 D. 5

2. Of the following, the wire size that is MOST commonly used for branch lighting circuits in homes is _____ A.W.G.

   A. #12 B. #8 C. #6 D. #4

3. When installing electrical circuits, the tool that should be used to pull wire through a conduit is a

   A. mandrel B. snake
   C. rod D. pulling iron

4. Of the following AC voltages, the LOWEST voltage that a neon test lamp can detect is _____ volts.

   A. 6 B. 12 C. 80 D. 120

5. Of the following, the BEST procedure to use when storing tools that are subject to rusting is to

   A. apply a thin coating of soap onto the tools
   B. apply a light coating of oil to the tools
   C. wrap the tools in clean cheesecloth
   D. place the tools in a covered container

6. If a 3 1/2 inch long nail is required to nail wood framing members together, the nail size to use should be

   A. 2d B. 4d C. 16d D. 60d

7. Of the four motors listed below, the one that can operate only on alternating current is a(n) _____ motor.

   A. series B. shunt
   C. compound D. induction

8. The sum of 1/3 + 2/5 + 5/6 is

   A. 1 17/30 B. 1 3/5 C. 1 15/24 D. 1 5/6

9. Of the following instruments, the one that should be used to measure the state of charge of a lead-acid storage battery is a(n)

   A. ammeter B. ohmmeter
   C. hydrometer D. thermometer

10. If three 1 1/2 volt dry cell batteries are wired in series, the TOTAL voltage provided by the three batteries is _____ volts.

    A. 1.5 B. 3 C. 4.5 D. 6.0

11. Taking into account time and one-half payment for time over 40 hours of work, the gross pay of an employee who works 43 hours in a week at a rate of pay of $10.68 per hour is

    A. $427.20 B. $459.24 C. $475.26 D. $491.28

12. The sum of 0.365 + 3.941 + 10.676 + 0.784 is

    A. 13.766 B. 15.666 C. 15.756 D. 15.766

13. In order to transmit mechanical power between two rotating shafts at right angles to each other, two gears are used. Of the following, the type of gears that should be used are _____ gears.

    A. herringbone
    B. spur
    C. bevel
    D. rack and pinion

14. To properly ground the service electrical equipment in a building, a ground connection should be made to _____ the building.

    A. the waste or soil line leaving
    B. the vent line going to the exterior of
    C. any steel beam in
    D. the cold water line entering

15. The area of the triangle shown at the right is _____ square inches.
    A. 120
    B. 240
    C. 360
    D. 480

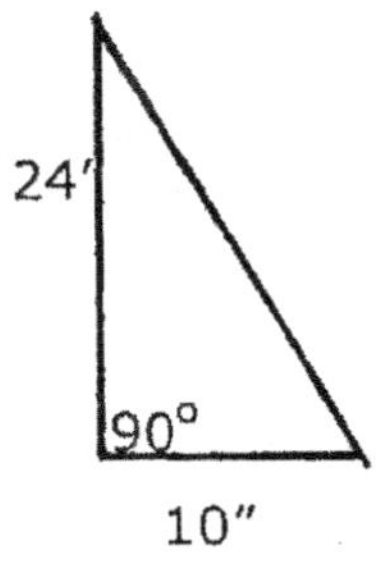

Questions 16-25.

DIRECTIONS: Questions 16 through 25 are to be answered on the basis of the tools shown on the next page. The tools are not shown to scale. Each tool is shown with an identifying number alongside it.

3 (#2)

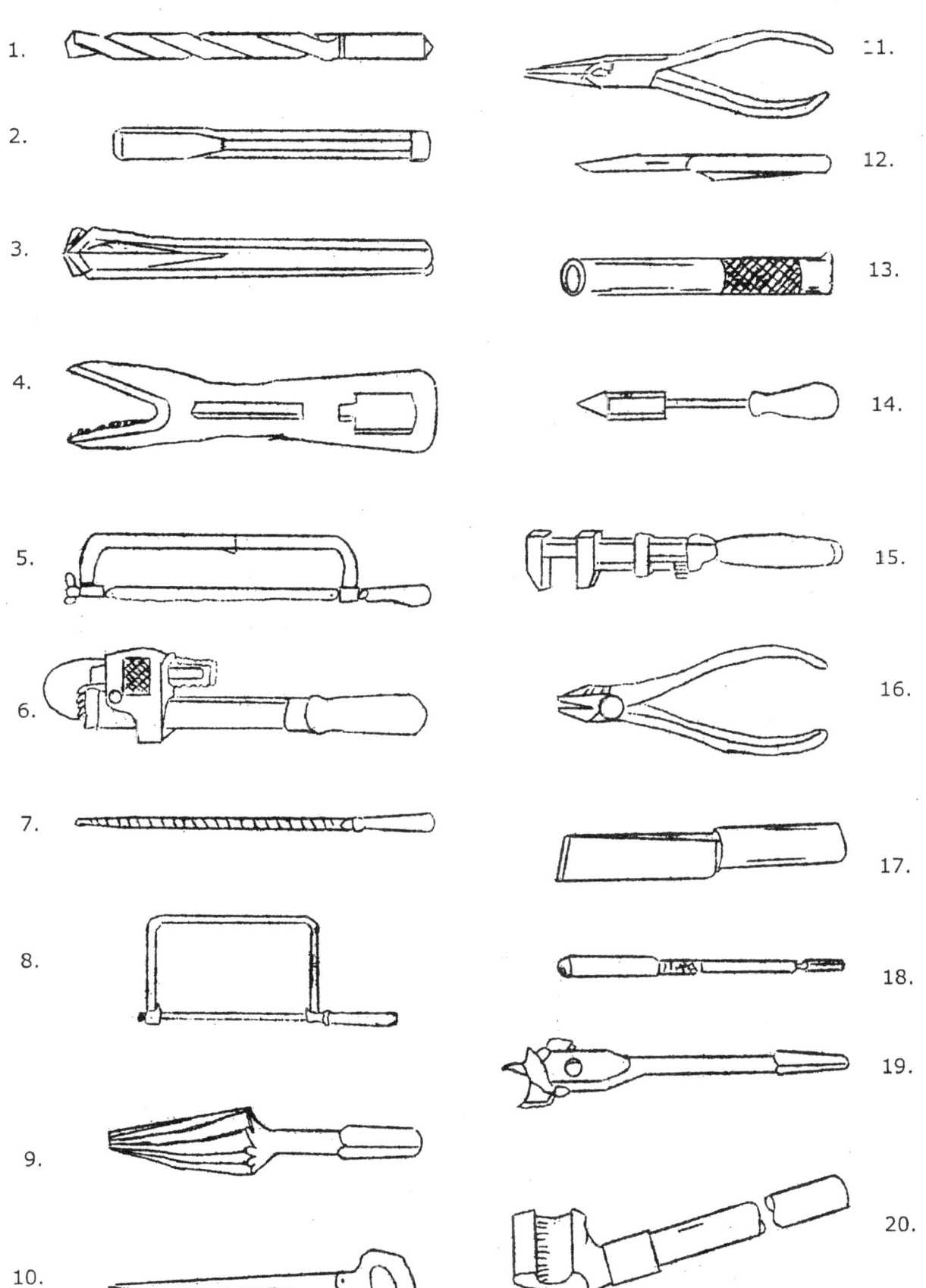

129

16. The tool that should be used for cutting thin wall steel conduit is Number 16._____
    A. 5   B. 8   C. 10   D. 16

17. The tool that should be used for cutting a 1 7/8 inch diameter hole in a wood joist is Number 17._____
    A. 3   B. 9   C. 14   D. 19

18. The tool that should be used for soldering splices in electrical wire is Number 18._____
    A. 3   B. 7   C. 13   D. 14

19. After cutting off a piece of 3/4 inch diameter electrical conduit, the tool that should be used for removing a burr from the inside of the conduit is Number 19._____
    A. 9   B. 11   C. 12   D. 14

20. The tool that should be used for turning a coupling onto a threaded conduit is Number 20._____
    A. 6   B. 11   C. 15   D. 16

21. The tool that should be used for cutting wood lathing in plaster walls is Number 21._____
    A. 5   B. 7   C. 10   D. 12

22. The tool that should be used for drilling a 3/8 inch diameter hole in a steel beam is Number 22._____
    A. 1   B. 2   C. 3   D. 9

23. Of the following, the BEST tool to use for stripping insulation from electrical hook-up wire is Number 23._____
    A. 11   B. 12   C. 15   D. 20

24. The tool that should be used for bending an electrical wire around a terminal post is Number 24._____
    A. 4   B. 11   C. 15   D. 16

25. The tool that should be used for cutting electrical hookup wire is Number 25._____
    A. 5   B. 12   C. 16   D. 17

KEY (CORRECT ANSWERS)

1. B
2. A
3. B
4. C
5. B

6. C
7. D
8. A
9. C
10. C

11. C
12. D
13. C
14. D
15. A

16. A
17. D
18. D
19. A
20. A

21. C
22. A
23. B
24. B
25. C

TEST 3

DIRECTIONS: Each question or incomplete statement is followed by several suggested answers or completions. Select the one that BEST answers the question or completes the statement. *PRINT THE LETTER OF THE CORRECT ANSWER IN THE SPACE AT THE RIGHT.*

1. An electric circuit has current flowing through it. The panel board switch feeding the circuit is opened, causing arcing across the switch contacts.
   Generally, this arcing is caused by

   A. a lack of energy storage in the circuit
   B. electrical energy stored by a capacitor
   C. electrical energy stored by a resistor
   D. magnetic energy induced by an inductance

   1.____

2. MOST filter capacitors in radios have a capacity rating given in

   A. microvolts   B. milliamps
   C. millihenries   D. microfarads

   2.____

3. Of the following, the electrical wire size that is COMMONLY used for telephone circuits is _____ A.W.G.

   A. #6   B. #10   C. #12   D. #22

   3.____

Questions 4-9.

DIRECTIONS: Questions 4 through 9 are to be answered on the basis of the electrical circuit diagram shown below, where letters are used to identify various circuit components.

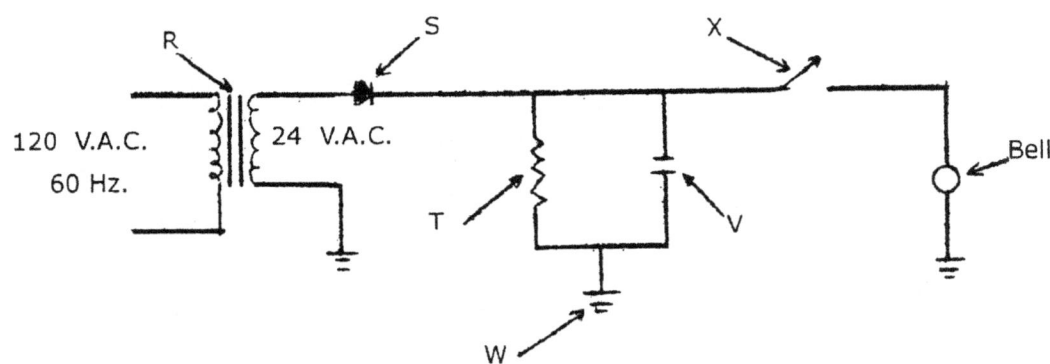

4. The device indicated by the letter R is a

   A. capacitor   B. converter
   C. resistor   D. transformer

   4.____

5. The device indicated by the letter S is a

   A. transistor   B. diode
   C. thermistor   D. directional relay

   5.____

132

6. The devices indicated by the letters T and V are used together to _____ components of the secondary current.

   A. reduce the AC
   B. reduce the DC
   C. transform the AC
   D. invert the AC

7. The letter W points to a standard electrical symbol for a

   A. wire
   B. ground
   C. terminal
   D. lightning arrestor

8. Closing switch X will apply the following type of voltage to the bell:

   A. 60 Hz. AC
   B. DC
   C. pulsating AC
   D. 120 Hz. AC

9. The circuit shown contains a _____ rectifier.

   A. mercury-arc
   B. full-wave
   C. bridge
   D. half-wave

10. A bolt specified as 1/4-28 means the following:
    The

    A. bolt is 1/4 inch in diameter and has 28 threads per inch
    B. bolt is 1/4 inch in diameter and is 2.8 inches long
    C. bolt is 1/4 inch long and has 28 threads
    D. threaded portion of the bolt is 1/4 inch long and has 28 threads per inch

11. When cutting 0.045-inch thickness sheet metal, it is BEST to use a hacksaw blade that has _____ teeth per inch.

    A. 7
    B. 12
    C. 18
    D. 32

12. To accurately tighten a bolt to 28 foot-pounds, it is BEST to use a(n) _____ wrench.

    A. pipe
    B. open end
    C. box
    D. torque

13. When bending a 2-inch diameter conduit, the CORRECT tool to use is a

    A. hickey
    B. pipe wrench
    C. hydraulic bender
    D. stock and die

14. When soldering two #20 A.W.G. copper wires together to form a splice, the solder that SHOULD be used is _____ solder.

    A. acid-core
    B. solid-core
    C. rosin-core
    D. liquid

15. A bathroom heating unit draws 10 amperes at 115 volts.
    The hot resistance of the heating unit should be _____ ohms.

    A. .08
    B. 8
    C. 11.5
    D. 1150

16. Of the following materials, the one that is NOT suitable as an electrical insulator is

    A. glass
    B. mica
    C. rubber
    D. platinum

17. An air conditioning unit is rated at 1000 watts. The unit is run for 10 hours per day, five days per week.
If the cost for electrical energy is 5 cents per kilowatt-hour, the weekly cost for electricity should be

   A. 25¢   B. 50¢   C. $2.50   D. $25.00

18. If a fuse is protecting the circuit of a 15 ohm electric heater and it is designed to blow out at a current exceeding 10 amperes, the MAXIMUM voltage from among the following that should be applied across the terminals of the heater is _____ volts.

   A. 110   B. 120   C. 160   D. 600

19. Before opening a pneumatic hose connection, it is important to remove pressure from the hose line PRIMARILY to avoid

   A. losing air
   B. personal injury
   C. damage to the hose connection
   D. a build-up of pressure in the air compressor

20. If the scale on a shop drawing is 1/4 inch to the foot, then a part which measures 3 3/8 inches long on the drawing has an ACTUAL length of _____ feet _____ inches.

   A. 12; 6   B. 13; 6   C. 13; 9   D. 14; 9

21. The function that is USUALLY performed by a motor controller is to

   A. start and stop a motor
   B. protect a motor from a short circuit
   C. prevent bearing failure of a motor
   D. control the brush wear in a motor

22. Of the following galvanized sheet metal electrical outlet boxes, the one that is NOT a commonly used size is the _____ box.

   A. 4" square
   B. 4" octagonal
   C. 4" x 2 1/8"
   D. 4" x 1"

23. When soldering a transistor into a circuit, it is MOST important to protect the transistor from

   A. the application of an excess of rosin flux
   B. excessive heat
   C. the application of an excess of solder
   D. too much pressure

24. When installing BX type cable, it is important to protect the wires in the cable from the cut ends of the armored sheath.
The APPROVED method of providing this protection is to

   A. use a fiber or plastic insulating bushing
   B. file the cut ends of the sheath smooth
   C. use a connector where the cable enters a junction box
   D. tie the wires into an Underwriter's knot

25. While lifting a heavy piece of equipment off the floor, a person should NOT

    A. twist his body
    B. grasp it firmly
    C. maintain a solid footing on the ground
    D. bend his knees

26. It is important that metal cabinets and panels that house electrical equipment should be grounded PRIMARILY in order to

    A. prevent short circuits from occurring
    B. keep all circuits at ground potential
    C. minimize shock hazards
    D. reduce the effects of electrolytic corrosion

27. A foreman explains a technical procedure to a new employee. If the employee does not understand the instructions he has received, it would be BEST if he were to

    A. follow the procedure as best he could
    B. ask the foreman to explain it to him again
    C. avoid following the procedure
    D. ask the foreman to give him other work

28. Of the following, the BEST connectors to use when mounting an electrical panel box directly onto a concrete wall are

    A. threaded studs
    B. machine screws
    C. lag screws
    D. expansion bolts

29. Of the following, the BEST instrument to use to measure the small gap between relay contacts is

    A. a micrometer
    B. a feeler gage
    C. inside calipers
    D. a plug gage

30. A POSSIBLE result of mounting a 40 ampere fuse in a fuse box for a circuit requiring a 20 ampere fuse is that the 40 ampere fuse may

    A. provide twice as much protection to the circuit from overloads
    B. blow more easily than the smaller fuse due to an overload
    C. cause serious damage to the circuit from an overload
    D. reduce power consumption in the circuit

KEY (CORRECT ANSWERS)

1.	D	16.	D
2.	D	17.	C
3.	D	18.	B
4.	D	19.	B
5.	B	20.	B
6.	A	21.	A
7.	B	22.	D
8.	B	23.	B
9.	D	24.	A
10.	A	25.	A
11.	D	26.	C
12.	D	27.	B
13.	C	28.	D
14.	C	29.	B
15.	C	30.	C

EXAMINATION SECTION
TEST 1

DIRECTIONS: Each question or incomplete statement is followed by several suggested answers or completions. Select the one that BEST answers the question or completes the statement. *PRINT THE LETTER OF THE CORRECT ANSWER IN THE SPACE AT THE RIGHT.*

1. The cathode of a phototube is USUALLY coated with a thin layer of _____ oxide.   1._____

    A. magnesium   B. cesium   C. titanium   D. zinc

2. The capacitor on a capacitor motor is connected in _____ winding.   2._____

    A. parallel with the starting
    B. series with the running
    C. parallel with the running
    D. series with the starting

3. The refrigerant used in MOST modern home electric cooling appliances is   3._____

    A. neon   B. argon   C. zenon   D. freon

4. Splicing compound is USUALLY referred to as   4._____

    A. cable varnish   B. friction tape
    C. rubber tape   D. varnish cambric

5. The filament supports of an incandescent lamp are affixed to the   5._____

    A. button rod   B. lead-in wires
    C. steam seal   D. ceramic insulator

6. A non-tamperable fuse is known as a   6._____

    A. fusetron   B. fusetat
    C. circuit breaker   D. Kirkman tamp-lock

7. The wall plate used to cover two toggle switches mounted side by side in a wall box is known as a _____ plate.   7._____

    A. multiple toggle   B. duplex
    C. two gang   D. double

8. Building wire with a thermoplastic insulation is called type   8._____

    A. T.P.   B. R.H.   C. T.W.   D. RH-RW

9. A repulsion-start induction motor operates on   9._____

    A. 4 wire A.C.   B. single phase A.C.
    C. D.C. - 110V-220V   D. A.C. - D.C.

10. A *fish tape* is used to   10._____

    A. pull wires through a conduit   B. weatherproof a splice
    C. test a grounded circuit   D. support long cable runs

137

2 (#1)

11. The color code of a 3 wire #12 cable is

    A. white black green   B. blue black red
    C. white black red   D. red white green

12. The motor that has no brushes or commutator is known as a _____ motor.

    A. split phase   B. capacitor
    C. compound   D. shunt

13. The temperature of a well-designed continuously run motor, delivering its full rated horsepower, should NOT increase by more than _____ Fahrenheit.

    A. 40°   B. 52°   C. 60°   D. 72°

14. A floodlight operating at a point 500 feet from the meter, wired with #14 wire whose resistance is 2.575 ohms per 1000', has a voltage drop of *approximately* _____ volts.

    A. 5.7   B. 11.33   C. 12.74   D. 15.37

15. The grid in the vacuum tube was introduced by

    A. Fauere   B. Oersted   C. De Forest   D. Le Lanche

16. In an element for an electric range, the material that insulates the wire from the tube is

    A. magnesium oxide
    B. asbestos
    C. high temperature fibre glass
    D. titanium oxide

17. Most thermostats and relays that are used to activate and control a home heating system operate on _____ volts.

    A. 6   B. 24   C. 32   D. 46

18. The revolutions per minute of an electric motor can be determined by using a(n)

    A. hydrometer   B. tachometer
    C. pulse indicator   D. prony brake

19. A record player pick-up arm, equipped with a phono cartridge that contains Rochelle-Salts, will produce a voltage known as

    A. phono-electric   B. bio-electric
    C. piezoelectric   D. pyrometric

20. The device that controls the flow of electrons in a solid is the

    A. electron tube   B. transistor
    C. anode   D. cathode

21. Fluorescent lamps are designed to operate on

    A. the rated voltage that appears on the lamp
    B. a rectifier controlled voltage
    C. a 115 volt or 230 volt circuit
    D. a circuit where the voltage fluctuation does not exceed 5%

22. The efficiency of a 3 horsepower motor that requires 2.4 kilowatts to drive it is   22.____

    A. 74%   B. 82%   C. 90%   D. 94%

23. The magnetic resistance that opposes the flow of magnetic current is   23.____

    A. inductance   B. reluctance
    C. reactance   D. impedance

24. The output in lumens per watt for an incandescent lamp (filament type) is _____ to _____ lumens.   24.____

    A. 14; 23   B. 30; 55   C. 50; 57   D. 58; 75

25. The voltage of a battery cell depends upon   25.____

    A. the number of lines cut per second
    B. the size of the plates and the distance they are set apart
    C. material that the plate is made of and the electrolyte used
    D. area of the zinc container

26. Most window-type air conditioners, such as used in the home, are equipped with a(n) _____ motor.   26.____

    A. synchronous   B. R-I
    C. seal-vac   D. hermetically sealed

27. Light that contains only a single color and also a single wave length is known as the _____ light.   27.____

    A. spectrum   B. laser
    C. aurora   D. sodium vapor

28. The *Edison effect* led to the development of the   28.____

    A. mercury vapor lamp   B. radio tube
    C. phonograph   D. fluorescent lamp

29. A device for producing high tension induced current is the _____ coil.   29.____

    A. Ruhmkorff   B. Solenoid   C. Thury   D. Choke

30. In a triode tube, the element placed between the cathode and the plate is called   30.____

    A. rectifier   B. controlled grid
    C. S C C   D. D C C

KEY (CORRECT ANSWERS)

1. B	11. C	21. C
2. D	12. A	22. D
3. D	13. D	23. B
4. C	14. C	24. A
5. A	15. C	25. C
6. B	16. A	26. D
7. C	17. B	27. B
8. C	18. B	28. B
9. B	19. C	29. A
10. A	20. B	30. B

TEST 2

DIRECTIONS: Each question or incomplete statement is followed by several suggested answers or completions. Select the one that BEST answers the question or completes the statement. *PRINT THE LETTER OF THE CORRECT ANSWER IN THE SPACE AT THE RIGHT.*

1. A fixture hickey is used to

   A. bend pipe
   B. suspend a ceiling light
   C. make a 60° offset in BX
   D. ground a fixture

   1.____

2. Nichrome wire is used in electrical heating devices because it

   A. is non-magnetic
   B. has a low melting point
   C. is cheaper than copper wire
   D. has a high resistance

   2.____

3. The letters *E M T* in conduit work refer to

   A. underwriters approval B. thin wall conduit
   C. A.C. use only D. ready for first inspection

   3.____

4. A 120 volt three-way incandescent lamp bulb has

   A. one filament B. two filaments
   C. three filaments D. a variable resistor

   4.____

5. When an object to be copperplated is immersed in its electrolyte, it should be connected to the

   A. anode B. cathode
   C. right terminal D. electrolyte

   5.____

6. A voltmeter consists of a milliammeter and a high resistance which are connected in

   A. multiple B. parallel C. series D. shunt

   6.____

7. A device for producing electricity directly from heat is called a

   A. turbine B. thermocouple
   C. transformer D. rheostat

   7.____

8. The combined resistance of a circuit containing five 40 ohm resistances in parallel is _____ ohms.

   A. 8 B. 20 C. 40 D. 200

   8.____

9. An alternator differs from a D.C. generator because it has no

   A. brushes B. commutator
   C. field poles D. rotor

   9.____

10. The resistance of a wire 1/16 inch in diameter is one OHM. A wire of the same length, but twice the diameter, has a resistance of ohms.

    A. 1/4 B. 1/2 C. 1 D. 2

    10.____

141

11. A device that measures energy consumption of electricity is called a

    A. wattmeter
    B. kilowatthourmeter
    C. kilowatt meter
    D. ammeter

12. A *universal* motor is a(n) _____ motor.

    A. shunt
    B. induction
    C. series
    D. synchronous

13. In a three phase, four wire, 208 volt distribution system, the voltage between any phase wire and the neutral is _____ volts.

    A. 0
    B. 120
    C. 208
    D. 240

14. Of the following, the motor that does NOT have a commutator is

    A. universal
    B. series
    C. repulsion induction
    D. split phase

15. An incandescent lamp rated at 130 volts-100 watts, and operated at 115 volts will

    A. consume more wattage and impair the life of the filament
    B. increase lamp life and reduce wattage consumed
    C. produce fewer lumens per watt and increase lamp efficiency
    D. have no effect on the lamp

16. A 2 horsepower 75% efficient D.C. motor operating at full load draws *approximately* _____ watts.

    A. 1000
    B. 1500
    C. 2000
    D. 3000

17. An insulating material that withstands heat better than wire with more ordinary insulation is

    A. rubber
    B. plastic
    C. rubber with cotton covering
    D. varnished cambric

18. Electrical resistance can be measured with a(n)

    A. voltmeter and an ammeter
    B. A.C. wattmeter
    C. thermocouple
    D. induction coil

19. The property of a circuit that enables it to store electrical energy in the form of an electrostatic field is called

    A. inductance
    B. reactance
    C. resistance
    D. capacitance

20. If a 50 ohm resistance draws two amperes from a circuit, the power it uses is

    A. 0.2 KW
    B. 25 watts
    C. 100 watts
    D. none of the above

21. The world's FIRST central light and power plant was developed by 21.____
    A. Samuel F.B. Morse   B. Lee De Forest
    C. Edwin H. Armstrong   D. Thomas A. Edison

22. A *tuner* circuit consists of a 22.____
    A. zener diode and tunnel transistor
    B. capacitor and inductance coil
    C. resistor and R.F. amplifier tube
    D. resistor and capacitor

23. A hotplate having a resistance of 30 ohms, connected to a 120 volt outlet, would draw a current of _____ amperes. 23.____
    A. 4   B. 90   C. 150   D. 3600

24. Of the following, the term that does NOT relate to magnetism is 24.____
    A. reluctance   B. oersted
    C. coulomb   D. magneto-motive force

25. A basic difference between radio waves and sound waves is that radio waves are 25.____
    A. of a different frequency   B. electrical currents
    C. molecules of air in motion   D. electromagnetic waves

26. An object that has a positive electrostatic charge would have an excess of 26.____
    A. electrons   B. protons
    C. neutrons   D. omega minus particles

27. Of the following, the statement that does NOT apply to a capacitor is that it can 27.____
    A. store electrons
    B. pass alternating current
    C. pass direct current
    D. be used to smooth out pulsating direct current

28. The section of a radio transmitter or receiver that causes a stream of electrons to vibrate back and forth at high frequencies is known as a(n) 28.____
    A. modulator   B. oscillator   C. amplifier   D. detector

29. The separation of speech or music from a radio wave carrying music or speech is referred to as 29.____
    A. audio filtration   B. separation
    C. demodulation   D. tracing

30. A circuit used to smooth out the surges of pulsating direct current from a rectifier is called a 30.____
    A. filter   B. multiplexer
    C. demodulator   D. local oscillator

KEY (CORRECT ANSWERS)

1.	B	11.	B	21.	D
2.	D	12.	C	22.	B
3.	B	13.	B	23.	A
4.	B	14.	D	24.	C
5.	B	15.	B	25.	D
6.	C	16.	C	26.	B
7.	B	17.	D	27.	C
8.	A	18.	A	28.	B
9.	B	19.	D	29.	C
10.	A	20.	A	30.	A

TEST 3

DIRECTIONS: Each question or incomplete statement is followed by several suggested answers or completions. Select the one that BEST answers the question or completes the statement. *PRINT THE LETTER OF THE CORRECT ANSWER IN THE SPACE AT THE RIGHT.*

1. The simple motor found in an electric clock is called a(n) _____ motor. 1.____
   - A. synchronous
   - B. induction
   - C. rotor
   - D. D.C.

2. The amperage of a fully charged car storage battery is USUALLY near _____ amps. 2.____
   - A. 10
   - B. 100
   - C. 1000
   - D. 10,000

3. To prevent the initial surge of current drawn by an electric motor from *burning out* the fuse in the circuit, one uses a 3.____
   - A. cartridge fuse
   - B. circuit breaker
   - C. plug fuse
   - D. fusetron

4. The many radio waves striking the antenna of a receiver are tuned-in with the 4.____
   - A. transformer
   - B. choke coil
   - C. variable condenser
   - D. diode detector

5. The starting motor of an automobile engine is shifted into mesh with the flywheel gear by a 5.____
   - A. vibrator
   - B. solenoid
   - C. bendix
   - D. starter button

6. The picture tube of a television set is also referred to as a _____ tube. 6.____
   - A. cathode-ray
   - B. power beam
   - C. oscilliscope
   - D. photo-electric

7. Generators that have two or more sets of field poles and require fewer revolutions to generate a 60-cycle-per second current are called 7.____
   - A. duo-dynamos
   - B. vibrators
   - C. poly-phase generators
   - D. alternators

8. A bar that has been artificially magnetized can be demagnetized by 8.____
   - A. quenching it in hot oil
   - B. pounding it with a heavy hammer
   - C. bending it into a *U* shape
   - D. wrapping it in insulating tape

9. The part of a generator which determines if it is a direct current generator is the 9.____
   - A. stator
   - B. field
   - C. commutator
   - D. brush

10. The term which refers to pressure or force in electric current is 10.____
    - A. amperage
    - B. voltage
    - C. ohms
    - D. electrons

11. Nichrome wire is MOST likely to be found in a(n)

    A. T.V. circuit
    B. electric motor
    C. electric clock
    D. electric heater

12. Electromagnetic waves are changed into pulses capable of producing sound waves in a radio by means of a

    A. transformer
    B. speaker
    C. detector
    D. oscillator

13. The SIMPLEST form of electronic tube is called

    A. cathode
    B. diode
    C. plate
    D. triode

14. Of the following, the one that is NOT a part of a radio tube is the

    A. envelope
    B. plate
    C. condenser
    D. filament

15. The speed of a simple electric motor can be controlled with the use of a

    A. variable resistor
    B. electrolytic condenser
    C. variable condenser
    D. prony-brake

16. A single wet cell can be made from a copper penny and a *zinc* penny attached to two copper leads immersed in

    A. mineral oil
    B. salt-water solution
    C. distilled water
    D. chromate of soda

17. The MINIMUM gauge wire for house circuits should be

    A. 10
    B. 18
    C. 14
    D. 22

18. The safety device used in a house wiring circuit to protect against an overload is a

    A. circuit breaker
    B. knife switch
    C. cut-off
    D. mercury switch

19. To prevent the generator from burning out at high speeds, the battery circuit of the automobile employs a

    A. choke coil
    B. variable resistor
    C. voltage regulator
    D. current trap

20. An interrupted current of 6 volts flows in the primary circuit of an induction coil of 100 turns of wire. If the secondary coil has 1,000 turns, the theoretical voltage output is

    A. .6
    B. 60
    C. 600
    D. .06

21. A 200 watt bulb in a 100 volt circuit uses _____ ampere(s).

    A. .2
    B. .02
    C. 2
    D. 20

22. A 220 volt air conditioner drawing 15 amperes of current operates 10 hours a day. The total cost of operation for four weeks at the rate of 4 cents per kilowatt hour would be

    A. $18.48
    B. $55.44
    C. $26.40
    D. $36.96

23. If a dry cell battery is capable of supplying a force of two volts and ten amperes of current, connecting five such batteries in parallel will result in a total capacity of _____ volts with _____ amperes.

   A. 2; 50 B. 20; 10 C. 10; 50 D. 10; 10

23._____

24. To calculate the number of turns of wire needed to make a step-up or step-down transformer when the voltages are known, and one set of windings is determined, we use the following formula:

   A. $\dfrac{\text{Primary turns}}{\text{Secondary turns}} = \dfrac{\text{Primary volts}}{\text{Secondary volts}}$

   B. $\dfrac{\text{Primary turns}}{\text{Primary volts}} = \dfrac{\text{Secondary volts}}{\text{Secondary turns}}$

   C. $\dfrac{\text{Primary turns}}{\text{Secondary volts}} = \dfrac{\text{Primary volts}}{\text{Secondary turns}}$

   D. $\dfrac{\text{Primary turns}}{\text{Secondary volts}} = \dfrac{\text{Primary volts}}{\text{Secondary turns}}$

24._____

25. To measure the specific gravity of the contents of a storage battery, one uses a

   A. hygrometer B. galvanometer
   C. ammeter D. hydrometer

25._____

26. Lightning is _____ electricity.

   A. induced B. ionized C. static D. magnetic

26._____

27. A lodestone is related to

   A. magnetism B. resistance
   C. conductivity D. reluctance

27._____

28. The term related to a storer of electricity is

   A. milliampere B. microfarad
   C. megohm D. microvolt

28._____

29. The thermostat as a switch employs the use of a

   A. diode tube B. tungsten filament
   C. bimetallic strip D. thermocouple

29._____

30. In servicing electrical apparatus, it is necessary to know the values of amperage, voltage, and resistance. When two of the factors are known, the third may be found by applying *Ohm's Law*.
   Of the following formulas, the one that does NOT apply is

   A. I = R/E B. R = E/I C. E = IR D. I = E/R

30._____

KEY (CORRECT ANSWERS)

1.	A	11.	D	21.	C
2.	B	12.	C	22.	D
3.	D	13.	B	23.	A
4.	C	14.	C	24.	A
5.	B	15.	A	25.	D
6.	A	16.	B	26.	C
7.	D	17.	C	27.	A
8.	B	18.	A	28.	B
9.	C	19.	C	29.	C
10.	B	20.	B	30.	A

TEST 4

DIRECTIONS: Each question or incomplete statement is followed by several suggested answers or completions. Select the one that BEST answers the question or completes the statement. *PRINT THE LETTER OF THE CORRECT ANSWER IN THE SPACE AT THE RIGHT.*

1. The effect of a capacitor on direct current is to _____ it. 1._____

    A. modulate
    B. block
    C. pass
    D. demodulate

2. Factors which determine the resistance of a wire are: 2._____

    A. Diameter, insulating material, length, strands
    B. Length, diameter, material, temperature
    C. Material, light factor, pressure, circumference
    D. Pressure, magnetism, binding, length

3. Current flow in a triode vacuum tube may be controlled by the 3._____

    A. plate and the grid
    B. filament and the plate
    C. grid and the heater
    D. cathode and the filament

4. If the resistance in a parallel circuit is *increased,* the voltage drop across a resistor would 4._____

    A. *increase*
    B. vary proportionally
    C. *decrease*
    D. remain the same

5. In parallel and series circuits, current is 5._____

    A. inversely proportional to resistance and directly proportional to voltage
    B. directly proportional to resistance and inversely proportional to voltage
    C. not affected by voltage
    D. not affected by resistance

6. The process of mixing audio waves with radio waves is called 6._____

    A. rectification
    B. attenuation
    C. modulation
    D. superimposition

7. Transistors are made of three parts: a base, a collector, and an emitter. When compared to a vacuum tube, the collector is comparable to the 7._____

    A. grid   B. plate   C. cathode   D. filament

8. Resistance wire used in electrical appliances is *usually* an alloy of 8._____

    A. tungsten, chromium, brass
    B. nickel, chromium, iron
    C. copper, nickel, tungsten
    D. iron, copper, molybdenum

9. A meter with terminals connected in series and across the line is a 9._____

    A. voltmeter   B. ammeter   C. ohmmeter   D. wattmeter

10. One hundred volts will push _____ milliamperes through 20k ohms of resistance. 10._____

    A. 2   B. 5   C. 50   D. 2000

11. A resistor having bands of orange, red, yellow, and silver would have a resistance value of _____ ohms.

    A. 32k B. 320k C. 2.3 meg D. 43 meg

12. A flashbulb used for photographic purposes contains

    A. aluminum and oxygen B. tungsten and helium
    C. aluminum and hydrogen D. tungsten and argon

13. A generator having a cummutator produces _____ current.

    A. alternating B. direct
    C. synchronous D. modulating

14. A step-down transformer has 1,200 turns on the primary. 90 volts is applied to the primary, and the second is to produce 15 volts.
    How many turns should be wound on the secondary?

    A. 200 B. 600 C. 7,200 D. 108,000

15. In a radio circuit, a transformer CANNOT be used to

    A. step-up a-c voltage
    B. isolate part of a circuit
    C. step-down d-c voltage
    D. couple part of a circuit to another

16. A transformer has 200 turns of #14 wire wound on primary and 1,000 turns of #14 wire wound on the secondary.
    A voltmeter attached to the secondary terminals would indicate _____ volts if 50 volts were attached to the
    primary.

    A. 0 B. 10 C. 250 D. 600

17. Service entrance cable for the typical home is usually made up of three wires. The *hot* wires are usually No.

    A. 4 or No. 6 B. 8 or No. 10
    C. 12 or No. 14 D. 16 or No. 18

18. In the PNP type transistor, the collector is *normally*

    A. negative B. positive
    C. shorted out D. not needed

19. In a beam power tube, the screen grid is

    A. the plate B. positive
    C. the suppressor D. negative

20. A silicon controlled rectifier is

    A. a nuvistor B. a CRT
    C. thermally operated D. a semi-conductor

21. In copper plating a metallic object, it should be placed at the   21.____

    A. anode   B. switch   C. cathode   D. electrolyte

22. At five cents per kilowatt hour, a 100-watt lamp which is operated for one hundred (100)   22.____
    hours would use energy that would cost

    A. 5 cents   B. less than 10 cents
    C. 50 cents   D. 5 dollars

23. A galvanometer may be converted to a voltmeter by adding a   23.____

    A. shunt in series   B. multiplier in series
    C. multiplier in parallel   D. shunt in parallel

24. The counter emf of an inductance coil is measured in   24.____

    A. milliamperes   B. microfarads
    C. henrys   D. millivolts

25. A fluorescent lamp lights when the   25.____

    A. ballast coil produces a high-voltage charge
    B. starter switch is placed in parallel with the filament
    C. mercury forms minute droplets on the filament
    D. ballast changes the A.C. to D.C. in the tube

26. The electrolyte used in a dry cell is composed of   26.____

    A. carbon, magnesium oxide, ammonia, sodium chloride
    B. sodium, manganese dioxide, alumina, zinc sulphate
    C. carbon, manganese dioxide, sal ammoniac, zinc chloride
    D. sodium, magnesium sulphate, arsenic, zinc oxide

27. A variable capacitor has its capacitance *increased* when the   27.____

    A. plates are open
    B. rotor is attached to the stator
    C. plates are meshed
    D. dielectric is given a full charge

28. The gas mixture commonly used in incandescent lamps is   28.____

    A. nitrogen and argon   B. nitrogen and helium
    C. helium and argon   D. hydrogen and oxygen

29. A motor with a high-starting torque and rapid acceleration is a(n) _____ motor.   29.____

    A. D.C. shunt wound   B. D.C. series wound
    C. A.C. synchronous   D. A.C. split phase

30. Dry cells used for powering cordless electric razors are usually _____ cells.   30.____

    A. manganese alkaline   B. nickel cadmium
    C. nickel silver   D. zinc carbon

KEY (CORRECT ANSWERS)

1. B	11. B	21. C
2. B	12. A	22. C
3. A	13. B	23. B
4. D	14. A	24. C
5. A	15. C	25. A
6. C	16. A	26. C
7. B	17. A	27. C
8. B	18. A	28. A
9. D	19. B	29. B
10. B	20. D	30. B

EXAMINATION SECTION
TEST 1

DIRECTIONS: Each question or incomplete statement is followed by several suggested answers or completions. Select the one that BEST answers the question or completes the statement. *PRINT THE LETTER OF THE CORRECT ANSWER IN THE SPACE AT THE RIGHT.*

1. The saw fitting operation that is likely to set up new strains in a circular saw blade and disturb the tension of the blade is known as

    A. hooking   B. fleaming   C. gumming   D. jointing

2. A gauge used by saw manufacturers to indicate the thickness of circular saw blades is the

    A. Washburn & Moen
    B. wickwire
    C. Stubbs
    D. Browne & Sharpe

3. Jointer knives are USUALLY beveled at an angle of

    A. 15 to 20°   B. 30 to 50°   C. 45 to 50°   D. 50 to 55°

4. In a gear train, the intermediate gear changes the _____ of the _____ gear(s).

    A. direction; follower
    B. velocity; driving and follower
    C. velocity; driving
    D. velocity; follower

5. The bevel angle for a 1 1/2" wood turning gouge is

    A. 30°   B. 45°   C. 50°   D. 60°

6. The number of standard v-belt cross-section sizes is

    A. 3   B. 5   C. 6   D. 8

7. Vegetable and animal greases and oils are NOT suitable for use as bearing lubricants because they have a tendency to

    A. act as a lapping compound
    B. develop free acid
    C. seep through housings
    D. break down under low temperatures

8. Each of the numbered main divisions on the thread chasing dial represents carriage travel equal to _____ inch.

    A. 1/4   B. 1/2   C. 3/4   D. 1

9. To cut a left-hand thread, it is necessary to

    A. reverse the direction of the spindle
    B. engage the bull-gear pin
    C. reverse the direction of the lead screw so that the carriage will travel from the head stock to the tail stock
    D. reverse the direction of the lead screw so that the carriage will travel from the tail stock to the head stock

10. The standard pitches for both straight and diamond knurls are

    A. 12-24-36   B. 14-20-36   C. 16-18-24   D. 18-24-36

11. On a band saw, the clearance between each guide block and the blade is APPROXIMATELY _____ of an inch.

    A. .003   B. .007   C. .010   D. .013

12. A good etching fluid for carbon steel consists of _____ part(s) of _____ acid and _____ part(s) of water.

    A. 1; hydrofluoric; 2   B. 1; nitric; 4
    C. 2; sulphuric; 1   D. 4; acetic ;1

13. The face of the chuck body that has concentric grooves marked at regular intervals is the _____ chuck.

    A. universal   B. independent
    C. three-jaw   D. standard

14. The side clearance for a right-hand facing tool is APPROXIMATELY

    A. 8°   B. 12°   C. 14°   D. 15°

15. The center head has an angle of

    A. 30°   B. 45°   C. 60°   D. 90°

16. The file that lends itself BEST for filing against a filleted shoulder or a rounded corner of a hole is known as a _____ file.

    A. crochet   B. hard   C. crossing   D. slitting

17. If seven grooves are to be cut on a 4" cylinder, using the standard index head on a milling machine, the number of turns of the index crank that must be made for each indexing is

    A. 3 1/3   B. 4 1/2   C. 5 5/7   D. 7 1/7

18. The raker tooth on a hollow ground saw is

    A. 1/64 of an inch longer than the scoring teeth
    B. the same height as the scoring teeth
    C. 1/64 of an inch shorter than the scoring teeth
    D. set .003 to .005 of an inch to prevent binding

19. Spelter is a compound of

    A. copper-zinc-tin   B. babbitt-lead-antimony
    C. tin-lead-zinc   D. zinc-lead-antimony

20. The recommended tempering color for a carbon steel screwdriver blade is

    A. light straw   B. deep straw
    C. bronze   D. deep blue

KEY (CORRECT ANSWERS)

1.	C	11.	A
2.	C	12.	B
3.	B	13.	B
4.	A	14.	A
5.	A	15.	D
6.	B	16.	A
7.	B	17.	B
8.	D	18.	C
9.	C	19.	A
10.	A	20.	D

TEST 2

DIRECTIONS: Each question or incomplete statement is followed by several suggested answers or completions. Select the one that BEST answers the question or completes the statement. *PRINT THE LETTER OF THE CORRECT ANSWER IN THE SPACE AT THE RIGHT.*

1. The term that is used to describe the axial advance of a screw thread is

   A. pitch
   B. lead
   C. helix
   D. number of threads per inch

2. In a standard bolt designated 3/4"-10 NC-2, the 2 stands for

   A. length of bolt below head
   B. length of bolt including head
   C. number of bolts required
   D. classification of fit

3. The radius of a circle will step around the circumference _____ times.

   A. three   B. four   C. six   D. eight

4. In a standard bolt designated 3/4"-10 NC-2, the *NC* stands for

   A. national coarse   B. nickel-carbon
   C. notched capscrew   D. non-chamfered head

5. A circle is dimensioned by giving the

   A. radius   B. diameter
   C. center line   D. circumference

6. The angle made by the isometric axes is

   A. 90°   B. 30°   C. 45°   D. 120°

7. Quarter size scale is represented by _____ = 1'0".

   A. 1/8"   B. 1/4"   C. 1"   D. 3"

8. The BEST all-around pencil for the draftsman is

   A. 2B   B. HB   C. H   D. 3H

9. Referring to double threads, the term lead is

   A. another name for the pitch
   B. applied to the taper on a pipe thread
   C. the distance that the thread advances axially in one turn
   D. the distance between two corresponding points on two adjacent threads

10. The joints connecting the vertical and horizontal members of a door are usually

    A. mitered   B. half-lap
    C. dove-tail   D. mortise and tenon

11. Whetting a wood chisel means 11._____
    A. dipping it in water
    B. paring sap wood
    C. sharpening it on an oil stone
    D. oiling it to prevent rust

12. The part of a plane that breaks the shavings is the 12._____
    A. cap iron   B. plane iron
    C. lever cap   D. plane mouth

13. The throat adjustment in the jack, smooth and jointer plane is 13._____
    A. set
    B. made by means of the thumbscrew
    C. made by means of the lateral adjustment
    D. made by moving the frog

14. The adjustable bit used to bore holes of different sizes is called _____ bit. 14._____
    A. the extension   B. multiple
    C. expansive   D. Forstner

15. The length of the average hand saw is _____ inches. 15._____
    A. 26   B. 18   C. 22   D. 30

16. An auger bit marked 8 on the tang will bore a hole _____ in diameter. 16._____
    A. 1"   B. 1/4"   C. 1/2"   D. 3/4"

17. A brad is similar in shape to a 17._____
    A. box nail   B. common nail
    C. tack   D. finishing nail

18. A wood much used in the United States which has to be imported is 18._____
    A. mahogany   B. gum wood   C. poplar   D. birch

19. Kiln-dried lumber, as compared with air-dried lumber, 19._____
    A. is stronger   B. is heavier
    C. resists decay better   D. contains less moisture

20. The back saw resembles the _____ saw. 20._____
    A. rip   B. mitre   C. compass   D. turning

KEY (CORRECT ANSWERS)

1. B
2. D
3. C
4. A
5. B

6. D
7. D
8. D
9. C
10. D

11. C
12. A
13. D
14. C
15. A

16. C
17. D
18. A
19. D
20. B

TEST 3

DIRECTIONS: Each question or incomplete statement is followed by several suggested answers or completions. Select the one that BEST answers the question or completes the statement. *PRINT THE LETTER OF THE CORRECT ANSWER IN THE SPACE AT THE RIGHT.*

1. A kerf is a

    A. joint
    B. fastener
    C. saw cut
    D. broken edge

    1._____

2. Shellac is thinned by adding

    A. alcohol
    B. linseed oil
    C. turpentine
    D. benzine

    2._____

3. The cutting principle of a rip saw is that of

    A. chipping   B. scoring   C. slicing   D. boring

    3._____

4. The layer of wood between the sapwood and the bark of a tree is called the

    A. heartwood   B. cambium   C. pith   D. medullary

    4._____

5. Linseed oil is made from

    A. flaxseed
    B. oak leaves
    C. pine tar
    D. petroleum

    5._____

6. Of the following, the BEST wood for exposure to the weather is the

    A. cypress   B. maple   C. gumwood   D. poplar

    6._____

7. The FIRST operation in the sharpening of a dull scraper is

    A. filing
    B. grinding
    C. burnishing
    D. whetting

    7._____

8. If a saw continues to run away from a line, the trouble may be caused by one of the following:
The

    A. wood is *green*
    B. wood has been improperly seasoned
    C. saw blade is too long
    D. saw teeth are set unevenly

    8._____

9. The purpose of using stain on wood is to

    A. imitate some more expensive wood
    B. preserve the wood
    C. fill the pores
    D. give a finished surface

    9._____

10. The modern safety head for a jointer has

   A. two knives in a square head
   B. three knives in a cylindrical head
   C. three knives in a square head
   D. lock nuts

11. A T-bevel is also known as a _____ square.

   A. bevel
   B. miter
   C. T-
   D. combination

12. Which of the following determines the thickness, width, and length of a piece of wood?

   A. Size
   B. Position
   C. Shape
   D. Grain

13. On a piece of stock, the dimension measured from edge to edge is called the

   A. length
   B. breadth
   C. width
   D. thickness

14. The usual position of the operator of a circular saw is to stand

   A. to the right and behind the saw
   B. to the left and behind the saw
   C. directly behind the saw
   D. on the left side of the saw table

15. One should file at right angles to the blade when sharpening a _____ saw.

   A. cross-cut
   B. rip
   C. back
   D. buck

16. The hollow where two teeth of a saw meet is called a

   A. valley
   B. raker
   C. land
   D. gullet

17. A mortise gauge has

   A. a depth stop
   B. an adjustable stop
   C. two spurs
   D. two adjustable beams

18. An anti-freeze having a low boiling point is

   A. zerex
   B. alcohol
   C. prestone
   D. glycerine

19. The S.A.E. number of a winter engine oil is

   A. 50
   B. 60
   C. 40
   D. 10

20. In using a common 1 in. shop micrometer caliper, one complete revolution of the thimble causes the spindle to move _____ in.

   A. 1/25
   B. .040
   C. 1/40
   D. 1/100

KEY (CORRECT ANSWERS)

1.	C	11.	A
2.	A	12.	D
3.	A	13.	C
4.	B	14.	B
5.	A	15.	B
6.	A	16.	D
7.	A	17.	C
8.	D	18.	B
9.	A	19.	D
10.	B	20.	C

EXAMINATION SECTION

TEST 1

DIRECTIONS: Each question or incomplete statement is followed by several suggested answers or completions. Select the one that BEST answers the question or completes the statement. *PRINT THE LETTER OF THE CORRECT ANSWER IN THE SPACE AT THE RIGHT.*

1. A gap of several thousandths of an inch between two parts is MOST accurately measured with a
   A. divider
   B. feeler gage
   C. vernier caliper
   D. gage block

2. For a very high-speed reduction the type of gear generally used is the
   A. worm and gear
   B. spur gear
   C. bevel gear
   D. herringbone gear

3. The spiral flutes on a twist drill are provided to
   A. remove the chips
   B. form a clearance hole
   C. prevent the drill from wobbling
   D. save material

4. The tool whose size is specified by weight is a
   A. cold chisel
   B. hammer
   C. wrench
   D. pair of pliers

5. Ball bearings are USUALLY made of
   A. steel
   B. brass
   C. cast iron
   D. babbit

6. An item which has the LEAST value in promoting general shop safety is
   A. plenty of overtime
   B. safety posters
   C. skilled employees
   D. expensive equipment

7. It would be MOST necessary to provide a metal cover for a container used for
   A. machine shop scrap
   B. floor sweepings
   C. oily rags and waste
   D. broken glass

8. A helper is NOT expected to assume responsibility. This means that
   A. he should not report defective equipment unless asked
   B. his supervisors have a low opinion of his ability
   C. he never does important work
   D. generally other employees are assigned to make the decisions

9. A sheet metal screw differs from an ordinary machine screw in that it
   A. requires a special nut
   B. always requires a special screwdriver
   C. is self-tapping
   D. is made only in short lengths

10. In moving heavy equipment or materials with an overhead traveling crane, a good procedure is to have the crane operator take operating signals from only a single designated person on the floor. This is important because it
    A. avoids the necessity of more than one person knowing the signals
    B. prevents overloading the crane with too much load
    C. requires fewer men
    D. avoids the danger of conflicting signals

11. Protective goggles should NOT be worn when
    A. descending a ladder after finishing a job
    B. dusting off machinery
    C. chipping concrete
    D. sharpening a cold chisel on a grinding wheel

12. The GREATEST danger in the use of ladders, stairways, floors and platforms made of iron is that they
    A. are difficult to maintain
    B. are slippery when greasy and wet
    C. have sharp edges causing injuries
    D. are too rigid and cause fatigue

13. Compressed air should NOT be used directly from a hose for dusting off work clothing mainly because
    A. the air may contain considerable moisture
    B. the dust may blow into machinery
    C. it may cause personal injury
    D. it is too noisy

14. The term which CORRECTLY refers to a machine screw is
    A. 8-24   B. #2 head   C. 10-penny   D. 1/2 by 3/4

15. Artificial respiration is applied when an accident has caused
    A. broken limbs   B. scalding
    C. breathing difficulties D. loss of blood

16. Lock washers are used PRINCIPALLY with
    A. wood screws   B. lag screws
    C. self-tapping screws D. machine screws

17. All employees receive a copy of the book "Rules and Regulations." The MOST likely reason for issuing this book is to
    A. give the answers to all technical questions
    B. relieve management of responsibility for accidents that may occur
    C. improve the employees' skills
    D. acquaint employees with their duties and responsibilities

18. If, when you are using an extension light with a long cord, the light should go out unexpectedly, you should FIRST
    A. inspect the cord for a broken wire
    B. replace the bulb with a new one
    C. check the fuses in the supply circuit
    D. check if the plug is still in the outlet

19. The MOST common danger in working around rotating machinery is from
    A. the suction effect created
    B. static electricity
    C. flying particles
    D. catching clothing on the moving parts

20. Acetylene is commonly used
    A. in cutting steel with a torch
    B. as a rust remover
    C. for extinguishing fires
    D. as a solvent for cleaning instruments

21. In drilling a hole which is to be tapped for a 3/8" screw, the twist drill size is
    A. 1/8" B. 5/16' C. 3/8" D. 7/16"

22. The material which is an alloy is
    A. aluminum B. tin C. zinc D. bronze

23. Cold chisels with "mushroomed" heads are repaired by
    A. cutting with hacksaw   B. turning
    C. grinding   D. hammering

24. In a first aid kit, you would NOT expect to find
    A. bandages   B. absorbent cotton
    C. splints for a broken leg   D. band-aids

25. In treating injuries it is MOST important that any bandages used be
    A. clean B. damp C. large D. waterproof

KEY (CORRECT ANSWERS)

1. B	11. A	21. B
2. A	12. B	22. D
3. A	13. C	23. C
4. B	14. A	24. C
5. A	15. C	25. A
6. A	16. D	
7. C	17. D	
8. D	18. D	
9. C	19. D	
10. D	20. A	

TEST 2

DIRECTIONS: Each question or incomplete statement is followed by several suggested answers or completions. Select the one that BEST answers the question or completes the statement. *PRINT THE LETTER OF THE CORRECT ANSWER IN THE SPACE AT THE RIGHT.*

Questions 1-9 refer to the figures below:

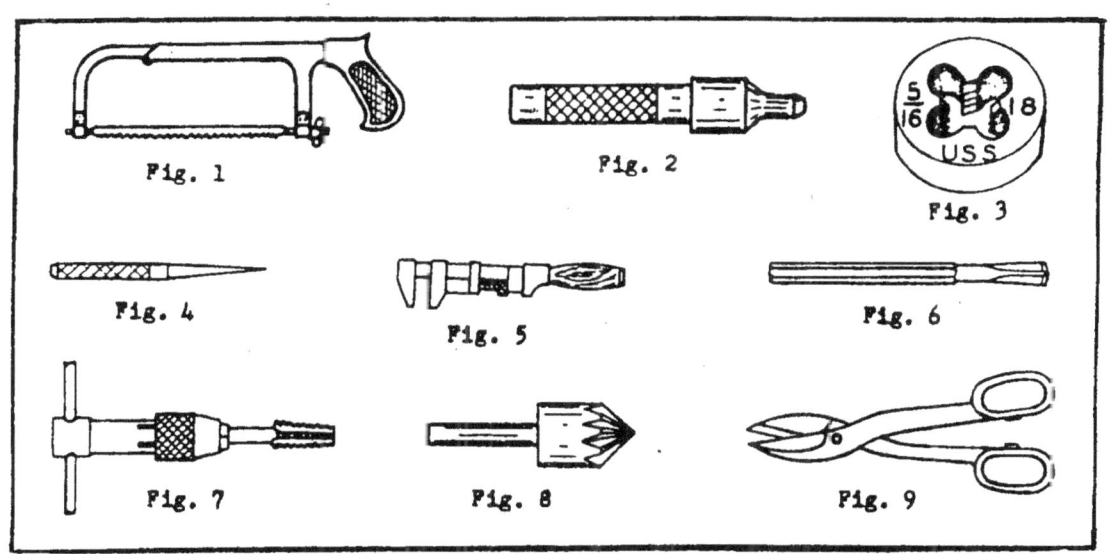

1. To thread a rod the tool to use is that shown in figure
   A. 3 B. 6 C. 7 D. 8

   1._____

2. The tool shown in figure 9 ordinarily would NOT be used to cut a
   A. sheet of aluminum
   B. sheet of copper
   C. sheet of paper
   D. tin plate

   2._____

3. In figure 5 there is shown a(n) _____ wrench.
   A. monkey B. stillson C. strap D. open-end

   3._____

4. The PROPER use for the tool shown in figure 4 would be as a
   A. center punch
   B. drift pin
   C. pick
   D. scriber

   4._____

5. The tool shown in figure 7 is used in
   A. broaching B. drilling C. tapping D. reaming

   5._____

6. The tool shown in figure 8 is used in
   A. reaming
   B. countersinking
   C. counterboring
   D. cutting concrete

   6._____

2 (#2)

7. A star drill is shown in figure
   A. 2 B. 6 C. 7 D. 8

8. The number "18" shown on the tool of figure 3 indicates
   A. type of thread
   B. size of opening
   C. depth of opening
   D. threads per inch

9. The tool to use to properly flare one end of copper tubing is shown in figure
   A. 2 B. 4 C. 6 D. 8

10. The instrument COMMONLY used to measure speed of rotation is called a
    A. manometer
    B. tachometer
    C. chronometer
    D. planimeter

11. When making a piping installation, the steel pipe is BEST turned by a _____ wrench.
    A. monkey
    B. adjustable open-end
    C. alligator
    D. stillson

12. The MAIN purpose of periodic inspections and tests made on equipment which is in constant use is to
    A. familiarize the operating men with the equipment
    B. keep the maintenance men busy during otherwise slack periods
    C. discover minor faults before they develop into serious breakdowns
    D. encourage the men to take better care of the equipment

13. A large oil storage tank has several manholes for easy access to the interior for periodic cleaning. You would NOT expect any of the manhole cover plates to be fastened to the tank by means of
    A. hinges and bolts
    B. rivets
    C. studs and nuts
    D. swing bolts and nuts

14. Compound used on threaded pipe joints should be applied on
    A. the piece that is threaded on the outside
    B. the joint edge after tightening
    C. both threaded pieces
    D. the piece that is threaded on the inside

15. When installed on moving machinery or shafting, set screws are often recessed so that no part of the screw sticks up above the surface MAINLY for
    A. strength B. appearance C. balance D. safety

16. When using a portable extension cord and lamp, an important safety precaution to take is to make sure that the cord
    A. is not too long
    B. does not kink
    C. does not create a tripping hazard
    D. does not lie in dirt

16._____

17. If a machine screw does NOT turn easily with the screwdriver you are using, you should try one with a
    A. sharper tip
    B. wider tip
    C. longer blade
    D. thicker handle

17._____

18. The presence of lubricating oil on shop floors is
    A. good because it lays the dust
    B. bad because it causes accidents
    C. good because it absorbs moisture and prevents dampness
    D. bad because it injures cement floors

18._____

19. The fastening at the points marked "X" in the steel drum shown below is MOST commonly done with

19._____

    A. rivets
    B. machine screws
    C. lag screws
    D. bolts

20. A piece is to be cut out of the angle iron in order to make the right angle bracket shown. Angle "X" should be _____ degrees.

20._____

    A. 30
    B. 45
    C. 60
    D. 90

21. A screwed fitting bypass is shown without valves. In making up this bypass the gap would be occupied by a standard   21._____

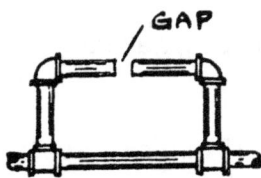

   A. coupling   B. expansion joint
   C. close nipple   D. union

22. The 2" pipe run shown has a pitch of 1/4" per foot. The total rise in 25' is   22._____

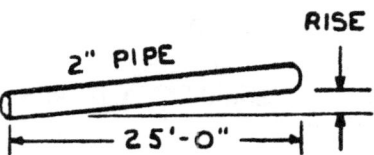

   A. 4 1/4"   B. 5 1/4"   C. 6 1/4"   D. 8 1/4"

23. The pitch (or distance between centers) of the evenly spaced tubes is   23._____

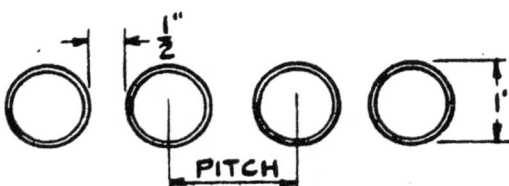

   A. 2 1/2"   B. 1 1/2"   C. 1"   D/ 3/4"

24. The flange bolts should be pulled up with a pair of   24._____

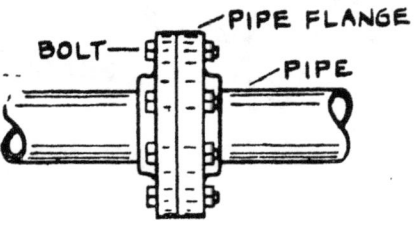

   A. monkey wrenches   B. stillson wrenches
   C. strap wrenches   D. open-end wrenches

25. The distance "X" between the centers of the two end holes is   25._____

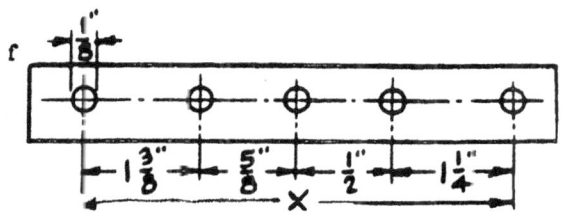

A. 3 3/4"   B. 3 1/2"   C. 3"   D. 2 3/4"

KEY (CORRECT ANSWERS)

1. A	11. D	21. D
2. C	12. C	22. C
3. A	13. B	23. B
4. D	14. A	24. D
5. C	15. D	25. A
6. B	16. C	
7. B	17. D	
8. D	18. B	
9. A	19. A	
10. B	20. D	

TEST 3

DIRECTIONS: Each question or incomplete statement is followed by several suggested answers or completions. Select the one that BEST answers the question or completes the statement. *PRINT THE LETTER OF THE CORRECT ANSWER IN THE SPACE AT THE RIGHT.*

1. Accident reports SHOULD be based on 1._____
   A. conclusions   B. facts   C. opinions   D. theories

2. The jaws of a vise close 3/16 of an inch for each turn of the screw. If the vise is open 6 inches, the number of turns required to close the jaw is 2._____
   A. 8   B. 16   C. 32   D. 64

3. Bolts are usually designated by 3._____
   A. diameter and length
   B. weight and diameter
   C. number per pound
   D. weight of each

4. To polish a steel rod, the BEST material to use would be 4._____
   A. sand paper
   B. emery cloth
   C. terry cloth
   D. crocus cloth

5. Alcohol is COMMONLY used as a(n) 5._____
   A. anti-freeze
   B. lubricant
   C. paint thinner
   D. rust remover

6. On a piece of round stock turning in a lathe it is POOR practice to use a file 6._____
   A. at all
   B. without a handle
   C. that has sharp teeth
   D. when the lathe is turning fast

7. Holes are usually countersunk for 7._____
   A. carriage bolts
   B. lag screws
   C. flat head screws
   D. square nuts

8. If the inside diameter of a pipe is 3/8 of an inch and the wall thickness is .091 inches, the outside diameter of the pipe is _____ inches. 8._____
   A. .193   B. .284   C. .466   D. .557

9. A tapered thread is used on a water pipe. The advantage of using a tapered thread is that 9._____
   A. it is easier to cut
   B. it helps make a tight joint
   C. no joint compound needs to be used
   D. it reduces the weight of the piping

10. The teeth of a hacksaw are generally set so as to make a cut wider than the saw blade. This is done MAINLY to
    A. permit easy movement of the blade
    B. strengthen the teeth
    C. prevent dulling the blade
    D. cool the blade

11. A hole has been drilled in a piece of metal and it is necessary to enlarge it by 0.010 of an inch to an exact size. The PROPER tool to use is a
    A. countersink   B. drill
    C. reamer   D. rat-tail file

Questions 12 through 23 refer to the figures shown below:

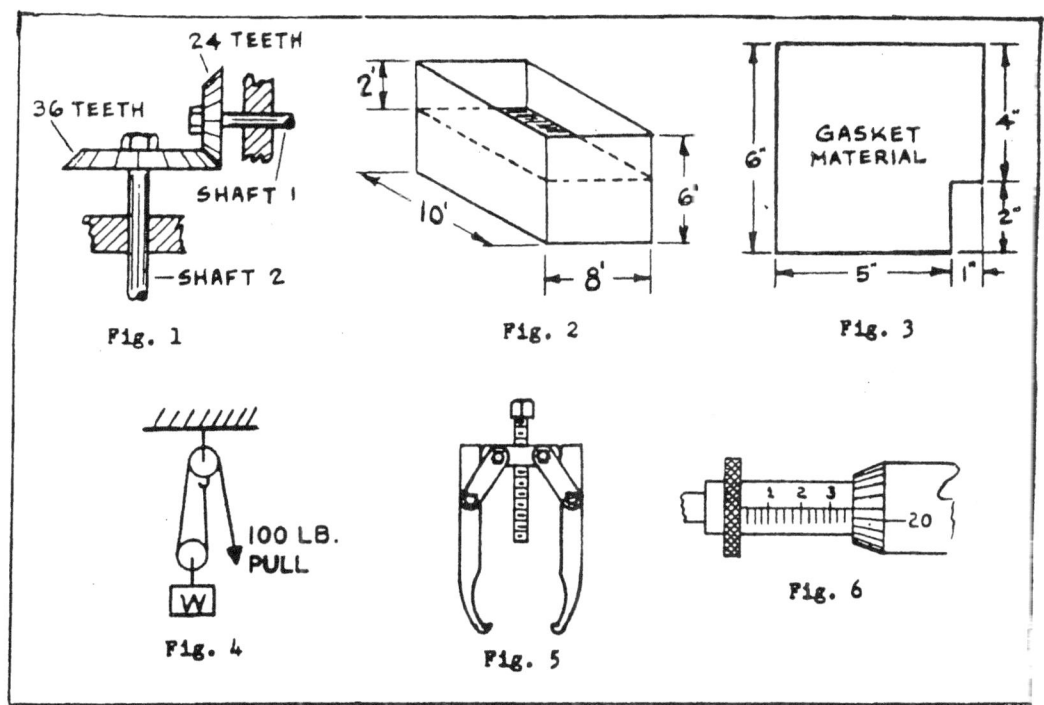

12. In figure 1 are shown two _____ gears.
    A. spur   B. herringbone   C. worm   D. bevel

13. In figure 1, when shaft 2 revolves at 150 rpm, shaft 1 revolves at ___ rpm.
    A. 225   B. 150   C. 100   D. 60

14. The TOTAL capacity of the partly filled tank in figure 2, in cubic feet, is
    A. 160   B. 240   C. 320   D. 480

15. The tank in figure 2, as shown, is _____ full.
    A. 1/3   B. 1/2   C. 2/3   D. 3/4

16. The diameter of the LARGEST circular gasket that may be cut from the gasket material in figure 3 is
    A. 2"   B. 4"   C. 5"   D. 6"

17. The area in square inches of the gasket material in figure 3 is
    A. 28   B. 32   C. 34   D. 36

18. The perimeter in inches of the gasket material in figure 3 is
    A. 18   B. 24   C. 30   D. 36

19. In figure 4 the MAXIMUM weight "W" that can be lifted as shown with a pull of 100 pounds is _____ lbs.
    A. 50   B. 100   C. 200   D. 300

20. The device shown in figure 5 is used
    A. to remove a pulley from the end of a shaft
    B. for punching holes in sheet metal
    C. as a jog in drilling
    D. to extract broken taps

21. In figure 5, to turn the bolt you would NOT use a(n) _____ wrench.
    A. stillson   B. monkey
    C. box   D. adjustable open-end

22. In figure 6 there is shown a
    A. vernier caliper   B. snap gauge
    C. micrometer caliper D. thread gauge

23. The reading on the instrument shown in figure 6 is
    A. 0.322"   B. 0.361"   C. 0.369"   D. 0.371"

24. If it is necessary for you to make some adjustment with your hands under a piece of heavy equipment, while a fellow worker lifts up and holds one end of it by means of a pinch bar, one important precaution you should take is to
    A. insert a temporary block to support the piece
    B. watch the bar to be ready if it slips
    C. wear gloves
    D. work as fast as possible

25. If a measurement scaled from a drawing is one inch, and the scale of the drawing is 1/4 inch to the foot, then the one-inch measurement would represent an actual length of
    A. 4 feet   B. 2 feet   C. 1/4 of a foot   D. 4 inches

KEY (CORRECT ANSWERS)

1. B	11. C	21. A
2. C	12. D	22. C
3. A	13. A	23. C
4. D	14. D	24. A
5. A	15. C	25. A
6. B	16. C	
7. C	17. C	
8. D	18. B	
9. B	19. C	
10. A	20. A	

TEST 4

DIRECTIONS: Each question or incomplete statement is followed by several suggested answers or completions. Select the one that BEST answers the question or completes the statement. *PRINT THE LETTER OF THE CORRECT ANSWER IN THE SPACE AT THE RIGHT.*

1. A circular disc is divided into 18 equal segments, each segment will have an angular section of
   A. 10°   B. 15°   C. 20°   D. 24°

   1._____

2. A lathe collar is BASICALLY a
   A. drill
   B. chuck
   C. mandrel
   D. knurling tool

   2._____

3. Babbitt hammers are used in machine shops PRINCIPALLY to
   A. protect workmen from flying chips
   B. prevent sparks
   C. prevent marring the work
   D. reduce noise

   3._____

4. A protractor is an instrument for measuring
   A. angles
   B. area
   C. the depth of drilled holes
   D. the thickness of sheet metal

   4._____

5. A ladder which is painted is a safety hazard MAINLY because the paint
   A. is slippery after drying
   B. may conceal weak spots in the rails and rungs
   C. causes the wood to crack more quickly
   D. peels and the wood starts to decay

   5._____

6. The MAIN reason for imbedding steel rods in concrete is to
   A. prevent the rods from rusting
   B. decrease the density of the concrete
   C. increase the strength of the concrete
   D. increase the weight of the concrete

   6._____

7. A department rule prohibits indulgence in intoxicating liquor, or being under its influence, while on duty. This rule is rigidly enforced in order to
   A. prevent an employee from endangering himself or others
   B. help promote temperance
   C. enable an employee to save money
   D. eliminate absenteeism

   7._____

8. Standard forms frequently call for entries on them to be printed. The MAIN reason for this practice is that printing, as compared to writing, is generally
    A. more compact
    B. more legal
    C. more legible
    D. easier to do

9. The instrument COMMONLY used to measure the diameter of a piece of work in a lathe is a
    A. micrometer caliper
    B. pair of outside calipers
    C. vernier caliper
    D. pair of dividers

10. The MOST important reason for roping off the work area when repairs are made is to
    A. prevent delays to the public
    B. protect the repair crew
    C. prevent distraction of the crew by the public
    D. protect the public

11. Copper liners are often put on the jaws of a vise to
    A. protect the jaws of the vise
    B. protect the work
    C. decrease noise
    D. grip the work tighter

12. If a coworker is in contact with a high-voltage circuit, the FIRST action taken should be to
    A. call a doctor
    B. use a resuscitation method on him
    C. call the foreman
    D. cut off power

13. The "gauge" of sheet metal indicates the sheet's
    A. width   B. thickness   C. length   D. area

14. When used in reference to pipe, the abbreviations I.D. and O.D. refer to the pipe
    A. density   B. diameters   C. length   D. weight

15. The BEST immediate first aid for a scraped knee is to
    A. apply plain Vaseline
    B. apply an ice pack
    C. apply heat
    D. wash it with soap and water

16. Of the sizes of sandpaper given, the FINEST is
    A. 1/2   B. 0   C. 00   D. 000

17. Powdered graphite is a good
    A. abrasive   B. achesive   C. insulator   D. lubricant

18. A particular casting will be LIGHTEST in weight if made of 18._____
    A. cast iron   B. aluminum   C. brass   D. steel

19. To prevent an ordinary steel nut from working loose under vibration, the 19._____
BEST device to use is a
    A. cotton pin   B. drop of solder
    C. fibre washer   D. lock washer

20. The head of a small rivet is readily formed with a 20._____
    A. ball peen hammer   B. claw hammer
    C. center punch   D. nail set

21. The machine used to bend sheet metal is called a 21._____
    A. brake   B. miller   C. planer   D. router

22. The word "plan" when used on a blueprint indicates 22._____
    A. a side elevation view   B. a top view
    C. a front elevation view   D. the order of assembly

23. Drilling must be done with special care when using any one of the very 23._____
small size twist drills because the
    A. drill speed may be too fast
    B. the drill is apt to break
    C. cut material will clog the drill
    D. drill may overheat

24. A parting tool is USUALLY used for work in a 24._____
    A. planer   B. milling machine
    C. lathe   D. shaper

25. Diagonal pliers are PROPERLY used to 25._____
    A. cut pipe   B. flatten steel tubing
    C. turn hexagonal nuts   D. cut wire

KEY (CORRECT ANSWERS)

1. C	11. B	21. A
2. B	12. D	22. B
3. C	13. B	23. B
4. A	14. B	24. C
5. B	15. D	25. D
6. C	16. D	
7. A	17. D	
8. C	18. B	
9. B	19. D	
10. D	20. A	

MECHANICAL APTITUDE EXAMINATION SECTION
TEST 1

MECHANICAL COMPREHENSION

DIRECTIONS: Questions 1 through 4 test your ability to understand general mechanical devices. Pictures are shown and questions asked about the mechanical devices shown in the picture. Read each question and study the picture. Each question is followed by four choices. For each question, choose the one BEST answer (A, B, C, or D). Then, *PRINT THE LETTER OF THE CORRECT ANSWER IN THE SPACE AT THE RIGHT.*

1.

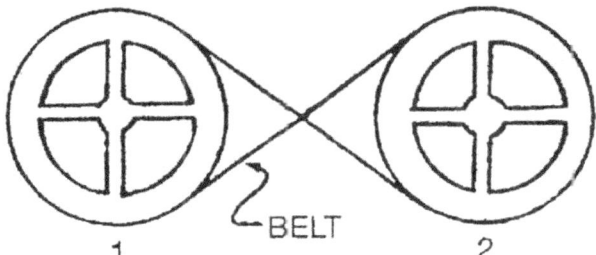

The reason for crossing the belt connecting these wheels is to
 A. make the wheels turn in opposite directions
 B. make wheel 2 turn faster than wheel 1
 C. save wear on the belt
 D. take up slack in the belt

1.____

2.

The purpose of the small gear between the two large gears is to
 A. increase the speed of the larger gears
 B. allow the larger gears to turn in different directions
 C. decrease the speed of the larger gears
 D. make the larger gears turn in the same direction

2.____

2 (#1)

3.

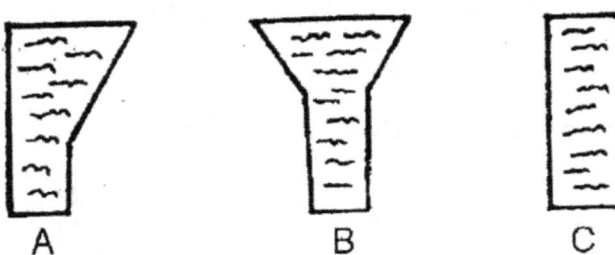

Each of these three-foot-high water cans have a bottom with an area of one square foot.
The pressure on the bottom of the cans is
   A. least in A   B. least in B   C. least in C   D. the same in all

4.

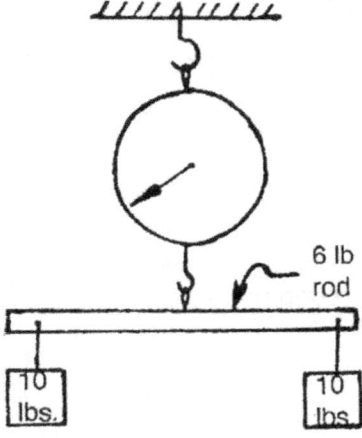

The reading on the scale should be
   A. zero   B. 10 pounds   C. 13 pounds   D. 26 pounds

KEY (CORRECT ANSWERS)

1. A
2. D
3. D
4. D

TEST 2

DIRECTIONS: Questions 1 through 6 test knowledge of tools and how to use them. For each question, decide which one of the four things shown in the boxes labeled A, B, C, or D normally is used with or goes best with the thing in the picture on the left. *PRINT THE LETTER OF THE CORRECT ANSWER IN THE SPACE AT THE RIGHT.*

NOTE: All tools are NOT drawn to the same scale.

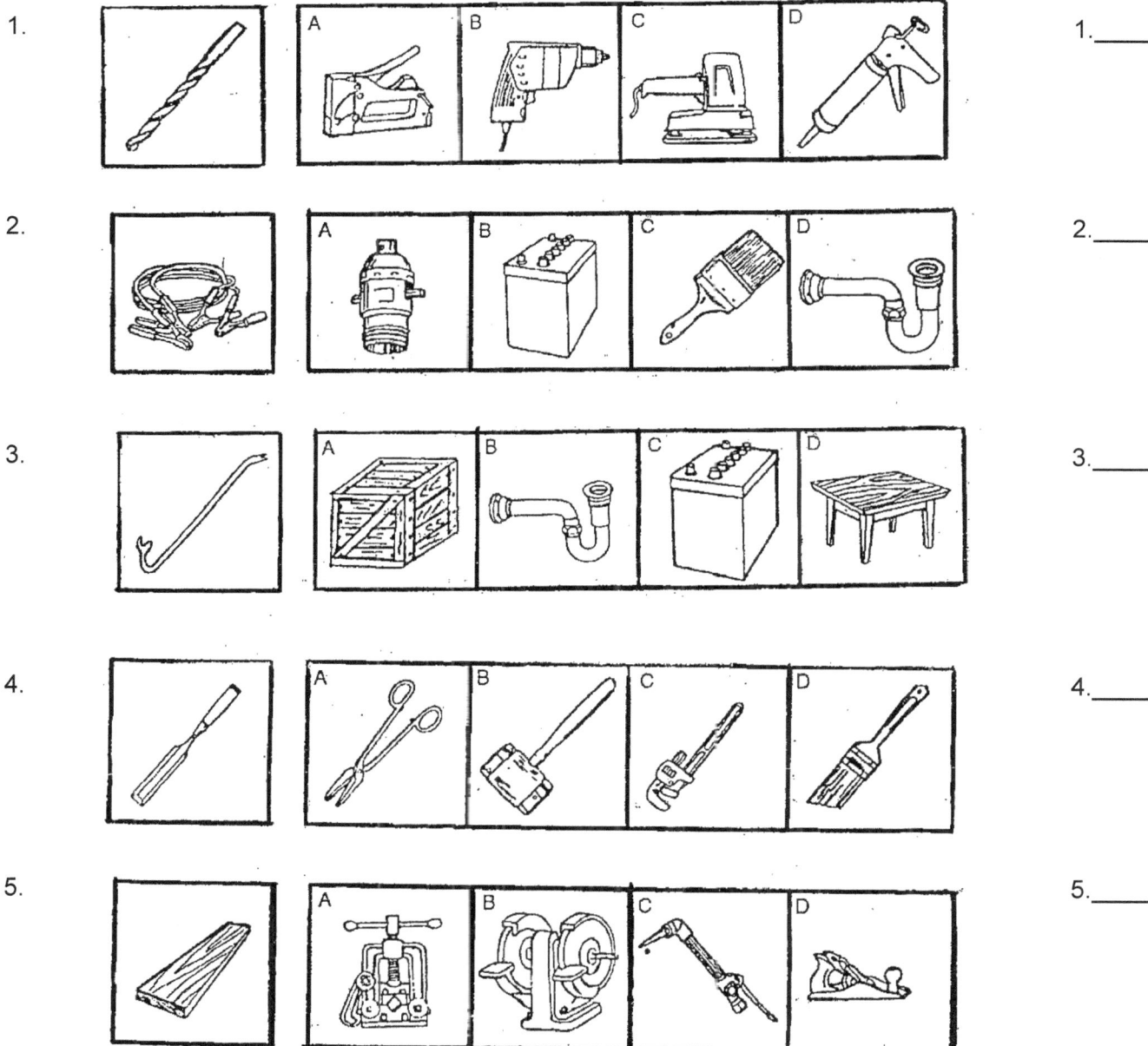

6. 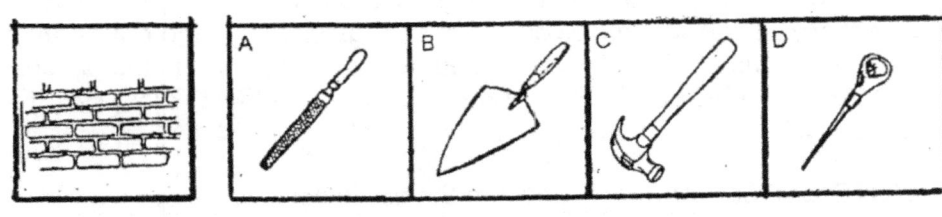 6._____

KEY (CORRECT ANSWERS)

1. B   4. B
2. B   5. D
3. A   6. B

MECHANICAL APTITUDE
EXAMINATION SECTION
TEST 1

DIRECTIONS: Questions 1 through 6 are questions designed to test your ability to distinguish identical forms from unlike forms. In each question, there are five drawings, lettered A, B, C, D, and E. Four of the drawings are alike. You are to find the one drawing that is different from the other four in the question. *PRINT THE LETTER OF THE CORRECT ANSWER IN THE SPACE AT THE RIGHT.*

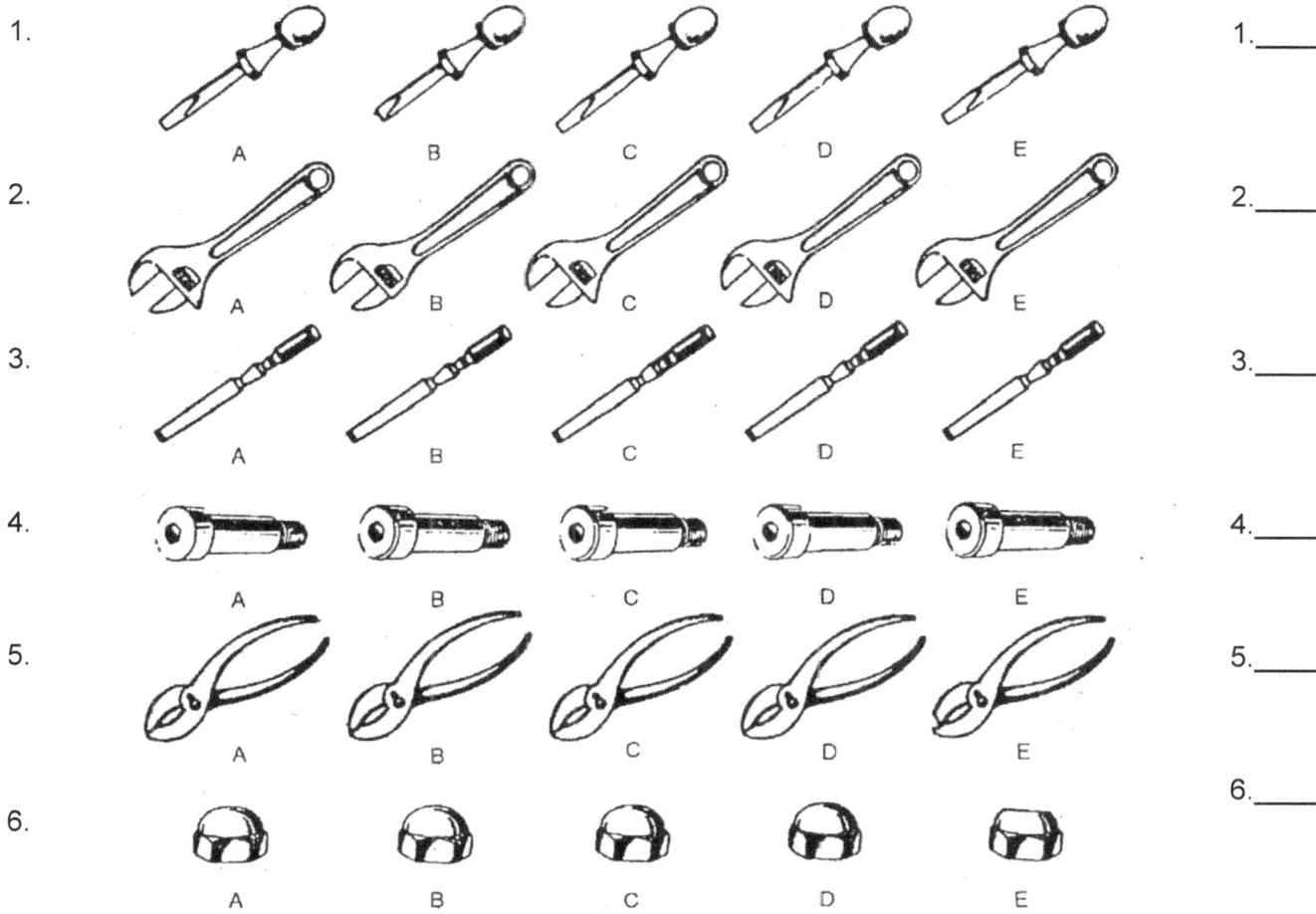

1._____

2._____

3._____

4._____

5._____

6._____

2 (#1)

Questions 7-8.

DIRECTIONS: Questions 7 and 8 are questions designed to test your knowledge of pattern matching. Questions 7 and 8 present problems found in making patterns. Each shows, at the left side, two or more separate flat pieces. In each question, select the arrangement lettered A, B, C, or D that shows how these pieces may be turned around or turned over in any way to make them fit together

7.  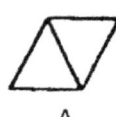    7.____
                                  A   B   C   D

From these pieces, which one of these arrangements can you make?

In Question 7, only the arrangement D can be made from the pieces shown at the left, so space choice D should be printed in the space at the right. (Note that it is necessary to turn the pieces around so that the short sides are at the bottom in the arrangement lettered D. None of the other arrangements show pieces of the given size and shape.)

8.  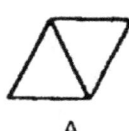   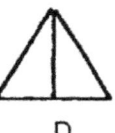 8.____
                                A   B   C   D

Questions 9-10.

DIRECTIONS: Questions 9 and 10 are questions designed to test your ability to identify forms of *Like* and *Unlike* proportions. In each of the questions, select from the drawings of objects labeled A, B, C, and D, the one that would have the TOP, Front, and Right views shown in the drawing at the left. Then, print the letter in the space at the right that has the same letter as your answer.

9. 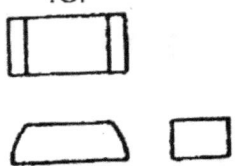  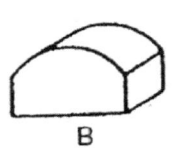  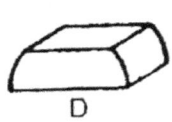 9.____

10. 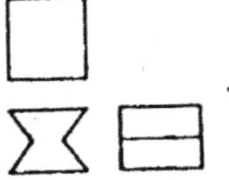 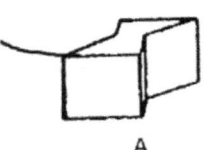 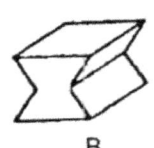 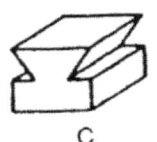 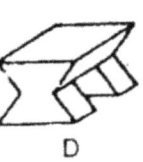 10.____

Questions 11-14.

Explanation and Commentary:
In each question, ONE rectangle is clearly wrong. For each question, use the measuring gage to check each of the rectangles and to find the WRONG one. Do this by putting the measuring gage rectangle on the question rectangle with the same letter so that the rectangles slightly overlap and the thin lines are parallel, like the one at the right. In this case, the height of the question rectangle exactly matches the height of the measuring gage rectangle, so the question rectangle is the right height.

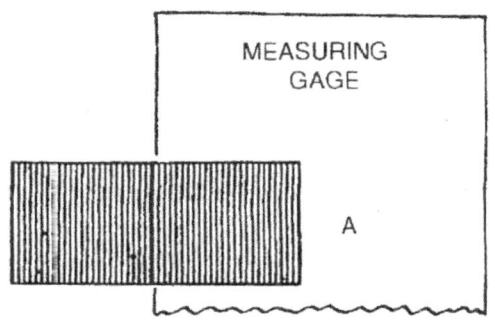

Once in every question when you put a measuring gage rectangle on a question rectangle, you will find that the heights do NOT match and that the question rectangle is clearly wrong, like the one at the right. In this case, you mark in the space at the right the same letter as the wrong rectangle. REMEMBER TO LINE UP THE MEASURING RECTANGLE WITH EACH QUESTION RECTANGLE SO THAT THE THIN LINES ARE EXACTLY PARALLEL.

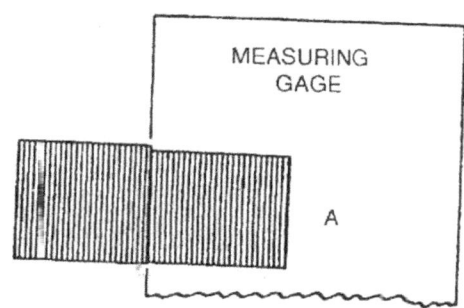

Now cut out the measuring gage on the last page and practice on the questions. The test will be limited, so practice doing them rapidly and accurately.

Questions 11 through 14 test how quickly and accurately you can check the heights of rectangles with a measuring gage. Each question has five rectangles of different heights. The height is the dimension that runs the same way as the thin lines.

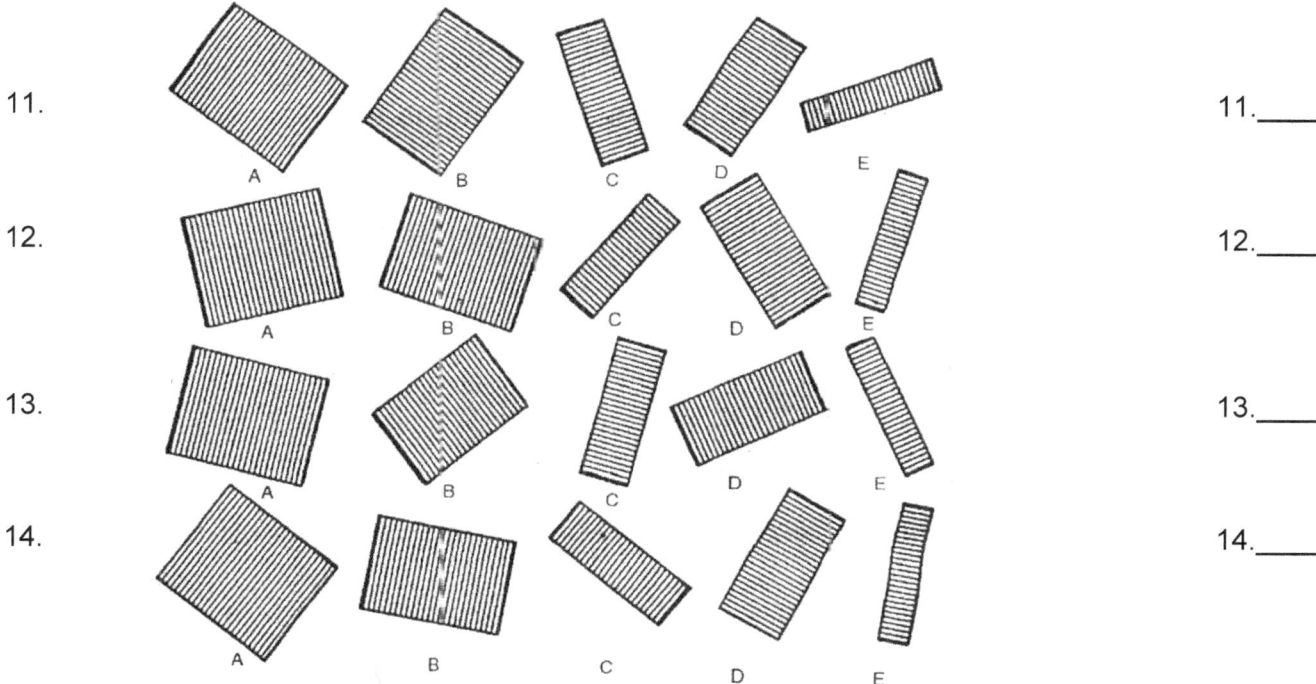

11._____

12._____

13._____

14._____

4 (#1)

MEASURING GAGE

 A

 B

 C

 D

 E

KEY (CORRECT ANSWERS)

1.	B	8.	B
2.	B	9.	D
3.	C	10.	B
4.	A	11.	D
5.	E	12.	C
6.	E	13.	B
7.	D	14.	A

ABSTRACT REASONING

COMMENTARY

The mathematical or quantitative ability of the candidate is generally measured through the form of questions and/or problems involving arithmetical reasoning, algebraic problem solving, and the interpretation of visual materials—graphs, charts, tables, diagrams, maps, cartoons, and pictures.

A more recent development, which attempts to assay facets of quantitative ability not ordinarily discernible or measurable, is the nonverbal test of reasoning of the type commonly designated as the figure analogy. Figure analogies are novel and differentiated measures of non-numerical mathematics reasoning.

Since intelligence exists in many forms or phases and the theory of differential aptitudes is now firmly established in testing, other manifestations and measurements of intelligence than verbal or purely arithmetical must be identified and measured.

Classification inventory, or figure classification, involves the aptitude of form perception, i.e., the ability to perceive pertinent detail in objects or in pictorial or graphic material. It involves making visual comparisons and discriminations and discerning slight differences in shapes and shading figures and widths and lengths of lines.

One aspect of this type of nonverbal question takes the form of a *positive* requirement to find the COMPATIBLE PATTERN (i.e., the one that *does* belong) from among two (2) sets of figure groups. The prescription for this question-type is as follows:

A group of three drawings lettered A, B, and C, respectively, is presented, followed on the same line by five (5) numbered alternative drawings labeled 1, 2, 3, 4, and 5, respectively.

The first two (2) drawings (A, B) in each question are related in some way.

The candidate is then to decide what characteristic *each* of the figures labeled A and B has that causes them to be related, and is then to select the one alternative from the five (5) numbered figures that is related to figure C in the same way that drawing B is related to drawing A.

Leading examples of presentation are the figure analogy and the figure classification. The Section that follows presents progressive and varied samplings of this type of question.

FIGURE ANALOGIES

Figure analogies are a novel and differentiated measure of non-numerical mathematics reasoning.

This question takes the form of, and, indeed, is similar to, the one-blank verbal analogy. However, pictures or drawings are used instead of words.

SAMPLE QUESTIONS AND EXPLANATIONS

DIRECTIONS: Each question in this part consists of 3 drawings lettered A, B, C, followed by 5 alternative drawings, numbered 1 to 5. The first 2 drawings in each question are related in some way. Choose the number of the alternative that is related to the third drawing in the same way that the second drawing is related to the first, and mark the appropriate space on your answer sheet.

1.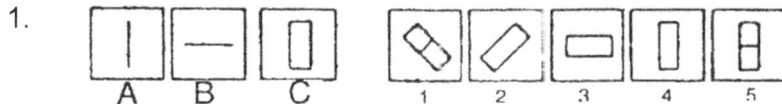

The CORRECT answer is 3. A vertical line has the same relationship to a horizontal line that a rectangle standing on its end has to a rectangle lying on its side.

2.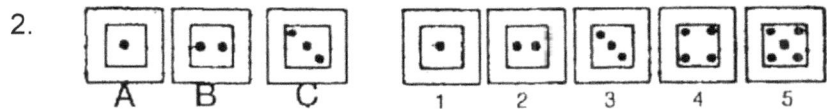

The second square has one more dot than the first square. Therefore, the CORRECT answer is alternative 4, which has one more dot than the third square.

3.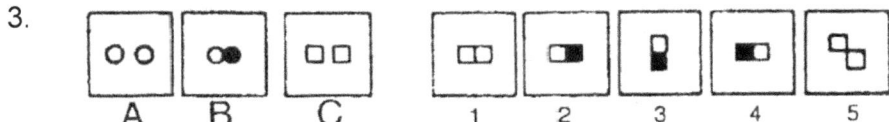

In the second drawing, the circles are moved together and the circle on the right darkened. Therefore, the CORRECT answer is 2, in which the squares are moved together and the right-hand square darkened.

4.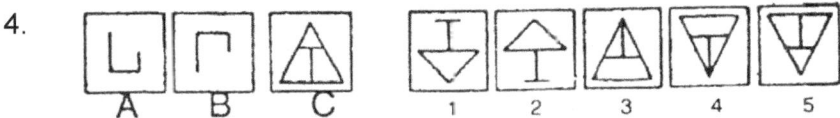

The CORRECT answer is 5. The second drawing is the inverted version of the first; alternative 5 is the inverted version of the third drawing.

5.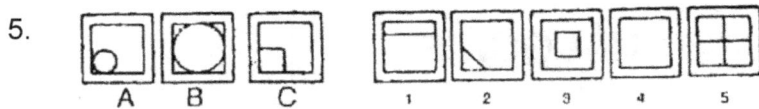

The CORRECT answer is 4. Drawing A has a small circle within a square; drawing B contains a circle completely filling the square. Drawing C has a small square within a square; in alternative 4, this small square has been magnified to its complete size within the outline of only one square.

6.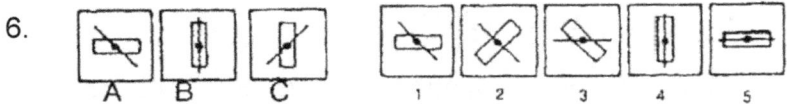

The CORRECT answer is 5. Drawing A appears in a horizontal position, with a diagonal line drawn through the center dot; drawing B appears in a vertical position, with a straight line drawn through the center dot. Drawing C is similar to drawing A, except that it appears in a vertical position; drawing 5 is similar to drawing B, except that it appears in a horizontal position. Our analogy may, therefore, be verbally expressed as

A : B : C : 5.

SUGGESTIONS FOR ANSWERING THE FIGURE ANALOGY QUESTION

1. In doing the actual questions, there can be little practical gain in rationalizing each answer that you attempt. What is needed is a quick and ready perceptive sense in this matter.

2. The BEST way to prepare for this type of question is to do the "Tests" in figure analogies that follow. By this method, you will gain enough functional skill to enable you to cope successfully with this type of question on the Examination.

SAMPLE TEST

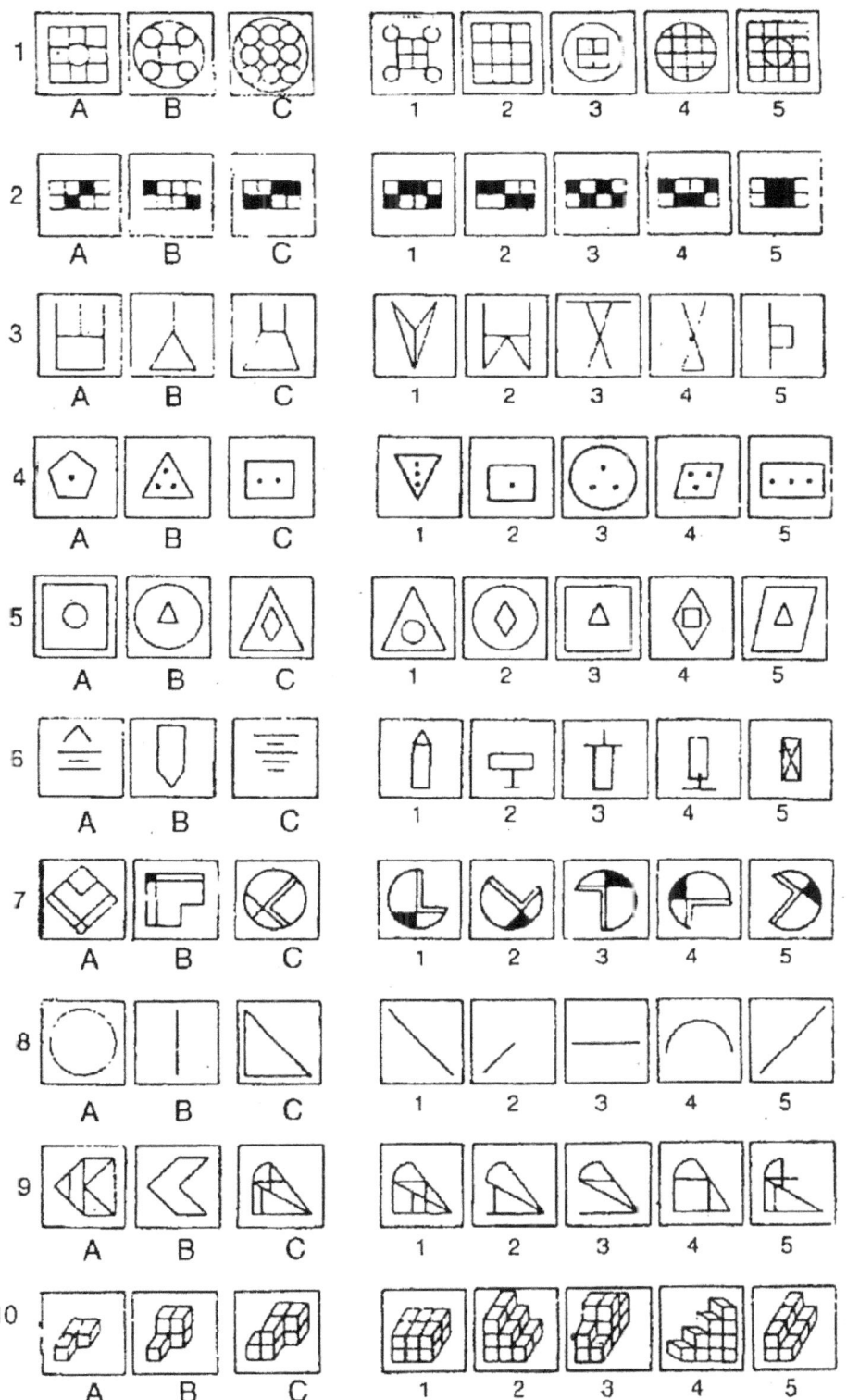

KEY (CORRECT ANSWERS)

1. 2   5. 4
2. 2   6. 3
3. 4   7. 3
4. 1   8. 2

EXPLANATION OF ANSWERS

1. In the second figure, the squares are changed to circles and the circles to squares.

2. In the second figure, the upper darkened area has moved two squares to the left, the lower, two squares to right.

3. The second figure has a flat base, like the first.

4. The sum and sides and dots in the second figure equals that of the first.

5. The outside part of the second figure is the inside part of the first.

6. The second figure is constructed from the lines given in the first.

7. The second figure is obtained from the first by rotating it 135° clockwise, darkening the smaller area and deleting the larger.

8. The second figure is the bisector of the area of the first.

9. The second figure is obtained from the first by deleting all the vertical lines.

10. The second figure contains two blocks more than the first.

FIGURE ANALOGIES
EXAMINATION SECTION
TEST 1

DIRECTIONS: Each question in this part consists of three drawings lettered A, B, C, followed by five alternative drawings, numbered 1 through 5. The first two drawings in each question are related in some way. Choose the number of the alternative that is related to the third drawing in the same way that the second drawing is related to the first and mark the appropriate space on your answer sheet

TEST 2

DIRECTIONS: Each question in this part consists of three drawings lettered A, B, C, followed by five alternative drawings, numbered 1 through 5. The first two drawings in each question are related in some way. Choose the number of the alternative that is related to the third drawing in the same way that the second drawing is related to the first and mark the appropriate space on your answer sheet.

TEST 3

DIRECTIONS: Each question in this part consists of three drawings lettered A, B, C, followed by five alternative drawings, numbered 1 through 5. The first two drawings in each question are related in some way. Choose the number of the alternative that is related to the third drawing in the same way that the second drawing is related to the first and mark the appropriate space on your answer sheet.

TEST 4

DIRECTIONS: Each question in this part consists of three drawings lettered A, B, C, followed by five alternative drawings, numbered 1 through 5. The first two drawings in each question are related in some way. Choose the number of the alternative that is related to the third drawing in the same way that the second drawing is related to the first and mark the appropriate space on your answer sheet.

11
TEST 5

DIRECTIONS: Each question in this part consists of three drawings lettered A, B, C, followed by five alternative drawings, numbered 1 through 5. The first two drawings in each question are related in some way. Choose the number of the alternative that is related to the third drawing in the same way that the second drawing is related to the first and mark the appropriate space on your answer sheet.

199

KEY (CORRECT ANSWERS)

TEST 1
1. 2
2. 4
3. 1
4. 5
5. 3
6. 2
7. 1
8. 3
9. 3
10. 5

TEST 2
1. 3
2. 1
3. 5
4. 2
5. 3
6. 2
7. 1
8. 4
9. 4
10. 1

TEST 3
1. 1
2. 3
3. 2
4. 4
5. 5
6. 2
7. 1
8. 4
9. 5
10. 3

TEST 4
1. 2
2. 5
3. 1
4. 3
5. 2
6. 5
7. 4
8. 3
9. 5
10. 4

TEST 5
1. 1
2. 3
3. 5
4. 2
5. 2
6. 5
7. 3
8. 1
9. 4
10. 4

FIGURE ANALOGIES/*INCOMPATIBLE PATTERN*

A form of the figure classification question is the nonverbal question which takes the form of finding the INCOMPATIBLE PATTERN from among two (2) sets of figure groups. The prescription for this question-type is as follows:

Two groups of four (4) figures each, labeled 1 and 2, are presented side by side. Then follows on the same line a third group of five (5) figures, labeled A, B, C, D, and E, respectively. The candidate is then to decide what characteristics EACH of the figure in group 1 has that NONE of the figures in group 2 has. Then select the lettered answer figure that has this characteristic.

SAMPLE QUESTIONS AND EXPLANATIONS

DIRECTIONS: Each of these problems consists of two groups of figures, labeled 1 and 2. These are followed by five (5) lettered answer figures. For each problem you are to decide what characteristic EACH of the figures in group 1 has that NONE of the figures in group 2 has. Then select the lettered answer figure that has this characteristic.

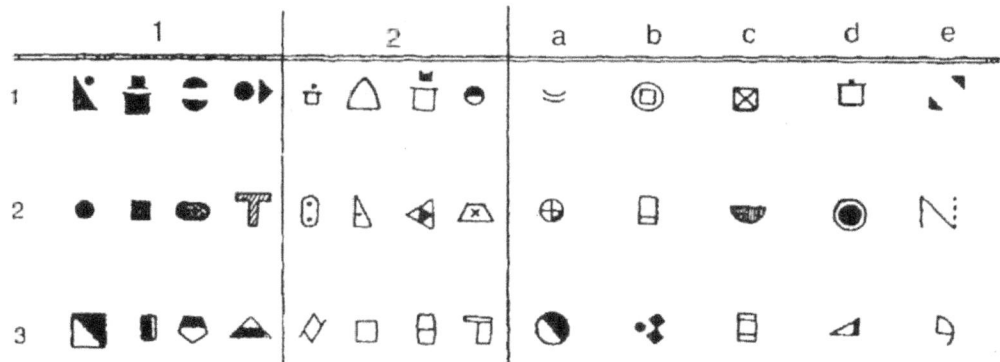

KEY
EXPLANATION OF ANSWERS

1. e Two figures completely blacked in.
2. c Shaded figure.
3. a A figure composed of solid line, partially shaded (blacked in).

TEST 1

TEST 2

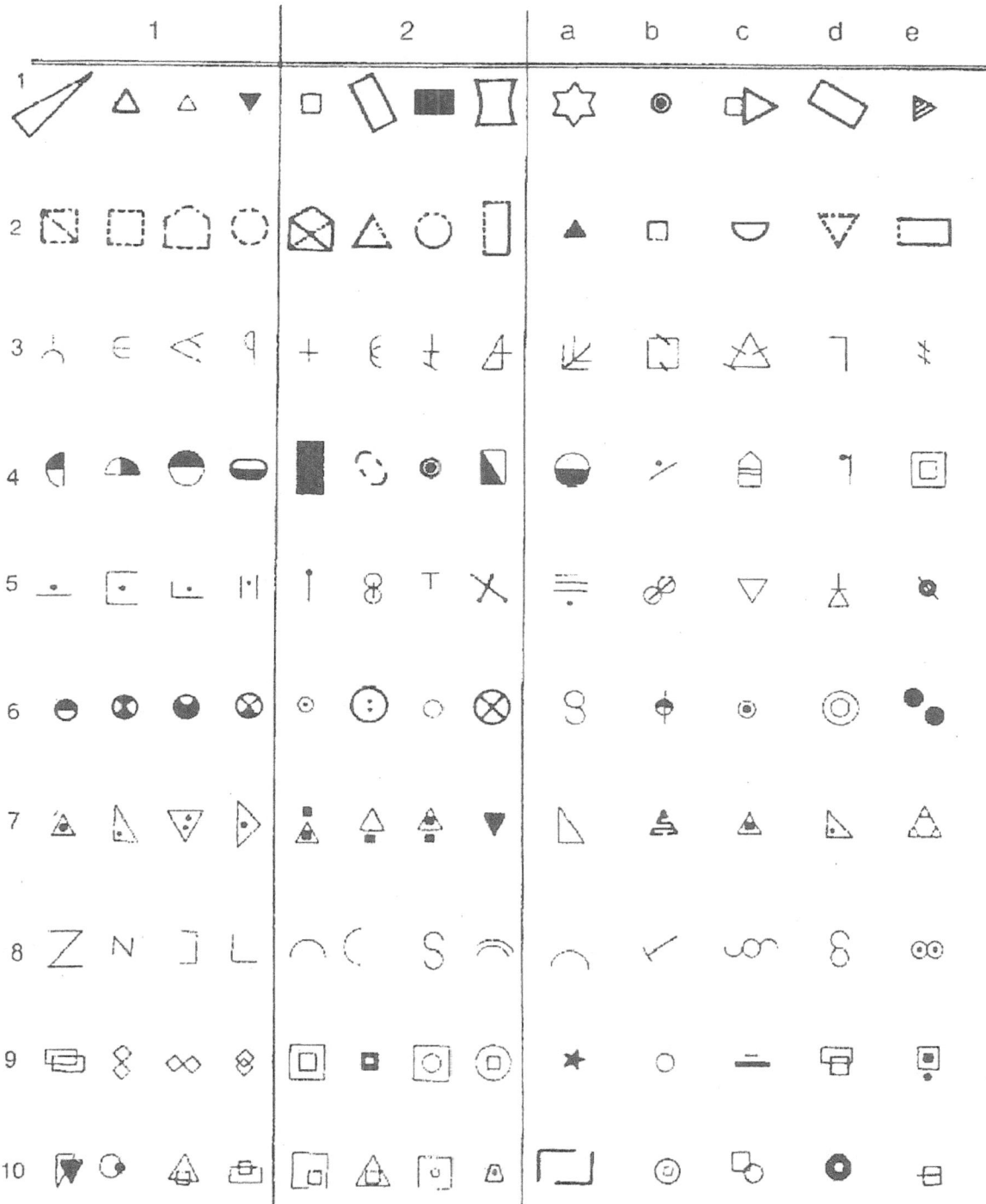

TEST 3

TEST 4

18
TEST 5

19

KEY (CORRECT ANSWERS)

EXPLANATION OF ANSWERS

TEST 1
1. e Solid circle
2. b Figure within a figure
3. c Square within a square, not filled in
4. e Dot within a figure
5. e Dot within a figure
6. c Open sided figure
7. e Open sided figure
8. a Overlapping figure
9. e Line extending from shape
10. b Shape within a shape

TEST 2
1. e Three-sided figure
2. d Completely broken-line figure
3. d Lines touch, but do not cross
4. a. Circular figure, half shaded
5. a Dot and straight line, not touching
6. b. Circular figure, partially shaded
7. d Triangular figure with dot inside
8. b Straight line figure
9. d Figures touch or overlap
10. c Two different figures, overlapping.

TEST 3
1. c Shaded (or lined) figure
2. a Completely broken outline with solid line center
3. c Smaller figure in conjunction with larger figure
4. d Three-sided figure
5. a Completely open figure
6. b Put together it makes a four-sided figure
7. e Cross ("X") inside of figure
8. d Shape made up of triangles
9. c Rounded (dotted) ends on star
10. e Part of center filled in solid

TEST 4
1. a Arrow with straight stem (not curved)
2. b Figure within a figure
3. a Overlapping lines
4. b Figure partially blacked in
5. e Complete line shape, not blacked in
6. b Circle and square overlapping
7. c Figure with curved line
8. a Star-shaped figure
9. e Figure within a figure
10. b Open-sided figure

TEST 5
1. b Completely blacked in figure
2. c Shaded figure
3. a Partially blacked in figure
4. d Dot within figure
5. a Figure within a figure
6. e Open-sided figure
7. d Figure with lines crossing
8. a Partially blacked in figure
9. c Broken line figure
10. e Figure with square

ABSTRACT REASONING

CLASSIFICATION INVENTORY SECTION
INCOMPLETE PATTERNS (NINE FIGURES)

The tests of incomplete patterns that follow consist of items which involve the visualization of nine figures arranged in sequence.

An incomplete pattern only is given. The candidate is to select from the five-lettered choices the correct figure for the last or ninth space.

DIRECTIONS: Each item in this test consists of an incomplete pattern. The complete pattern would be made up of nine figures arranged in sequence. The candidate is to determine the correct figure for the last or ninth space from the five-lettered choices given

SAMPLE QUESTIONS AND EXPLANATIONS

QUESTIONS

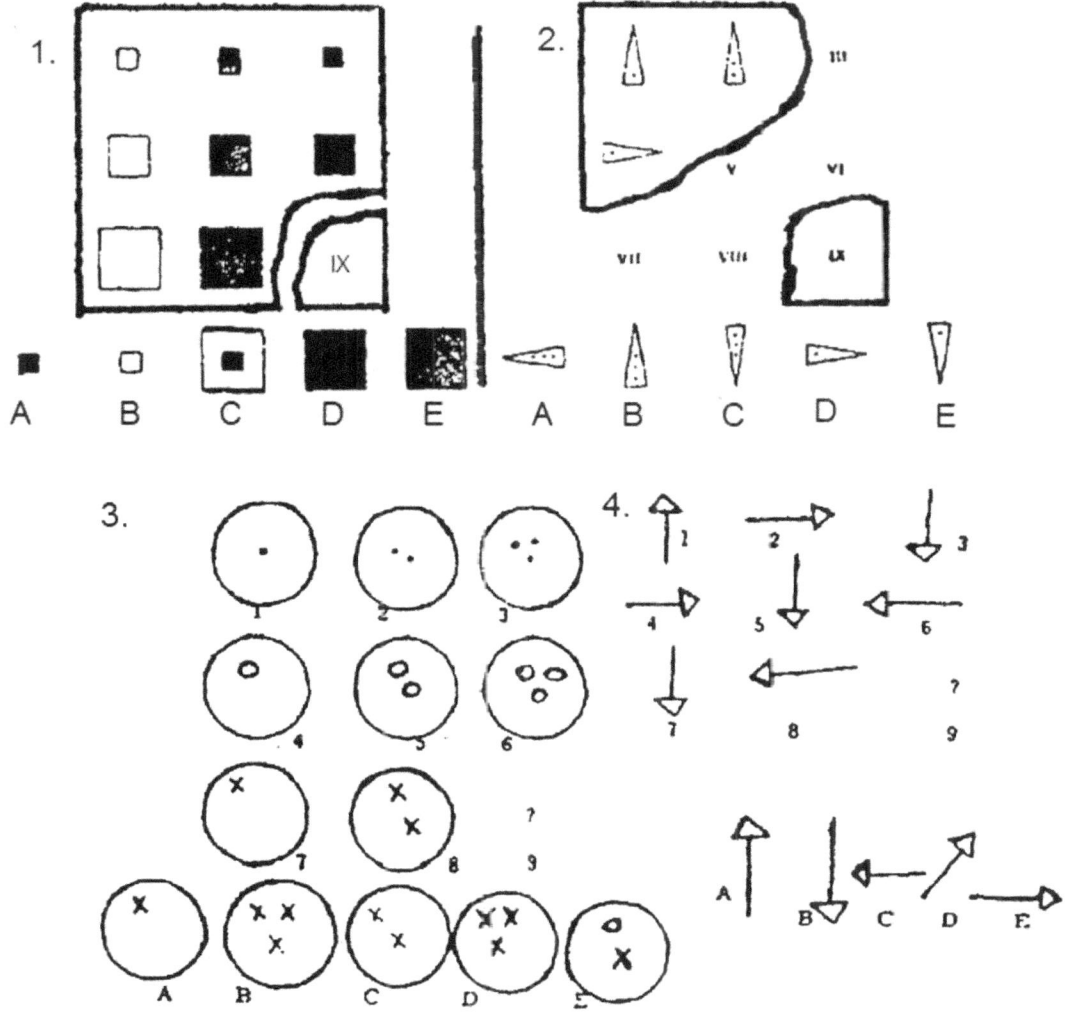

EXPLANATIONS: In Question 1, notice how the figures change as they go across each row of the pattern. They become darker. As they go down, the figures become larger. Therefore, the CORRECT figure for space IX is large is large and dark. Answer choice D is the CORRECT answer.

In Question 2, the figures acquire more dots as they go across the top row. As they go down, the point of the figure is rotated a quarter of a turn to the right. Therefore, the CORRECT answer figure for space IX has three dots and its point is directed downward toward the bottom of the page. Answer choice C is the CORRECT answer.

3. The correct answer is D. Each of the rows of circles has, exclusively, a number of ., o, or x's om ascending order. (Note that B is incorrect since the circle is larger than the given circles.)

4. The correct answer is A. Note that in row 1, two of the arrows (1,2) are turned to the right and one (3) is turned to the left. In row 2, one of the arrows (4) is turned to the right, and two (5,6) are turned to the left. In row three, two arrows are turned to the left (7,8). Therefore, one arrow (9) must be turned to the right in a similar way (answer A).

TESTS IN INCOMPLETE PATTERNS

TEST 1

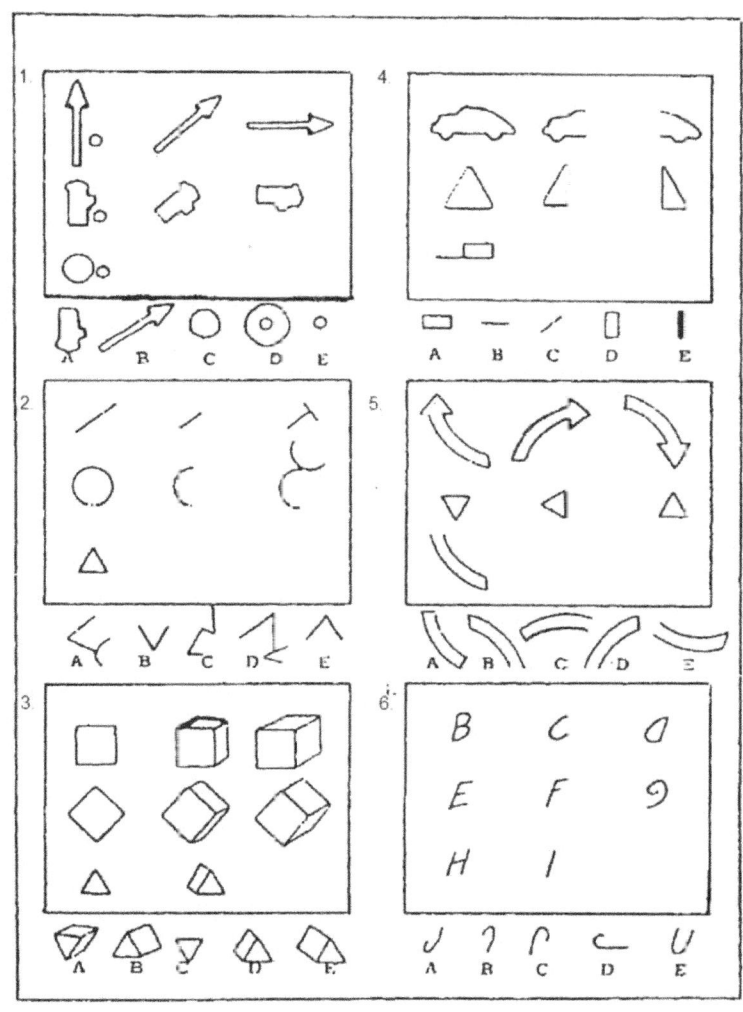

KEY (CORRECT ANSWERS)

1. C
2. C
3. E
4. A
5. B
6. C

TEST 2

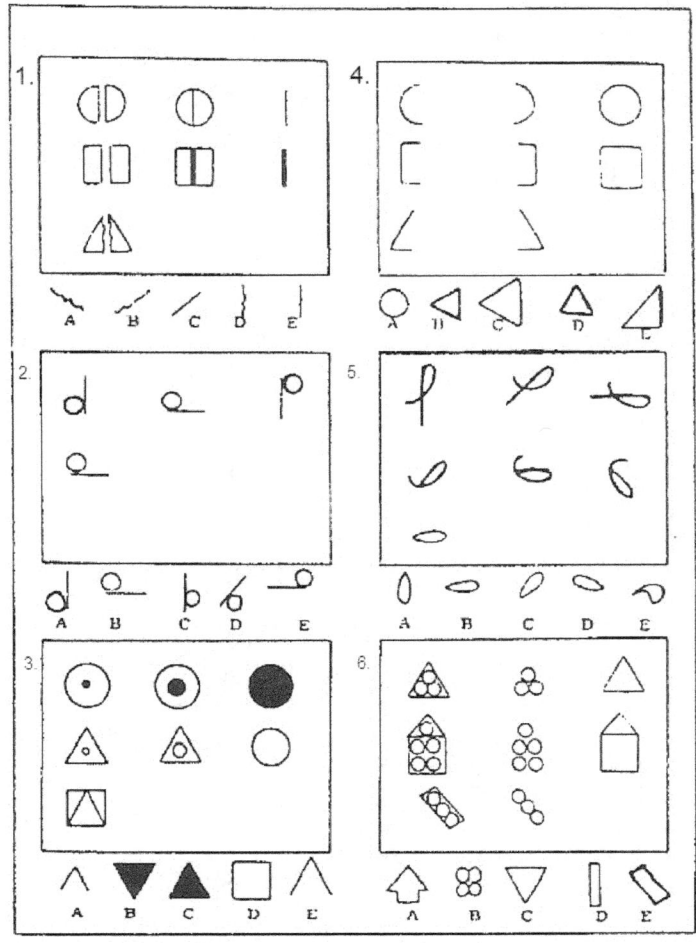

KEY (CORRECT ANSWERS)

1. D
2. A
3. E
4. C
5. A
6. E

TEST 3

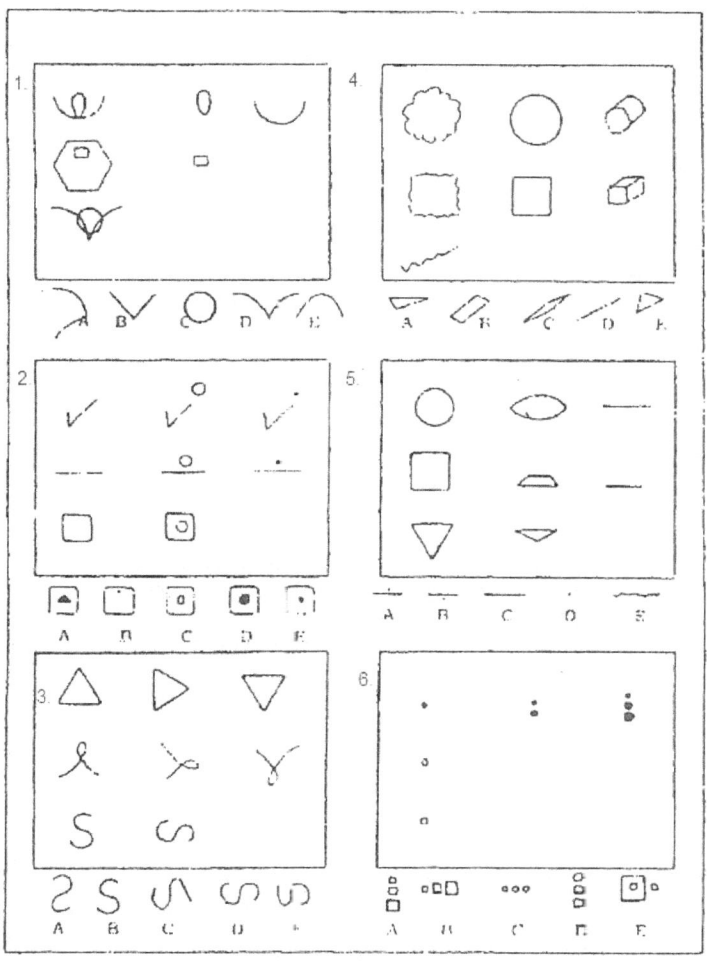

KEY (CORRECT ANSWERS)

1. D
2. E
3. B
4. C
5. C
6. A

TEST 4

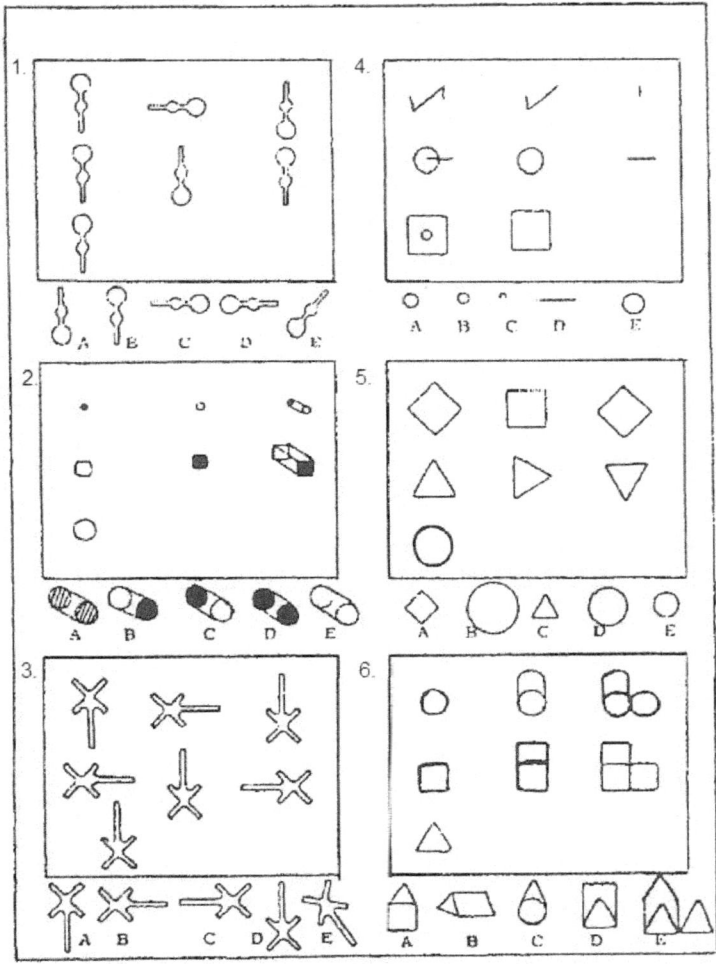

KEY (CORRECT ANSWERS)

1. A
2. B
3. A
4. B
5. D
6. E

7

TEST 5

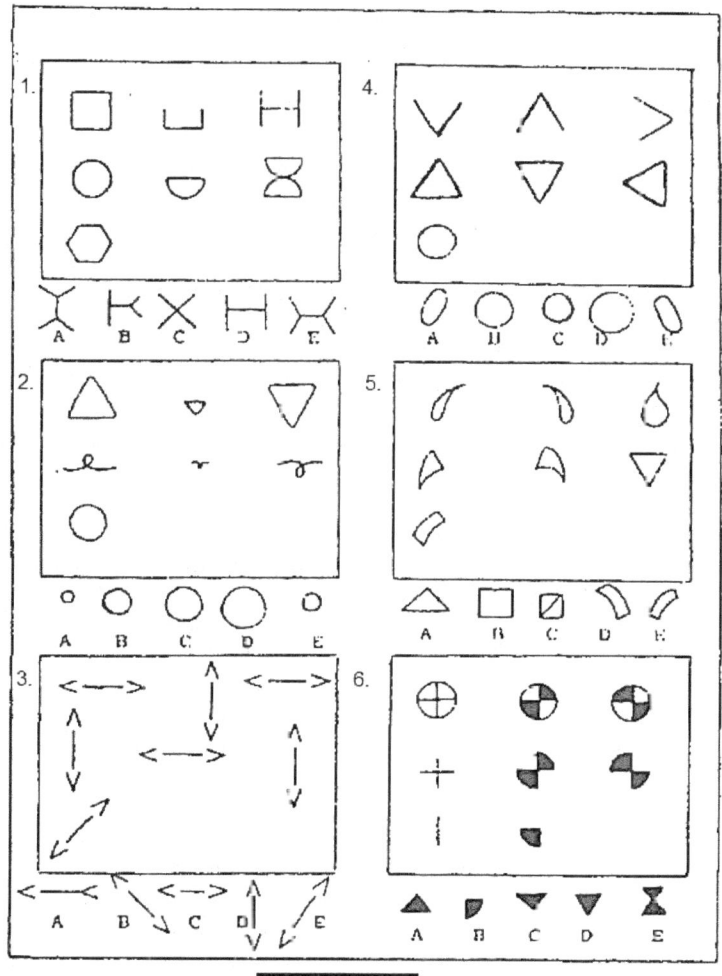

KEY (CORRECT ANSWERS)

1. E
2. C
3. E
4. B
5. B
6. B

PATTERN ANALYSIS (RIGHT SIDE ELEVATION
SAMPLE QUESTION

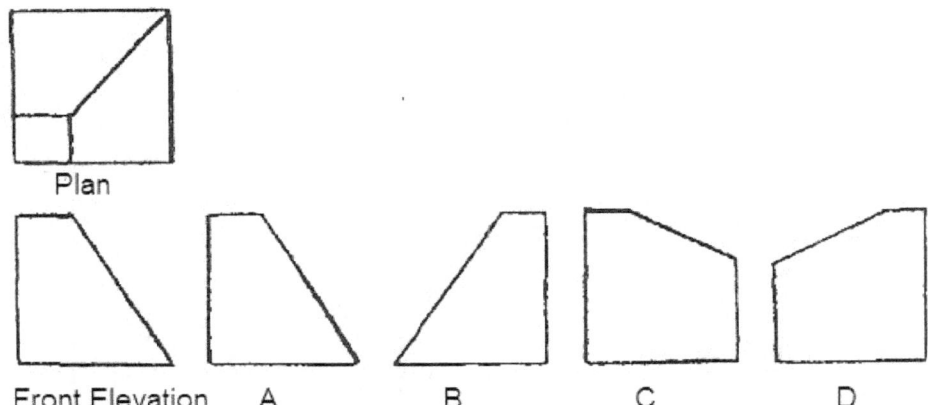

5. In the sample shown above, which figure CORRECTLY represents the right side elevation? 5.____
   1. A   2. B   3. C   4. D

The correct answer is 1.

TEST 1

Questions 1-5.

DIRECTIONS: In Questions 1 through 5 which follow, the plan and front elevation of an object are shown on the left, and on the right are shown four figures, one of which, and ONLY one, represents the right side elevation. Mark your answer in the space at the right the number which represents the right side elevation.

1. A   2. B   3. C   4. D

1.   1.____

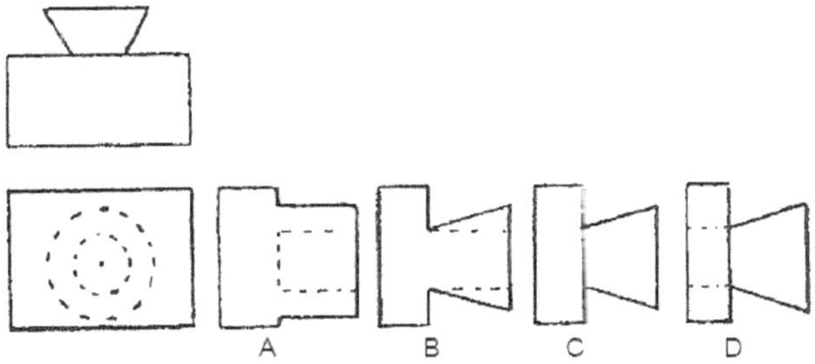

2.   2.____

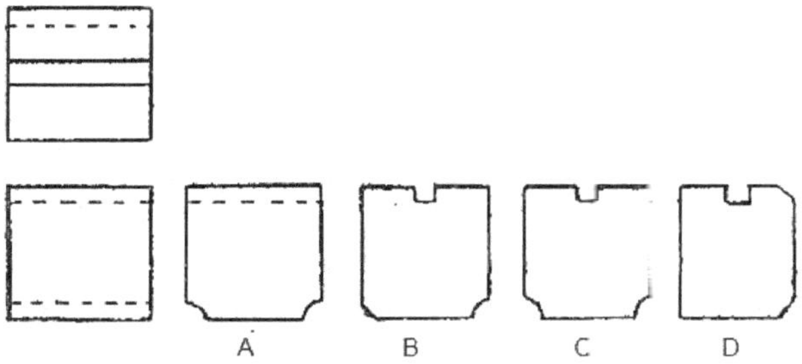

3.   3.____

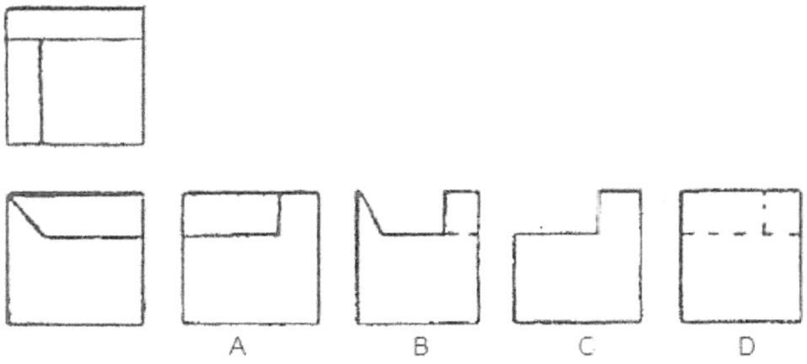

4.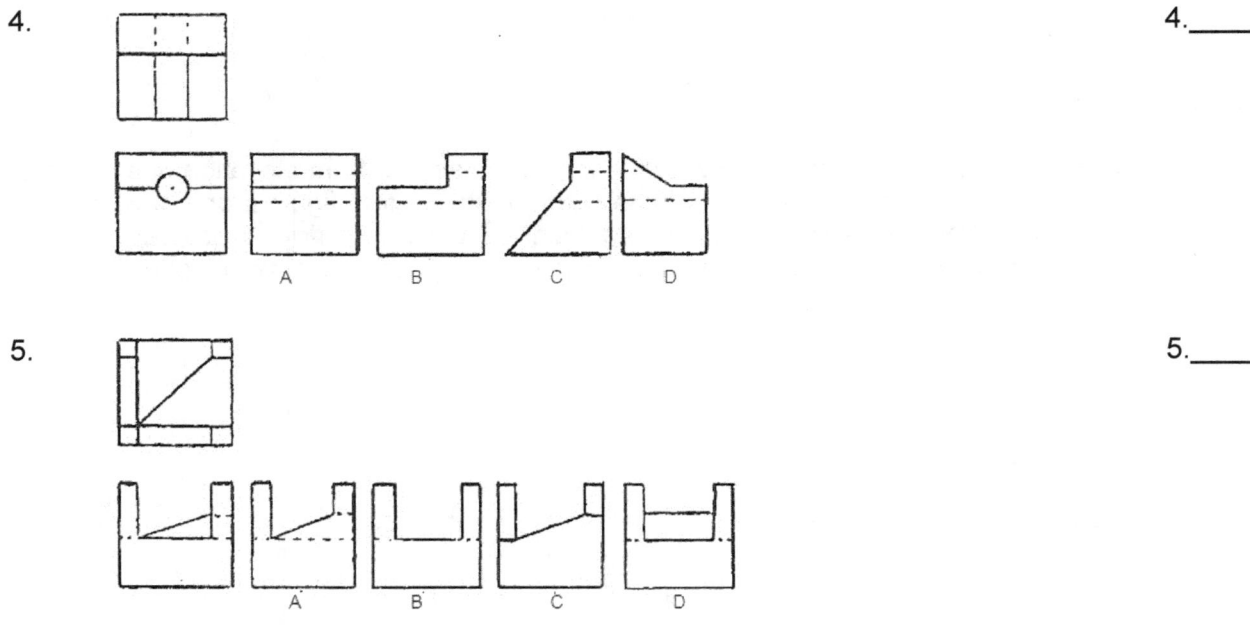

5.

KEY (CORRECT ANSWERS)

1. 4
2. 3
3. 3
4. 2
5. 2

PATTERN ANALYSIS (END ELEVATION)

Questions 1-5.

DIRECTIONS: In each of the following groups of drawings, the top view and front elevation of an object are shown at the left. At the right are four drawings, one of which represents the end elevation of the object as seen from the right. Select the drawing which represents the CORRECT end elevation. The first group is shown as a sample ONLY.

SAMPLE QUESTION

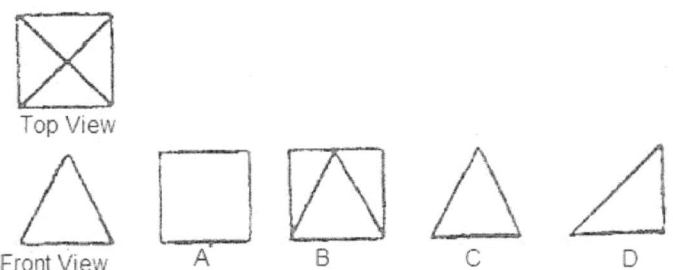

Which drawing represents the CORRECT end elevation?
1. A   2. B.   3. C   4. D

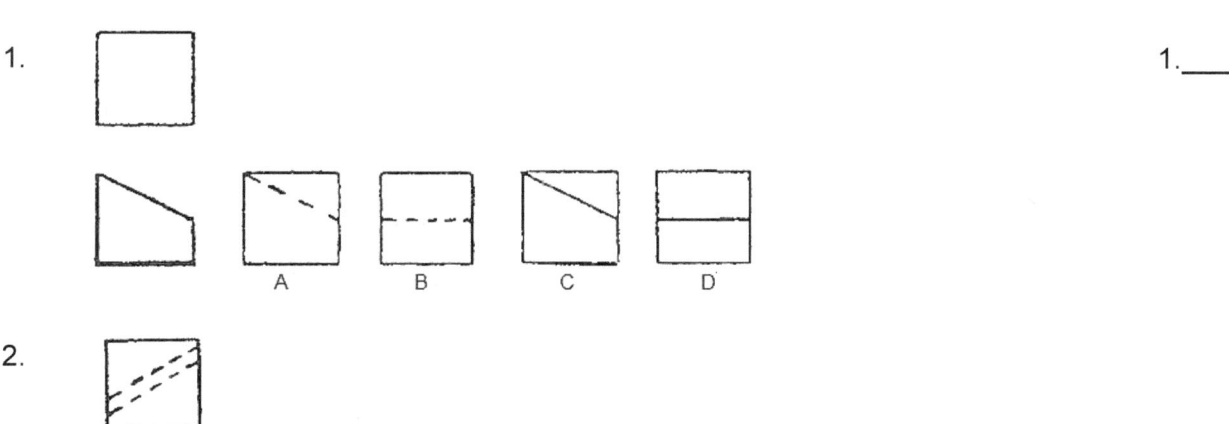

1. ____

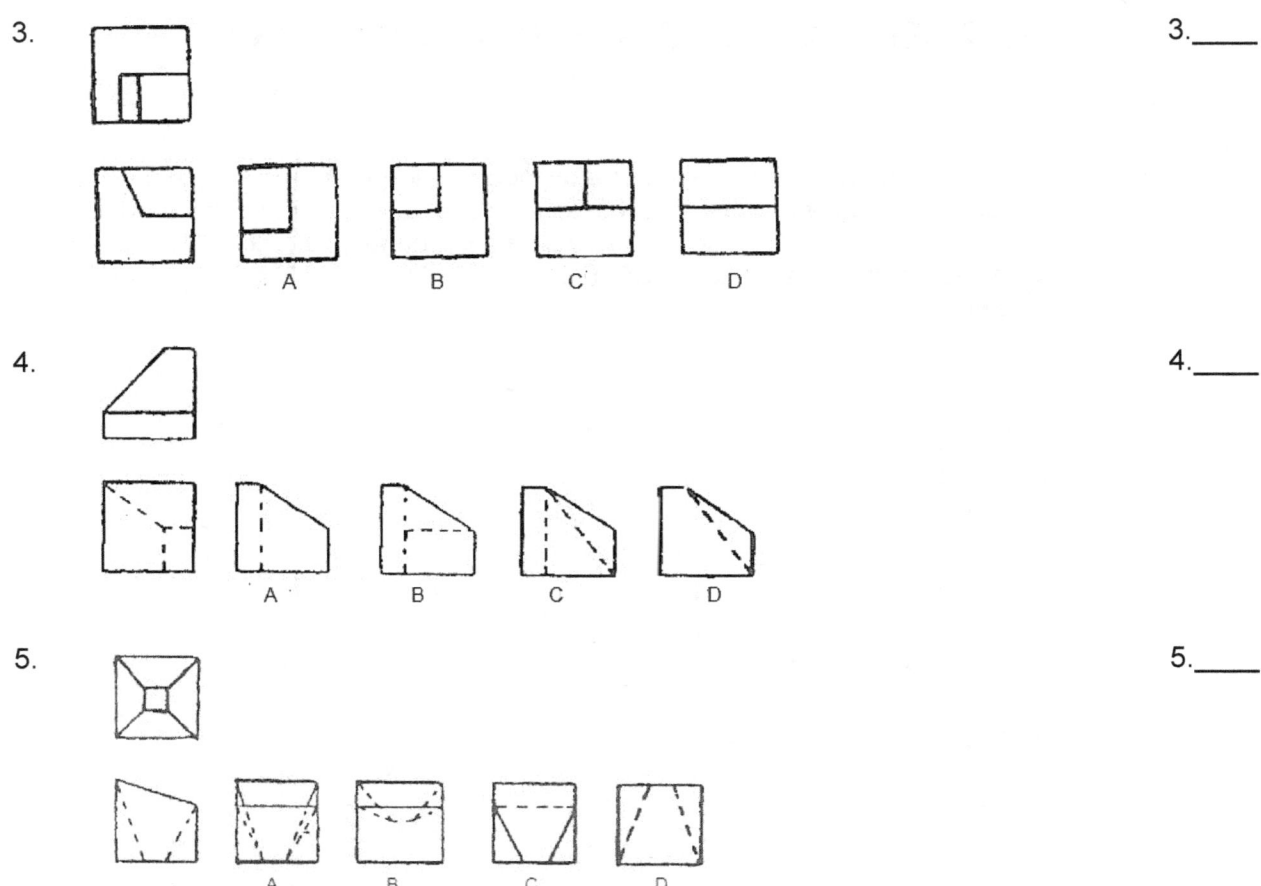

KEY (CORRECT ANSWERS)

1. 4
2. 3
3. 2
4. 1
5. 1

PATTERN ANALYSIS (RIGHT SIDE VIEW)

TEST 1

Questions 1-5.

DIRECTIONS: In each of Questions 1 to 5, inclusive, two views of an object are given. Of the views labeled A, B, C, and D, select the one that CORRECTLY represents the right side view of each object.

Which view represents the right side view? 1. A; 2. B. 3 C; 4. D.

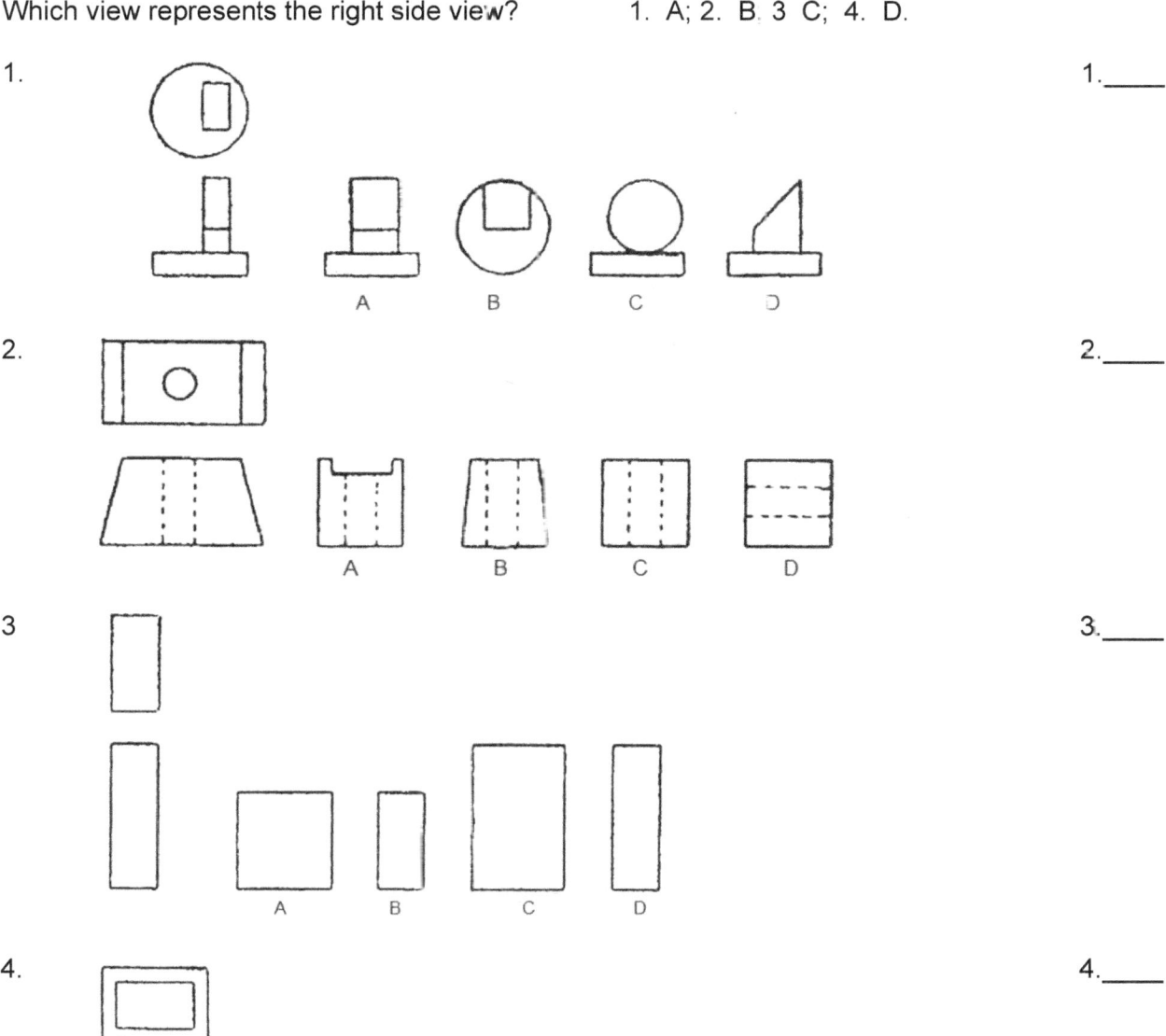

1.____

2.____

3.____

4.____

5.   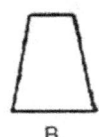  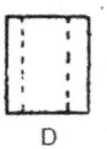   5.____

               A.   B.   C.   D.

KEY (CORRECT ANSWERS)

1. 4
2. 3
3. 3
4. 2
5. 2

SURVEY OF OTHER TYPES OF PATTERN ANALYSIS QUESTIONS

SOLID FIGURE TURNING

Questions 1-3.

DIRECTIONS: The following questions represent figures made up of cubes or other forms glued together. Select the ONE of the four figures lettered A, B, C, D which is the figure at the left turned in a different position and print the letter of the answer in the space at the right. (Note: You are permitted to turn over the figures, to turn them around and to turn them both over and around.)

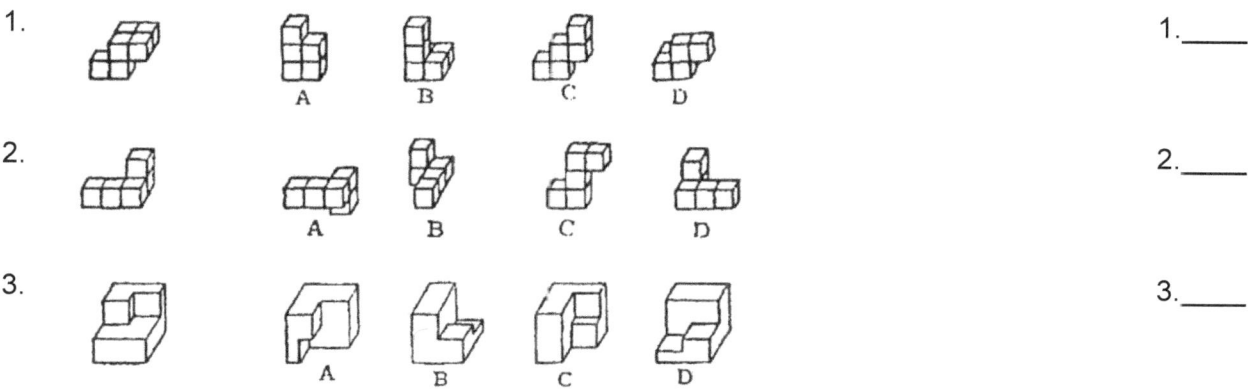

1.____

2.____

3.____

TOUCHING CUBES

Questions 4-7.

DIRECTIONS: Questions 4 and 5 are based on the group of touching cubes at the left, and Questions 6 and 7 on the group at the right.

All the cubes are exactly the same size, and there are only enough hidden cubes to support the ones you can see. The question number is on a cube in the group. You are to find how many cubes in that group touch the numbered cube. Note: A cube is considered to touch the numbered cube if ANY part, EVEN A CORNER, touches. Mark the answer in the space at the right to show how many cubes touch the numbered cube

    A.   if the answer is 1 or 6 or 11 cubes
    B.   if the answer is 2 or 7 or 12 cubes
    C.   if the answer is 3 or 8 or 13 cubes
    D.   if the answer is 4 or 9 or 14 cubes
    E.   if the answer is 5 or 10 or 15 cube

4.

5.

6.

7.

4.____

5.____

6.____

7.____

Questions 8-9.

DIRECTIONS: In each of the following questions, the drawing at the left represents a cube. There is a different design on each of the six faces of the cube. At the right are four other drawings of cubes lettered A, B, C, and D.

Select the ONE of the four which is actually the cube on the left turned to a different position and print the CORRECT answer in the space at the right. (Note: The cube at the left may have been turned over, it may have been turned may have been turned around, or it may have been turned both over and around, and faces not seen in the drawing on the left may have become visible.)

8.

A B C D

6.____

224

9.
    A   B   C   D

7.____

CUBE COUNTING

Questions 10-15.

DIRECTIONS: In each of the following questions, count the number of boxes or cubes represented in the drawing and print the letter of the correct answer in the space at the right.

10.

    A. 16   B. 26   C. 40   D. 22

10.____

11.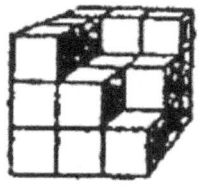

    A. 22   B. 16   C. 27   D. 24

11.____

12.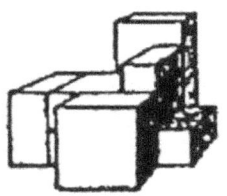

    A. 7   B. 8   C. 9   D. 10

12.____

13.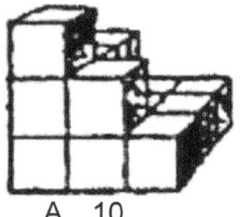

    A. 10   B. 13   C. 12   D. 14

13.____

14.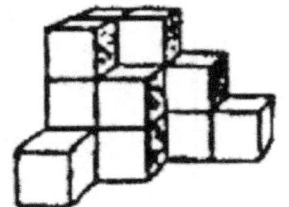

A. 15 B. 13 C. 12 D. 1-

14.___

15.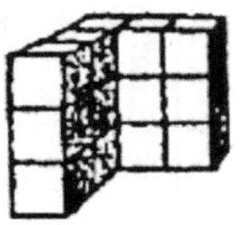

A. 16 B. 12 C. 10 D. 15

15.___

KEY (CORRECT ANSWERS)

1. D   6. B(7)   11. A
2. B   7. E(10)   12. B
3. D   8. B   13. .D
4. C(3) 9. A   14 A
5. A(6) 10. C   15. A

ARITHMETICAL REASONING

EXAMINATION SECTION

TEST 1

DIRECTIONS: Each question or incomplete statement is followed by several suggested answers or completions. Select the one that BEST answers the question or completes the statement. *PRINT THE LETTER OF THE CORRECT ANSWER IN THE SPACE AT THE RIGHT.*

1. A class decided to cultivate a garden. The principal gave them a piece of ground 40 feet long and 30 feet wide. There were 18 boys and 12 girls in the class. The class voted that each pupil should be allowed an equal amount of the space in the garden.
   The number of square feet which was set aside for the *exclusive* use of the boys was
   A. 30   B. 40   C. 480   D. 720

   1.____

2. The chef allowed 20 minutes cooking time per pound for a roast weighing 6 lbs. 12 ozs.
   If the roast was placed in the oven at 4:20 P.M., it *should be done* by
   A. 6:00 P.M.   B. 6:32 P.M.   C. 6:35 P.M.   D. 7:12 P.M.

   2.____

3. To check the correctness of the answer to a multiplication example, divide the
   A. product by the multiplier
   B. multiplier by the product
   C. multiplicand by the multiplier
   D. multiplier by the multiplicand

   3.____

4. Of the following correct ways to solve .125 × .32, the MOST efficient is to
   A. write .125 under .32, multiply, point off 5 places
   B. write .32 under .125, multiply, point off 5 places
   C. multiply 125 by 32 and divide by 1000 × 100
   D. divide .32 by 6

   4.____

5. If you were to eat each meal in a different restaurant in the city's eating places, assuming that you eat 3 meals a day, it would take you more than 19 years to cover all of the city's eating places.
   On the basis of this information, the BEST of the following choices is that the number of restaurants in the city
   A. exceeds 20,500
   B. is closer to 21,000 than 22,000
   C. exceeds 21,000
   D. does not exceed 21,500

   5.____

6. The cost of electricity for operating an 875-watt toaster, an 1100-watt steam iron, and four 75-watt lamps, each for one hour, at 7.5 cents per kilowatt hour (1 kilowatt equals 1000 watts) is
   A. 15 cents   B. 17 cents   C. $1.54   D. $1.71

   6.____

7. Of the following, the pair that is NOT a set of equivalents is:
   A. .021%, .00021
   B. ¼%, .0025
   C. 1.5%, 3/200
   D. 225%, .225

8. Assuming that the series will continue in the same pattern, the NEXT number in the series 3, 5, 11, 29......is
   A. 41   B. 47   C. 65   D. 83

9. If the total area of a picture measuring 10 inches by 12 inches plus a matting of uniform width surrounding the picture is 224 square inches, the WIDTH of the matting is
   A. 2 inches
   B. 2 4/11 inches
   C. 3 inches
   D. 4 inches

10. The *net price* of a $25 item after SUCCESSIVE discounts of 20% and 30% is
    A. 11   B. $12.50   C. $14   D. $19

KEY (CORRECT ANSWERS)

1.	D	6.	B
2.	C	7.	D
3.	A	8.	D
4.	D	9.	A
5.	A	10.	C

SOLUTIONS TO ARITHMETICAL REASONING

1. Answer: (D) 720

   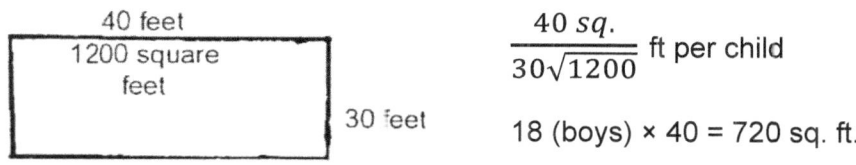

   18 (boys) × 40 = 720 sq. ft.

2. Answer: (C) 6:35 P.M.

   20 minutes per 1 lb.

   ```
   120
   +15
   135 minutes
   -120 minutes (2 hours
    15 minutes
   ```

   $\therefore \dfrac{12\ oz.}{16\ oz} = \dfrac{3}{4}$ lb.

   3/4 × 20 = 15 minutes
   20 × 6 = 120 minutes

   ```
    4:20 P.M.
   +2:15 (2 hours, 15 minutes)
    6:35 P.M.
   ```

3. Answer: (A) product by the multiplier

   12 (multiplicand
   ×2 (multiplier
   24 (product)

4. Answer: (D) divide .32 by 8

   The most efficient way is to divide .32 by 8.
   .125 = .12 ½ = 12 ½% = 1/8

   $1/8 \times .32 = \dfrac{.32}{8}$ $\dfrac{.04}{8\overline{)\,.32}}$
   $\phantom{1/8 \times .32 = \dfrac{.32}{8}\ \ \ \ }.32$

4 (#1)

5. Answer: (A) exceeds 20,500

    365 (days in 1 year)
    × 3 (meals)
    1095 (meals in 1 year)
    × 19 (number of years)
    20,805 (number of meals eaten in 19 years)   4 (leap-year days)
    +   12 (number of meals eaten in leap years)   × 3 (meals)
    20,817 (total)   12 (leap-year meals)

6. Answer: (B) 17 cents
875 + 1100 + 300 = 2275 watts
2275/1000 = 11/40 kilowatt hours
2 11/40 × 7.5 cents = $.17 approximately

7. Answer: (D) 225%, .225

    A. .021% = .00021   B. $1/4\% = \dfrac{1}{400} = .0025$

    C. $1.5\% = .015 + \dfrac{15}{1000} = \dfrac{3}{200}$ D. 225% = 2.25 (not .225)

8. Answer: (D) 83

Suggestions For Series Problems
1. Find the difference between the numbers (or squares of differences).
2. In this series, each difference is multiplied by 3 and added to the succeeding number.
    3,5:   the difference is 2; thus difference was multiplied by 3 giving 6, which was then added to 5, to make the next number in the series 11.
    5,11:   the difference is 6; this difference was multiplied by 3, giving 18, which was then added to 11, to make the next number in the series 29.
    11,29: the difference is 18; this difference should be multiplied by 3, giving 54, which, when added to 29, will give the next number in the series, 83.

9. Answer: (A) 2 inches

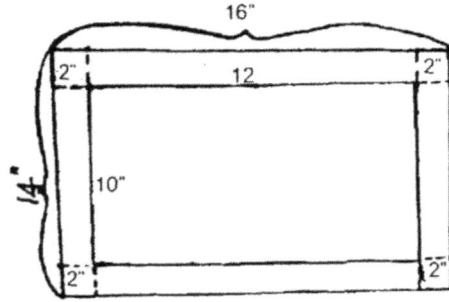

5 (#1)

The total area = 224 square inches (16 × 14).
If 2 inches are added to either side of the picture's width and to either side of the picture's length, we get a new width of 14 inches (10 + 4) and a new length of 16 inches (12 + 4).
Therefore, 14 × 16 = 224 square inches,
Or, a uniform matting width of 2 inches.

10. Answer: (C) $14

SOLUTION
Successful discounts
   20%   30%
1. Convert to decimals .2, .3
2. Subtract from 1.0, .8, .7
3. Multiply .8 × .7 = .56
4. 1.00 - .56 = .44
   25.00
   × .44
   100
   100
   $11.00
5. $25.00 - $11.00 = $14.00

ALTERNATE SOLUTION
$ 25
× .20
$5.00
$25 - $5 = $20
$ 20
× .30
$6.00
$20 - $6 = $14

TEST 2

DIRECTIONS: Each question or incomplete statement is followed by several suggested answers or completions. Select the one that BEST answers the question or completes the statement. *PRINT THE LETTER OF THE CORRECT ANSWER IN THE SPACE AT THE RIGHT.*

1. The cost of 63 inches of ribbon at 12 cent per yard is
   A. $.20   B. $.21   C. $.22   D. $.23

2. If 1½ cups of cereal are used with 4½ cups of water, the amount of water needed with ¾ of a cup of cereal is
   A. 2 cups   B. 2⅛ cups   C. 2¼ cups   D. 2½ cups

3. Under certain conditions, sound travels at about 1100 ft. per second. If 88 ft. per second is approximately equivalent to 60 miles per hour, the above condition is, of the following, CLOSEST to _____ miles per hour.
   A. 730   B. 740   C. 750   D. 760

4. Of the following, the MOST NEARLY accurate set of equivalents is
   A. 1 ft. equals 30.48 centimeters   B. 1 centimeter equals 2.54 inches
   C. 1 rod equals 3.28 meters   D. 1 meter equals 1.09 feet

5. If one angle of a triangle is three times a second angle and the third angle is 20 degrees more than the second angle, the SECOND ANGLE is
   A. 32°   B. 34°   C. 40°   D. 50°

6. Assuming that on a blueprint ¼ inch equals 12 inches, the ACTUAL length in feet of a steel bar represented on the blueprint by a line $3^3/_8$ inches long is
   A. $3^3/_8$ B. 6¾   C. 12½   D. 13½

7. A plane leaves Denver, Colorado, on June 1st at 1 P.M. Mountain Standard Time and arrives at New York City on June 2nd A.M. Eastern Daylight Saving Time.
   The ACTUAL time of flight was _____ hours.
   A. 10   B. 11   C. 12   D. 13

8. Of the following, the value CLOSEST to that of $\frac{42.10 \times .0003}{.002}$ is:
   A. .063   B. .63   C. 6.3   D. 63

9. If Mrs. Jones bought 3¾ yards of dacron at $1.16 per yard and $4^2/_3$ yards of velvet at $3.87 per yard, the amount of change she receives from $25 is
   A. $2.12   B. $2.28   C. $2.59   D. $2.63

10. The water level of a swimming pool, 75 feet by 42 feet, is to be raised 4 inches. 10.____
The number of gallons of water needed for this purpose is (1 cubic foot equals 7½ gallons)
   A. 140   B. 7,875   C. 31,500   D. 94,500

KEY (CORRECT ANSWERS)

1.	B	6.	D
2.	C	7.	A
3.	C	8.	C
4.	A	9.	C
5.	A	10.	B

SOLUTIONS TO ARITHMETICAL REASONING

1. Answer: (B) $.21

   SOLUTION

   $63" = \frac{63}{36}$ yds; $\frac{6.3}{3.6} \times \frac{.01}{.12} = 21¢$

   ALTERNATE SOLUTION

   12¢ per yard

   $\frac{12}{36} = \frac{1}{3}$ ¢ per inch; $\frac{63"}{1} \times \frac{1}{3} ¢ = \frac{63}{3} = 21¢$

2. Answer: (C) 2¼ cups

   SOLUTION

   From the data given, we form the proportion,

Proportion	Cereal	Water
1st mixture	1½ cups	4½ cups
2nd mixture	¾ cups	x cups

   ¾ is half of 1½; therefore, half of 4½ is ¼

   ALTERNATE SOLUTION

   From the data given, we form the proportion,
   1½ (cups of cereal): 4½ (cups of water) = ¾ (cup of cereal): x ∴ 3/2 : 9/2 = ¾ : x
   3/2x = 27/4
   x = 9/4 – 2¼ (cups of water)

3. Answer: (C) 750 miles per hour
   Speed of sound = 1100 ft. per second
   88 ft. per second = 60 miles an hour
   $\frac{1100}{88}$ = 12½ (the number of times the speed of sound is greater than 60 miles an hour)
   ∴ 60 × 12½ = 750 miles per hour (the speed of sound)

4. Answer: (A) 1 ft. equals 30.48 centimeters
   Taking each alternative in turn:
   1. A meter = 100 centimeters
      A meter = 39 in. (approx.) = 3¼ ft. (39/12 = 3¼)
      3 ¼ ft. = 1 meter = 100 centimeters
      ∴ 1 ft. = $\frac{100}{3\ 1/4}$ = 30.48 centimeters (approx.)
   2. 1 meter = 39 in. = 3 ¼ ft. (approx.)
   3. 1 centimeter = .39 in.
   4. 1 rod = 5½ yds. = 16½ ft.
      ∴ 1 rod = 5 meters (approx.) (see item 2 above)

4 (#2)

5. Answer: (A) 32°
   Let x = second angle
   Let 3x = first angle
   Let x + 20° = third angle
   5x + 20 = 180°
   x = 32°

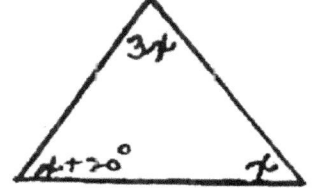

6. Answer (D) 13 ½

   $$\frac{1/4"}{12} = \frac{3\ 3/8"}{x}$$

   ¼ ÷ 12/1 = 27/8 ÷ x/1
   ¼ × 1/12 = 27/8 × 1/x

   $$\frac{1}{4} = \frac{27}{8x}$$

   8x = 48 × 27 = 1296
   x = 162 inches
     = 13½ ft.

7. Answer: (A) 10 hours
   TIME BELTS

   In traveling eastward, we set our clocks forward for each time zone.

   Plane left at 1 P.M.
   Traveled around clock 12 hours or 13 hours at 2 A.M.

   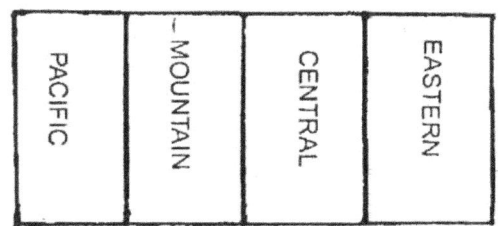

   4 A.M. 5 A.M. 6 A.M. 7 A.M. E.S.T.
                           8 A.M. D.S.T.

   Subtract 2 hours' difference between Mountain Time and Eastern Standard Time.
   Subtract another hour for Daylight Saving Time. That is, 13 – 3 = 10 hours.

8. Answer: (C) 6.3

   In 42.10, discard for practical purposes the .10 and perform as follows;

   $$\frac{42 \times .003}{.002} = \frac{.0125}{.002} = \frac{12.6}{2}\ 63$$

9. $1.16 $ 3.86 $18.06 $25.00
    × 3 3/4   × 4 2/3   + 4.35   - 22.41
    $4.35 $18.06 $22.42 $ 2.59

10. Answer: (B) 7,875
    42 × 75 × 1/3 ft. (4") = 1050 cu. ft.
    × 7 ½
    7,875 gallons

235

TEST 3

DIRECTIONS: Each question or incomplete statement is followed by several suggested answers or completions. Select the one that BEST answers the question or completes the statement. *PRINT THE LETTER OF THE CORRECT ANSWER IN THE SPACE AT THE RIGHT.*

1. The part of the total quantity represented by a 24-degree sector of a circle graph is
   A. $6^2/_3\%$ B. 12%   C. $13^1/_3\%$ D. 24%

   1.____

2. If the shipping charges to a certain point are 62 cents for the first 5 oz. and 8 cents for each additional ounce, the weight of a package for which the charges are $1.66 is
   A. 13 ounces   B. $1^1/_8$ lbs.   C. 1¼ lbs.   D. 1½ lbs.

   2.____

3. If 15 cans of food are needed for 7 men for 2 days, the number of cans needed for 4 men for 7 days is
   A. 15   B. 20   C. 25   D. 30

   3.____

4. The total saving in purchasing thirty 13-cent ice cream pops for a class party at a reduced rate of $1.38 per dozen is
   A. 35¢   B. 40¢   C. 45¢   D. 50¢

   4.____

5. The quotient for the division of 36 apples among 4 children may be correctly found by thinking
   A. 36 ÷ ¼   B. $36\overline{)4.0}$ C. ¼ of 36   D. 4/36

   5.____

6. The missing term in the equation 1/3 of ? = ½ of 90 is
   A. 45   B. 30   C. 15   D. 135

   6.____

7. The fraction CLOSEST to 4/5 is
   A. 2/3   B. 7/9   C. 8/11   D. 5/8

   7.____

8. Of the following, the one which may be used CORRECTLY to compute the value of 4 × 22½ is
   A. (4×45) + (4×1/2)
   B. (4×1/2) + (4×2)+(4×2)
   C. (1/2 if 4(+ (2×4)+(2×4)
   D. (4×20) + (4×2)+((4×1/2)

   8.____

9. 16 ½ ÷ ¼ may CORRECTLY be expressed as
   A. (1/4×16) + (1/4×1/2)
   B. (4×16) + 4×1/2)
   C. $4\overline{)16.5}$
   D. ¼ times 33/2

   9.____

10. In computation, ¾ may be CORRECTLY transformed into 6/8 for the same reason that
    A. 7(3+4) = 21 + 28
    B. 3 apples + 5 apples = 8
    C. $.2\overline{)3.4} = 2\overline{)34}$
    D. 3 + 4 = 4 + 3

    10.____

KEY (CORRECT ANSWERS)

1. A   6. D
2. B   7. B
3. D   8. D
4. C   9. B
5. C   10. C

SOLUTIONS TO ARITHMETICAL REASONING

1. Answer: (A) 6 2/3%

   $$\frac{24}{360} = \frac{2}{30} = \frac{1}{15} = .06\ 2/3 = 6\ 2/3\%$$

2. Answer: (B) 1 1/8 lbs.
   Total charges = $1.66
   Charge for 1st 5 oz. = .62
                         $1.04 (remaining charges at rate of .08/oz.)

   5 oz. + 13 oz. = 18 oz. (Total no. of oz. in weight of pkge.)
   OR $\frac{18}{16}$ 1 1/8 lb.

3. Answer: (D) 30
   If 15 cans of food are needed for 7 men for 2 days, therefore, 7½ cans are needed for these same 7 men for 1 day.
   7 ½ ÷ 7 = 15/14 the no. of cans needed by 1 man for 1 day.
   4 × 7 × 15/14 = 30, the number of cans needed by 4 men for 7 days.

4. Answer (C) 45¢
   $.13 × 30 = $3.90 (regular rate)
   30 = 2½ doz.; $1.38 × 2½ = $3.45 (reduced rate)
   Total saving = $.45 ($3.90 - $$3..45)

5. Answer: (C) ¼ of 36   36/4 = 9

6. Answer: (D) 135   1/3 of ? = ½ of 90
                    1/3x = 45
                    x = 3 × 45
                      = 135

7. Answer: (B) 7/9
   4/5 = .80   8/11 = .73
   2/3 = .66   5/8 = .63
   7/9 = .78

8. Answer: (D) (4 × 20) ÷ (4× 2) ÷ (4 × ½)

   22 ½
   ×4
   ───
   80   Choice (D) (4×20) + (4×2) + (4×1/2) = 80 + 8 + 2 = 90
    8   (This is an example of the Distribution Law which links the operations
    2   of addition and multiplication.)
   ──
   10

9. Answer: (B) (4×16) + (4×1/2)

   $16 ½ ÷ 4 = \dfrac{16\ 1/2}{4} = 16\ ½ × 4/1 = (4×16) ÷ (4×1/2)$

10. Answer: (C) $2\overline{)3.4} = 2\overline{)34}$

    $\dfrac{3}{4} = \dfrac{6}{8}\ ;\ \dfrac{3.4}{.2} = \dfrac{34}{2} = 17$

TEST 4

DIRECTIONS: Each question or incomplete statement is followed by several suggested answers or completions. Select the one that BEST answers the question or completes the statement. *PRINT THE LETTER OF THE CORRECT ANSWER IN THE SPACE AT THE RIGHT.*

1. The mathematical law of distribution is illustrated by all of the following EXCEPT:

    A. 15
        ×12
        150
         30
        180

    B. 15
        ×12
         30
        150
        180

    C. 15
        ×12
        180

    D. 15
        ×12
         30
         15
        180

    1._____

2. Of the following series of partial sums which might arise in the addition of 36 and 25, the one that is INCORRECT IS:
    A. 11, 31, 61   B. 11, 4, 6, 61   C. 11, 41, 61   D. 36, 56, 61

    2._____

3. Of the following, the one which equals one million is:
    A. ten hundred thousand
    B. 10^7
    C. 10×10×10×10×10×10×10
    D. 1 plus 6 zeros

    3._____

4. Of the following groups, the one containing four terms all associated with one algorismic process is:
    A. Added, quotient, dividend, divisor
    B. Dividend, quotient, divisor, minuend
    C. Dividend, quotient, addend; minuend
    D. Multiplicand, product, minuend, addend

    4._____

5. Depreciation of a certain machine is estimated, for any year, at 20% of its value at the beginning of the year.
   If the machine is purchased for $600, its estimated net value at the end of two years is CLOSEST to
    A. $325   B. $350   C. $375   D. $400

    5._____

6. Hats are purchased at the rate of $33 per dozen.
   If they are sold at a close-out sale for $2.50 each, the *percent loss* on the cost price is
    A. 3   B. 3 1/3   C. 9 1/11   D. 10

    6._____

7. The time, 3 hours, 58 minutes after 10:56 A.M. is
    A. 4:54 P.M.   B. 2:54 P.M.   C. 4:15 P.M.   D. 2:15 P.M.

    7._____

8. Mr. Brown had $20.00 when he took his three children on a bus trip. He spent $7.33 for the four tickets and bought each of the children a magazine costing 15¢, a candy bar costing 11¢, and a 5¢ package of chewing gum. His change from the $20.00 was
    A. $12.74   B. $11.43   C. $11.74   D. $12.84

    8._____

2 (#4)

9. The loan value on a life insurance policy at the end of 5 years is $30.19 per $1,000 of insurance.
   The LARGEST amount to the nearest dollar that can be borrowed on a $5,500 policy at the end of five years is
   A. $17   B. $151   C. $166   D. $1,660

10. Using cups that hold six ounces of milk, the number of cupfuls a person can obtain from 1 ½ gallons of milk is
    A. 16   B. 24   C. 32   D. 64

KEY (CORRECT ANSWERS)

1.	C	6.	C
2.	B	7.	B
3.	A	8.	C
4.	B	9.	C
5.	C	10.	C

3 (#4)

SOLUTIONS TO ARITHMETICAL REASONING

1. Answer: (C)
   15
   ×12
   ―――
   180

   The Distributive Law links the operations of addition and arithmetic.

2. Answer: (B) 11, 4, 6, 61

   Partial Sums

v36	(A) 11	(C) 11	(D) 36
+25	+20	+30	+20
61	31	41	56
	+30	+20	+5
	61	61	61

3. Answer: (A) ten hundred thousand 100,000 × 1,000,000

4. Answer: (B) dividend, quotient, divisor, minuend
   Division is repeated subtraction
   divisor   21   quotient
            12)256   dividend
              24
              16   minuend – partial dividend
              12
               4   partial dividend

36	multiplicand		
×45	multiplier		
180	partial product	5	addend
144	partial produce	+6	addend
1620	product	11	sum

7,485	minuend
2,648	subtrahend
4,837	remainder (difference)

5. Answer: (C) $375

$600	$480	$600	$480
× .20	× .20	-120	96
120.00	96.00	$480	$384 (approximately

4 (#4)

6. Answer: (C) 9 1/11
   Cost of one dozen
   Selling price of one dozen $33.00 $2.50
                                 30.00   ×   12
                                 $ 3.00 $30.00 sold at close-out sale

   $$\frac{L}{C} = \frac{\$3}{\$33} = \frac{1}{11} = 9\ 1/11\%$$

7. Answer: (B) 2:54 P.M.
   A simple way to do this is to add 4 minutes to 10:56 A.M., making 11:00 A.M. Adding 3 hours = 2:00 P.M.
   Adding 54 minutes (instead of 58 minutes, to compensate for the 4 minutes added to 10:56 A.M.) = 2:54 P.M.

8. Answer: (C) $11.74

15¢	31¢	$7.33	$20.00
11¢	×3	+.93	-8.26
5¢	93¢	$8.26	$11.74
31¢			

9. Answer: (C) $166
   $30.19 × 5 = $150.95 (loan value on $5,000 policy at end of 5 years))
   $150.95 ÷ 10 = $15.10 (approx.) (loan value on additional $500 at end of 5 years)
   ∴ $150.95 + $15.10 = $166 (approx.)

10. Answer: (C) 32
    We must know that 1 cup = 8 oz. and that 1 qt. = 4 cups or 32 oz.
    Since 1 gallon = 4 qts., 1 gallon = 128 oz. (4×32 oz.)
    ∴ ½ gallon = 64 oz. and 1 ½ gallon = 192 oz. (128 +64)
    Finally, 192 ÷ 6 = 32 (cups)

TEST 5

DIRECTIONS: Each question or incomplete statement is followed by several suggested answers or completions. Select the one that BEST answers the question or completes the statement. *PRINT THE LETTER OF THE CORRECT ANSWER IN THE SPACE AT THE RIGHT.*

1. A storekeeper purchased an article for $36. In order to include 10% of cost for overhead and to provide $9 of net profit, the MARKUP should be
   A. 25% B. 35% C. 37 ½ % D. 40%

   1._____

2. A rectangular carton has twice the height, one-third the length, and four times the width of a second carton.
   The ratio of the volume of the first carton to that of the second is
   A. 16 : 3 B. 3 : 1 C. 8 : 3 D. 3 : 8

   2._____

3. If a boy has a number of dimes and quarters in his pocket adding up to $3.10, the LARGEST possible number of dimes he can have is
   A. 16 B. 28 C. 26 D. 21

   3._____

4. In a number system using the base 10, the value represented by the first digit 3 reading from the left, in the number 82,364,371, is _____ times the value represented by the second digit 3.
   A. 30 B. 100 C. 1,000 D. 10,000

   4._____

5. The number of revolutions made by a bicycle wheel of 28-inch diameter in traveling ½ mile is CLOSEST to
   A. 720 B. 180 C. 360 D. 120

   5._____

6. Of the following, the property which is TRUE of all parallelograms is that the
   A. diagonals are equal
   B. diagonals meet at right angles
   C. sum of the interior angles is 180º
   D. diagonals bisect each other

   6._____

7.
   ```
        218
   32)6985
        64
        58
        32
       265
       256
         9
   ```

   7._____

Of the following explanations about steps in the above computation, the one which is LEAST meaningful or accurate is that the
- A. 64 represents 200 × 32
- B. 265 is the result of subtracting 320 from 585
- C. 9 is part of the quotient
- D. 256 symbolizes the subtraction of 32 eight times

8. Assuming that a system of meridians and parallels of latitude like that used on maps of the earth's surface, were designed for the moon's surface, the distance covered by a man traveling 1° on the moon, as compared to that covered in traveling 1° on the earth, would be
   - A. equal
   - B. less
   - C. greater
   - D. sometimes greater and sometimes less

9. 1958 may MOST correctly be expressed in Roman numerals as
   - A. MDCDLVIII
   - B. CMMLVIII
   - C. MCMLVIII
   - D. MCMLIIX

10. If the same positive quantity is added to both the numerator and the denominator of a proper fraction, the VALUE of the new fraction as compared to that of the original fraction will be
    - A. greater
    - B. less
    - C. equal
    - D. either greater or less

KEY (CORRECT ANSWERS)

1.	B	6.	D
2.	C	7.	C
3.	C	8.	B
4.	C	9.	C
5.	C	10.	A

SOLUTIONS TO ARITHMETICAL REASONING

1. Answer: (B) 35%
   Cost = $36
   Overhead = 10% of cost, OR $3.60
   Profit = $9.00 (Given)
   Selling Price = $48.60 (36 + 3.60 + 9)
   Markup = $12.60 (48.60 (S.P.) − 36 (Cost))

   Finally, $\dfrac{12.60 \text{ (markup)}}{36.00 \text{ (cost)}}$ = 35%

2. Answer: (C) 8 : 3

   First Carton

   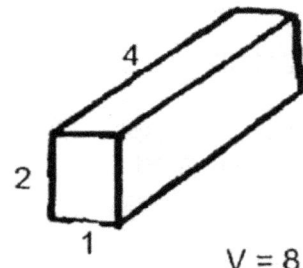

   V = 8

   Second Carton

   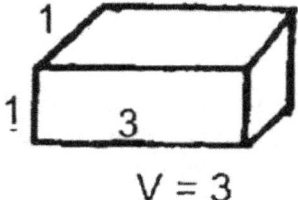

   V = 3

   $\dfrac{V1}{V2} = \dfrac{8}{3}$

3. Answer: (C) 26   26 × 10 = $2.60 + .50 = $3.10.

4. Answer: (C) 1,000 times the value represented by the second digit 3 (approximately)
   300 × 1,000 = 300,000

5. Answer: (C) 360

   C = πD
   C = 22/7 × 28 = 88"

   1 revolution of wheel covers 88"
   ½ × 5280 × 12/1 = traveling distance in inches

   6 × 5280 − 32680 inches

   ```
         360 revolutions
   88)31680
      264
      528
      528
   ```

4 (#5)

6. Answer: (D) diagonals bisect each other

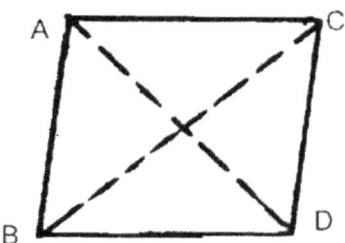

triangle = 180°

parallelogram = 360°

7. Answer: Answer (C) 9 is part of the quotient
Division is repeated subtraction
Below is a division "pyramid," which shows what actually happens when we divide.

```
         8
        10
       200
   32)6985   dividend        32 × 100 = 3200
      6400                   32 × 200 = 6400
       585   partial dividend  32 × 10 = 320
       320
       265   partial dividend
       256
         9   partial dividend
```

8. Answer: (B) less
Diameter of moon = 2000 mile; diameter of earth = 8000 miles

Moon   Earth

The larger the circle, the larger the arc.
1° of arc = 1/360 of circle

Circumference of earth = 25,000 miles
Circumference of moon = 6,200 miles (1/4 of earth)

```
         69+
   360)25,000            1° = 69+ miles on the equator (Earth)
       21 6              1° = 17+ miles (Moon)
        3 40
        3 24
          16
```

247

9. Answer: (C) MCMLVIII

   M   = 1000
   CM = 900
   L   = 50
   VIII =   8
          1958

10. Answer: (A) greater

    $\dfrac{2+2}{3+2} = \dfrac{4}{5} = \dfrac{12}{15}$ $\dfrac{2}{3} = \dfrac{10}{15}$

EXAMINATION SECTION
TEST 1

DIRECTIONS: Each question or incomplete statement is followed by several suggested answers or completions. Select the one that BEST answers the question or completes the statement. *PRINT THE LETTER OF THE CORRECT ANSWER IN THE SPACE AT THE RIGHT.*

Questions 1-5.

DIRECTIONS: Questions 1 through 5 are to be answered SOLELY on the basis of the following graph

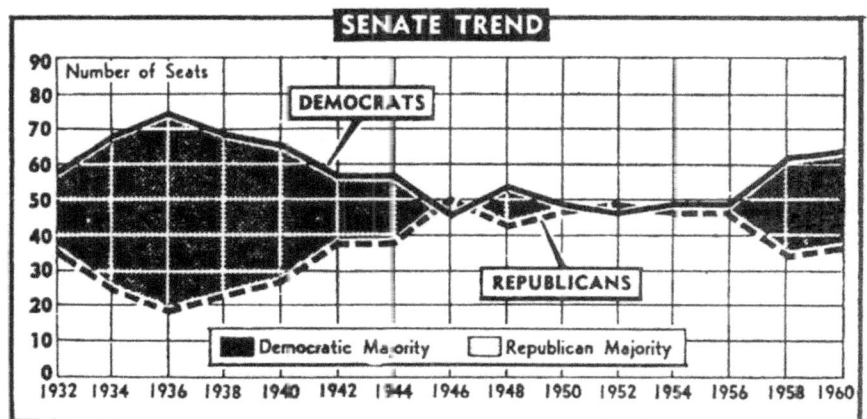

1. In which year were there the most Democratic Senators in the United States Senate?
    A. 1958   B. 1940   C. 1936   D. 1946   E. 1960

2. In which of the following years were there more Republican than Democratic Senators in the United States Senate?
    A. 1944   B. 1946   C. 1948   D. 1932   E. 1960

3. Approximately how many Democratic Senators were there in the United States Senate in 1958?
    A. 30   B. 40   C. 50   D. 60   E. 70

4. What was the approximate ratio of Democratic Senators to Republican Senators in the United States Senate in 1938?
    A. 3:2   B. 4:3   C. 5:1   D. 7:2   E. 7:4

5. In which of the following years were there the FEWEST Republican Senators in the United States Senate?
    A. 1938   B. 1958   C. 1948   D. 1932   E. 1944

Questions 6-10.

DIRECTIONS: Questions 6 through 10 are to be answered SOLELY on the basis of the following graph.

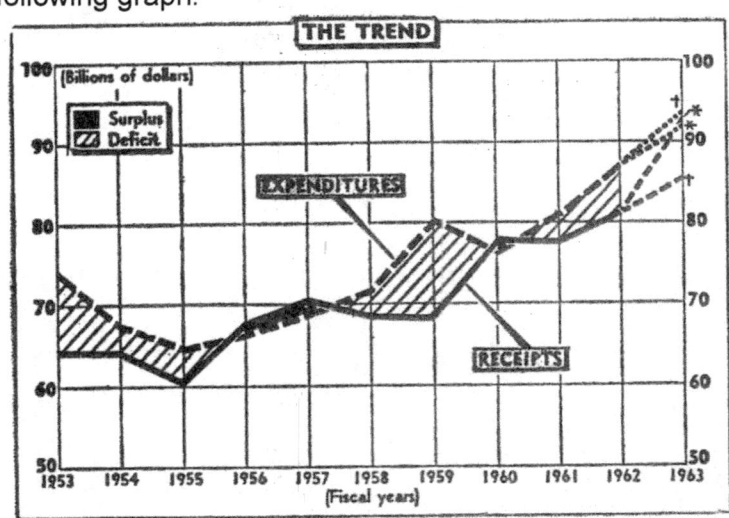

6. In which of the following years did federal government revenue exceed expenditures?
   A. 1954   B. 1957   C. 1962   D. 1959   E. 1953

7. In which of the following years was federal government revenue GREATEST?
   A. 1960   B. 1953   C. 1962   D. 1959   E. 1955

8. As shown on the graph, what was the LARGEST differential between federal government expenditures and income in any one year?
   Approximately _____ billion dollars.
   A. five   B. seven   C. eight and a half
   D. eleven and a half E. three

9. As shown on the graph, between which two years did federal government expenditures rise MOST sharply?
   A. 1961-1962   B. 1955-56   C. 1958-60
   D. 1961-1963   E. 1959-60

10. As shown on the graph, between which two years did federal government revenue decline MOST sharply?
    A. 1954-1955   B. 1959-1960   C. 1960-1961
    D. 1955-1566   E. 1957-1958

KEY (CORRECT ANSWERS)

1. C
2. B
3. D
4. D
5. A

6. B
7. C
8. D
9. C
10. A

TEST 2

DIRECTIONS: Each question or incomplete statement is followed by several suggested answers or completions. Select the one that BEST answers the question or completes the statement. *PRINT THE LETTER OF THE CORRECT ANSWER IN THE SPACE AT THE RIGHT.*

Questions 1-5.

DIRECTIONS: Questions 1 through 5 are to be answered SOLELY on the basis of the following graph.

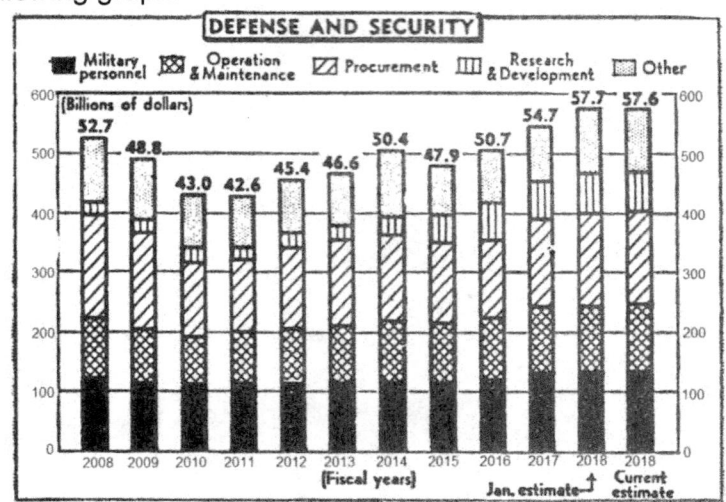

1. Which of the following statements about the graph is TRUE?
   A. The federal government has never spent less than ten billion dollars a year on research and development.
   B. Federal government expenditures for research and development have steadily declined.
   C. Federal government expenditures on military personnel have risen steadily over the past ten years.
   D. Federal government expenditures for military personnel have never been less than ten billion dollars.
   E. Total military expenditures by the federal government have risen steadily over the past ten years.

   1._____

2. In which of the following years did the federal government spend the MOST for military procurement?
   A. 2017   B. 2012   C. 2010   D. 2015   E. 2008

   2._____

3. Between which two years did total military expenditures by the federal government rise MOST sharply?
   A. 2009-2010   B. 2016-2017   C. 2011-2012
   D. 2014-2015   E. 2013-2014

   3._____

252

4. How much more did the federal government spend on defense and security in the year its expenditures were highest than in the year its expenditures were lowest, as reflected in the graph (excluding 2018).
   A. 100 billion dollars
   B. fifty and a half billion dollars
   C. eighty and three-quarter billion dollars
   D. one hundred thirty and one-fifth billion dollars
   E. one hundred twenty and one-tenth billion dollars

4.____

5. In which of the following years did the federal government spend more on research and development than on operation and maintenance?
   A. 2017   B. 2008   C. 2016
   D. 2015   E. None of the above

5.____

Questions 6-10.

DIRECTIONS: Questions 6 through 10 are to be answered SOLELY on the basis of the following graph.

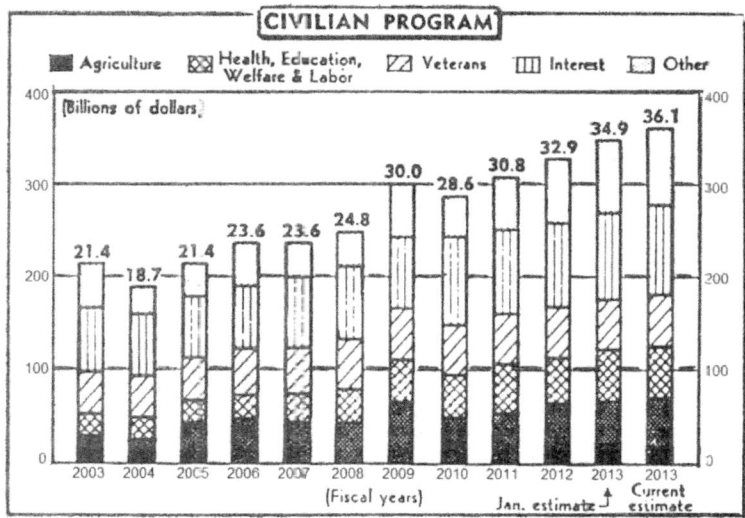

6. Which of the following statements about the graph is FALSE?
   A. Federal government expenditures on interest have always exceeded expenditures on health, education, and welfare.
   B. Federal government expenditures on veterans have never exceeded one hundred billions dollars a year.
   C. Federal government expenditures on agriculture have risen steadily over the last ten years.
   D. Total federal expenditures on civilian programs have not risen steadily over the last ten years.
   E. The federal government spent more on civilian programs in 2012 than in any other year.

6.____

7. Between which two years did federal government expenditures on civilian programs rise MOST sharply?
   A. 2004-2005
   B. 2008-2009
   C. 2011-2012
   D. 2005-2006
   E. 2010-2011

   7.____

8. In which of the following years were government expenditures on agriculture the HIGHEST?
   A. 2008   B. 2009   C. 2005   D. 2011   E. 2020

   8.____

9. How many times during the last ten years did total federal government expenditures on civilian programs decline from one year to the next?
   A. 1   B. 2   C. 3   D. 4   E. 5

   9.____

10. In which of the following years were the federal government's "other" civilian program expenses the HIGHEST?
    A. 2006   B. 2003   C. 2010   D. 2012   E. 2004

    10.____

KEY (CORRECT ANSWERS)

1.	D	6.	C
2.	C	7.	B
3.	B	8.	B
4.	E	9.	B
5.	E	10.	D

TEST 3

DIRECTIONS: Each question or incomplete statement is followed by several suggested answers or completions. Select the one that BEST answers the question or completes the statement. *PRINT THE LETTER OF THE CORRECT ANSWER IN THE SPACE AT THE RIGHT.*

Questions 1-5.

DIRECTIONS: Questions 1 through 5 are to be answered SOLELY on the basis of the following graph.

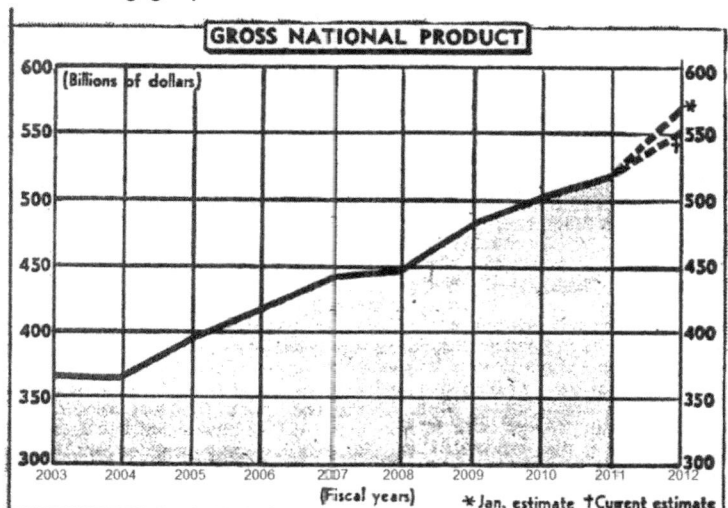

1. Between 2003 and 2011, how many times did the gross national product decline from one year to the next?   1.___
   A. 1   B. 2   C. 3   D. 4   E. 5

2. How many years did it take the gross national product to rise approximately one hundred billion dollars from 2005?   2.___
   A. 1   B. 2   C. 3   D. 4   E. 5

3. Between which two years was the rise in gross national product the SHARPEST?   3.___
   A. 2008-2009   B. 2007-2008   C. 2010-2011
   D. 2009-2010   E. 2003-2004

4. Between which two years was the rise in gross national product the SLIGHTEST?   4.___
   A. 2010-2011   B. 2004-2005   C. 2007-2008
   D. 2009-2010   E. 2005-2006

5. By approximately what percentage did gross national product rise between 2008 and 2010?   5.___
   A. Eight percent   B. Fifteen percent   C. Twenty-five percent
   D. Eleven percent   E. Nineteen percent

Questions 6-10.

DIRECTIONS: Questions 6 through 10 are to be answered SOLELY on the basis of the following graph.

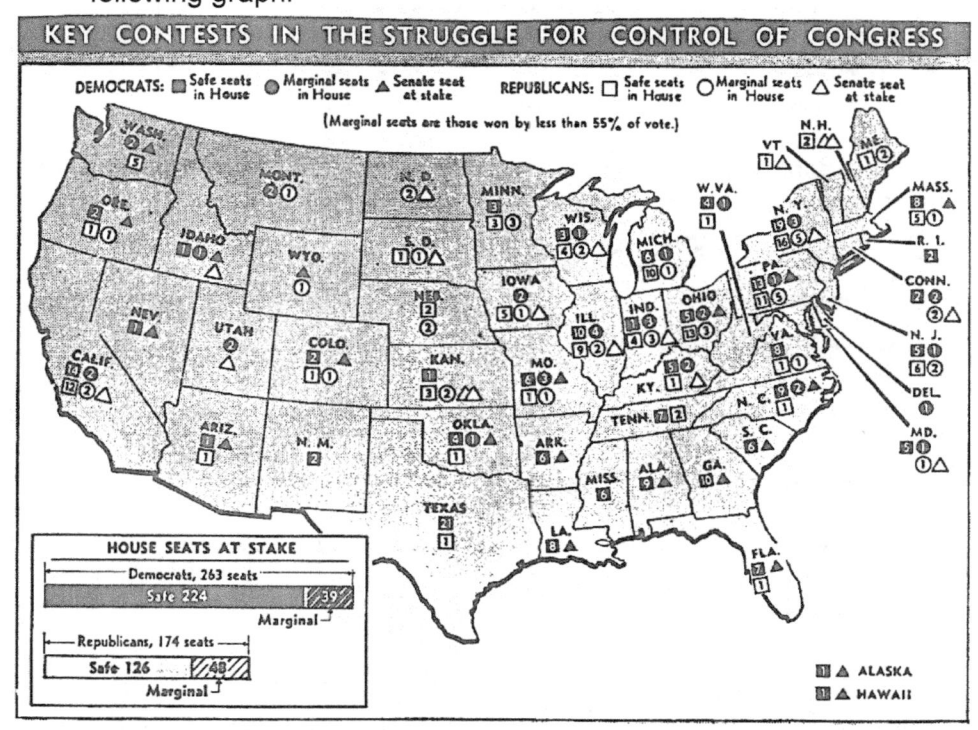

6. How many marginal seats in the House of Representatives did the Republicans control on the West Coast?
   A. 1   B. 2   C. 3   D. 4   E. 5

   6.____

7. How many safely Democratic House seats were there in New England?
   A. 6   B. 8   C. 10   D. 12   E. 14

   7.____

8. How many safe seats in the House of Representatives did both parties have in Pennsylvania?
   A. 14   B. 18   C. 12   D. 16   E. 24

   8.____

9. How many seats in the House of Representatives did both parties have in California?
   A. 4   B. 26   C. 14   D. 30   E. 16

   9.____

10. The ratio between the total of Democratic seats and the total Republican seats in the House of Representatives was APPROXIMATELY
    A. 4 to 3   B. 3 to 2   C. 5 to 4   D. 7 to 5   E. 9 to r

    10.____

KEY (CORRECT ANSWERS)

1. A
2. E
3. A
4. C
5. D
6. C
7. D
8. E
9. D
10. B

TEST 4

DIRECTIONS: Each question or incomplete statement is followed by several suggested answers or completions. Select the one that BEST answers the question or completes the statement. *PRINT THE LETTER OF THE CORRECT ANSWER IN THE SPACE AT THE RIGHT.*

Questions 1-5.

DIRECTIONS: Questions 1 through 5 are to be answered SOLELY on the basis of the following table.

English Language Daily and Sunday U.S. Newspapers (as of September 30, 2011)								
State	Morning Papers & Circulation		Evening Papers & Circulation		Total M & E & Circulation		Sunday Papers & Circulation	
Alabama	4	211,795	16	475,130	20	686,925	14	569,646
Alaska			6	53,514	6	53,514	1	4,102
Arizona	3	174,445	11	214,667	14	389,112	6	314,401
Arkansas	5	145,650	29	237,395	34	383,045	10	311,962
California	17	1,703,395	113	2,859,565	130	4,562,960	30	4,109,024
Colorado	3	215,664	21	424,383	24	640,047	8	640,701
Connecticut	6	225,318	19	581,487	25	806,805	6	472,853
Delaware	1	34,518	2	87,934	3	122,452		
District of Columbia	1	407,089	2	454,747	3	861,836	2	787,480
Florida	15	1,025,441	30	689,925	45	1,715,366	30	1,541,024
Georgia	6	394,854	23	522,285	29	917,139	11	824,233
Hawaii	1	70,097	4	137,558	5	207,655	3	208,274
Idaho[1]	4	70,080	12	81,905	15	151,985	5	115,918
Illinois	9	1,858,502	73	1,982,819	82	3,841,321	18	2,968,730
Indiana	10	446,928	80	1,195,272	90	1,642,200	18	1,095,571
Iowa[1]	4	292,665	41	655,009	44	947,674	9	841,827
Kansas[1]	5	232,428	47	427,714	51	680,142	14	413,565
Kentucky[1]	5	290,732	22	408,948	26	699,680	12	502,161
Louisiana	4	347,503	15	384,317	19	731,820	8	585,912
Maine	5	197,460	4	54,765	9	252,225	1	101,421
Maryland	4	224,967	8	524,332	12	749,299	3	658,952
Massachusetts[1]	6	804,594	45	1,431,978	50	2,386,572	8	1,492,880
Michigan	1	550,000	52	1,769,599	53	2,319,599	11	2,021,405
Minnesota	5	388,188	25	691,395	30	1,079,513	6	952,619
Mississippi	4	81,283	14	184,727	18	266,010	6	151,935
Missouri	7	762,909	47	1,063,583	54	1,826,492	13	1,461,555
Montana	4	106,559	12	62,952	16	169,511	9	154,169
Nebraska	3	167,697	17	304,312	20	472,009	5	349,462
Nevada	2	38,147	6	58,291	8	96,438	3	79,154
New Hampshire[1]	1	25,007	9	102,378	9	127,385	1	43,004
New Jersey	5	409,753	22	1,078,478	27	1,488,231	9	977,717
New Mexico	1	47,720	18	140,352	19	188,072	13	159,632
New York	22	5,033,688	66	3,711,276	88	3,744,964	20	9,198,327
North Carolina	9	548,473	38	562,890	47	1,111,363	15	743,038
North Dakota	8	35,481	9	127,046	11	162,527	2	88,600
Ohio	8	840,173	88	2,473,971	26	3,314,144	19	2,083,904
Oklahoma	7	319,374	44	430,476	51	749,850	41	669,934
Oregon	4	248,608	20	397,664	24	646,272	5	472,819
Pennsylvania[1]	28	1,415,099	95	2,785,703	120	4,200,802	12	2,866,417
Rhode Island	1	61,910	6	237,326	7	299,236	2	199,904
South Carolina	8	346,595	9	149,348	17	495,943	7	378,076
South Dakota	2	6755	11	164,514	13	171,269	4	116,440
Tennessee	7	497,545	23	573,733	30	1,071,278	11	784,155
Texas	26	1,251,207	91	1,708,992	117	2,960,199	79	2,601,166
Utah	1	101,201	4	141,201	5	242,402	4	239,139
Vermont	8	53,659	6	36,643	8	90,302	1	11,744
Virginia	9	410,129	22	493,243	31	503,372	12	601,824
Washington	6	337,231	21	640,658	27	977,889	10	842,684
West Virginia	10	233,010	21	250,151	31	483,161	9	364,540
Wisconsin	3	265,451	35	907,778	38	1,173,229	8	983,681
Wyoming	6	37,454	4	37,502	10	74,956	4	38,818
Total U.S., Sept. 30, 2011	312	24,094,361	1,458	35,167,103	1,761	59,261,464	558	48,216,499
Total U.S., Sept. 30, 2010	312	24,028,788	1,459	34,852,958	1,763	58,881,746	563	47,698,651
Total U.S., Sept. 30, 2009	306	23,547,046	1,455	34,752,677	1,755	58,299,723	564	47,848,477
Total U.S., Sept. 30, 2008	308	23,206,964	1,460	34,387,490	1,756	57,594,454	558	47,041,223
Total U.S., Sept. 30, 2007[2]	309	23,170,552	1,453	34,634,893	1,755	57,805,445	544	47,044,349
Total U.S., Sept. 30, 2006[2]	314	22,491,500	1,454	34,610,010	1,761	57,101,510	546	47,162,246
Total U.S., Sept. 30, 2005[2]	316	22,183,408	1,454	33,963,951	1,760	56,147,359	541	45,447,658

[1]"All-day" newspapers are listed in morning and evening columns, and their circulations are divided between morning and evening figures. Adjustments have been made in state and U.S. total figures.
[2]Excludes newspapers and circulations for Alaska and Hawaii

1. The circulation of morning newspapers is greater than that of evening newspapers in
   A. Massachusetts
   B. Pennsylvania
   C. Wyoming
   D. Florida
   E. North Carolina

   1._____

2. The circulation of Sunday newspapers is greater than that of the combined morning and evening newspapers in
   A. Alabama
   B. Virginia
   C. Connecticut
   D. West Virginia
   E. New York

   2._____

3. The FEWEST number of combined morning and evening newspapers are circulated in
   A. New Jersey and North Carolina
   B. Tennessee and Wisconsin
   C. Idaho and Nebraska
   D. Rhode Island and South Carolina
   E. Maryland and Nevada

   3._____

4. Which of the following statements is TRUE?
   A. Total morning newspaper circulation has increased steadily since 2005.
   B. Total evening newspaper circulation has increased steadily since 2005.
   C. Total combined morning and evening newspaper circulation has increased steadily since 2005.
   D. Total Sunday newspaper circulation has increased steadily since 2005.
   E. More evening newspapers are circulated in California than in Pennsylvania.

   4._____

5. The LARGEST increase in total Sunday newspaper circulation occurred between
   A. 2010 and 2011
   B. 2009 and 2010
   C. 2008 and 2009
   D. 2007 and 2008
   E. 2006 and 2007

   5._____

Questions 6-10.

DIRECTIONS: Questions 6 through 10 are to be answered SOLELY on the basis of the table shown on the following page.

CRIME
City Arrests, Distribution by Sex, 2018
(Data in this table are from reports furnished the FBI by 2,776 cities over 2,500 in population. This represents a total population of 85,158,360)

Offense Charged	Males	Females	Total
Criminal Homicide:			
Murder and nonnegligent manslaughter	3,791	834	4,625
Manslaughter by negligence	1,458	160	1,618
Forcible Rape	7,143		7,143
Robbery	31,563	1,612	33,175
Aggravated Assault	46,951	8,404	55,355
Burglary-breaking and entering	122,400	4,077	126,477
Larceny-theft	186,999	41,068	228,067
Auto theft	56,409	2,138	54,547
Other assaults	126,817	14,967	141,784
Embezzlement and fraud	28,548	5,738	34,286
Stolen Property; buying, receiving,, etc.	9,808	937	10,745
Forgery and counterfeiting	17,821	3,792	21,613
Prostitution and commercialized vice	7,563	19,280	26,843
Other sex offenses (includes statutory rape)	37,652	8,552	46,204
Narcotic Drug Laws	21,227	3,853	25,080
Weapons: Carrying, possessing, etc.	33,746	2,239	35,985
Offenses Against family and children	31,099	3,918	35,017
Liquor laws	84,790	14,258	99,048
Driving while intoxicated	153,462	10,760	164,222
Disorderly conduct	373,760	61,126	434,886
Drunkenness	1,286,309	112,984	1,399,293
Vagrancy	134,569	12,957	147,526
Gambling	99,529	9,042	108,571
All other offenses	403,757	76,342	480,099
Suspicion	110,692	14,924	125,616
TOTAL ARRESTS, 2018	3,417,863	433,962	3,851,825

6. Approximately how many times more men than women were arrested in American cities in 2018?

    A. 2   B. 4   C. 6   D. 8   E. 10

6._____

7. Which of the following statements if FALSE?
   A. More men than women were arrested for burglary in American cities in 2018.
   B. No women were arrested for forcible rape in American cities in 2018.
   C. About fourteen times as many men as women were arrested for drunken driving in American cities in 2018.
   D. More men than women were arrested for each classification of crime in American cities in 2018.
   E. More women were arrested for drunkenness in American cities in 2018 than for any other offense.

7._____

8. For which of the following offenses were the most men arrested in American cities in 2018?
   A. Murder and manslaughter   B. Larceny
   C. Forgery and counterfeiting   D. Auto theft
   E. Disorderly conduct

8._____

9. Which of the following offenses accounted for a larger percentage of the total female arrests than of the total male arrests in American cities in 2018?
   A. Auto theft
   B. Drunkenness
   C. Carrying and possessing weapons
   D. Burglary
   E. Disorderly conduct

10. Which of the following offenses accounted for a percentage of the total female arrests in American cities in 2018 which MOST closely approximates the percentage of the total male arrests for the same offense?
    A. Offenses against family and children
    B. Auto theft
    C. Carrying and possessing weapons
    D. Prostitution and commercialized vice
    E. Drunken driving

KEY (CORRECT ANSWERS)

1.	D	6.	D
2.	E	7.	D
3.	C	8.	E
4.	A	9.	E
5.	C	10.	A

TEST 5

DIRECTIONS: Each question or incomplete statement is followed by several suggested answers or completions. Select the one that BEST answers the question or completes the statement. *PRINT THE LETTER OF THE CORRECT ANSWER IN THE SPACE AT THE RIGHT.*

Questions 1-5.

DIRECTIONS: Questions 1 through 5 are to be answered SOLELY on the basis of the following table.

MARRIAGE AND DIVORCE
(New statutory enactments and recent judicial decisions or interpretation may affect the following summary, therefore, government officials or an attorney should be consulted for advice.)
MARRIAGES AND DIVORCES IN THE UNITED STATES, 1940-2011

Year	Marriage Number	Rate[1]	Divorce Number	Rate[1]	Year	Marriage Number	Rate[1]	Divorce Number	Rate[1]
1940	570,000	9.0	33,461	.5	1986	1,369,000	10.7	236000	1.8
1945	620,000	8.9	40,387	.6	1987	1,451,296	11.3	249000	1.9
1950	709,000	9.3	55,751	.7	1988	1,330,780	10.3	244000	1.9
1955	842,000	10.0	67,976	.8	1989	1,403,633	10.7	251000	1.9
1960	948,166	10.3	83,045	.9	1990	1,595,879	12.1	264000	2.0
1965	1,007,595	10.0	104,298	1.0	1991	1,695,999	12.7	293000	2.2
1966	1,075,775	10.6	114,000	1.1	1992	1,772,132	13.2	321000	2.4
1967	1,144,200	11.1	121,564	1.2	1993	1,577,050	11.7	359000	2.6
1968	1,000,109	9.7	116,254	1.1	1994	1,452,394	10.9	400000	2.9
1969	1,150,186	11.0	141,527	1.3	1995	1,612,992	12.2	485000	3.5
1970	1,274,476	12.0	170,505	1.6	1996	2,291,945	16.4	610000	4.3
1971	1,163,863	10.7	159,580	1.5	1997	1,991,878	13.9	483000	3.4
1972	1,134,151	10.3	148,815	1.4	1998	1,811,155	12.4	408000	2.8
1973	1,229,784	11.0	165,096	1.5	1999	1,579,798	10.6	397000	2.7
1974	1,184,574	10.4	170,952	1.5	2000	1,667,231	11.1	385144	2.6
1975	1,188,334	10.3	175,449	1.5	2001	1,594,694	10.4	381000	2.5
1976	1,202,574	10.2	184,678	1.6	2002	1,539,318	9.9	392000	2.5
1977	1,201,053	10.1	196,292	1.6	2003	1,546,000	9.8	390000	2.5
1978	1,182,497	9.8	200,176	1.7	2004	1,490,000	9.2	379000	2.4
1979	1,232,559	10.1	205,876	1.7	2005	1,531,000	9.3	377000	2.3
1980	1,126,856	9.2	195,961	1.6	2006	1,585,000	9.5	382000	2.3
1981	1,060,914	8.6	188,003	1.5	2007	1,518,000	8.9	381000	2.2
1982	981,903	7.9	164,241	1.3	2008	1,451,000	8.4	368000	2.1
1983	1,098,000	8.7	165,000	1.3	2009	1,494,000	8.5	395000	2.2
1984	1,302,000	10.3	204,000	1.6	2010	1,527,000	8.5	391000	2.2
1985	1,327,000	10.4	218,000	1.7	2011	1,547,000	8.5	([4])	2.2

[1]Per 1,000 population. Divorce rates for 1967-69 and 1991-96 are based on population including armed forces overseas. Marriage rates are based on population excluding armed forces overseas.
[2]Includes annulments. [3]Provisional. [4]Not available.
NOTE: Figures for marriages for all years include partial or complete estimates for some states; figures for divorces are estimated, except for 1950, 1955, and 1972-32.

1. In 1997, there was one divorce in the U.S. for approximately every _____ marriage(s). 1.____
   A. 1 B. 2 C. 3 D. 4 E. 5

2. In 1945, there was one divorce in the U.S. for approximately every _____ 2.____
   A. 5 B. 10 C. 15 D. 20 E. 25

3. Approximately how many times higher than the divorce rate in 1940 was the divorce rate in 1995?
   A. 6   B. 11   C. 5   D. 15   E. 7

   3._____

4. According to the table, in which year was there the second largest number of divorces in the U.S.?
   A. 1995
   B. 1996
   C. 2010
   D. 1997
   E. None of the above

   4._____

5. According to the table, in which year was the second largest number of marriages in the U.S.?
   A. 1996
   B. 1998
   C. 1991
   D. 1992
   E. None of the above

   5._____

Questions 6-10.

DIRECTIONS: Questions 6 through 10 are to be answered SOLELY on the basis of the following table.

		Distribution of U.S. Population by Race, 1900-2010					
			Non-white				
Year	White	Black	Indian	Japanese	Chinese	All Other	Total Non-White
1900	19,553,068	3,638,808					3,638,808
1910	26,922,537	4,441,830	44,021		34,933		4,520,784
1920	33,589,377	4,880,009	25,731	55	63,199		4,968,994
1930	43,402,970	6,580,793	66,407	148	105,465		6,752,813
1940	55,101,258	7,488,676	248,253	2,039	107,488		7,846,456
1950	66,809,196	8,833,994	237,196	24,326	89,863		9,135,379
1960	81,731,957	9,827,763	265,683	72,157	71,531	3,175	10,240,309
1970	94,820,915	10,463,131	244,437	111,010	61,639	9,488	10,839,705
1980	110,286,740	11,891,143	332,397	138,834	74,954	50,978	12,438,306
1990	118,214,870	12,865,518	333,969	126,947	77,504	50,467	13,454,405
2000	134,942,028	15,042,236	343,410	141,768	117,629	110,240	15,755,333
2010	158,831,732	18,871,831	523,591	464,332	237,292	394,397	20,491,443
Urban	110,428,332	13,807,640	145,593	381,114	226,577	280,000	14,840,418
Rural	48,403,400	5,064,191	377,998	83,218	10,715	68,299	5,651,025

6. Approximately how many times more white persons were there than non-white in the U.S. in 2010?
   A. 2   B. 4   C. 6   D. 8   E. 10

   6._____

7. Between which two years was there the GREATEST increase in the number of non-whites in the U.S.?
   A. 1900 and 1910
   B. 1910 and 1940
   C. 1940 and 1970
   D. 1990 and 2000
   E. 2000 and 2010

   7._____

8. Between which two years was there the GREATEST percentage of Japanese in the U.S.?
   A. 1970 and 1980
   B. 1940 and 1950
   C. 2000 and 2010
   D. 1960 and 1970
   E. 1950 and 2000

   8._____

9. Between which two years was there the GREATEST increase in the number of whites in the U.S.?
   A. 1930 and 1940   B. 1900 and 1910   C. 2000 and 2010
   D. 1960 and 1980   E. 1940 and 1960

10. During how many decades has the Chinese population of the U.S. declined?
    A. 1   B. 2   C. 3   D. 4   E. 5

KEY (CORRECT ANSWERS)

1.	D	6.	D
2.	C	7.	E
3.	E	8.	C
4.	A	9.	D
5.	E	10.	C

DATA SUFFICIENCY

To further extend and measure the mathematical or quantitative ability of the candidate, a novel item, the test of data sufficiency, has been added to the mathematical aptitude section of the examination.

The candidate is presented with a problem for which two (2) facts (statements) are given. Then, he is to evaluate, without *necessarily* solving the problem, the relevance or irrelevance of the relationship of each or both of the statements to the actual solution of the problem. The directions for choice of decision in this matter are five (5) in number and are fundamentally more intricate and complicated than the actual solutions and/or comprehension of the problem.

The problems themselves are fairly simple in nature, alternating between arithmetical and algebraic foundations. Note that it is *NOT* the solution itself that is sought here but, rather, an indication by the candidate that he knows how to proceed to solve the problem. That is, a show of problem-solving technique rather than of computational skill is the desired outcome in this case. The basis is apparently the attempt to essay the ability of the candidate to think and to outline directions of procedure on his own.

The directions and sample questions with answers that follow serve to definitively delimn this question-type. In addition, six (6) Tests of Data Sufficiency, consisting of sixty (60) questions, together with solutions, are presented to challenge the candidate and to assure his overlearning of this novel question-type.

SAMPLE QUESTIONS AND ANSWERS

DIRECTIONS: Each of the questions below is followed by two statements, labeled (1) and (2), in which certain data are given. In these questions you do not actually have to compute an answer, but rather you have to decide whether the data given in the statements are *sufficient* for answering the question. Using the data given in the statements *plus* your knowledge of mathematics and everyday facts (such as the number of days in July), you are to blacken the box on the answer sheet under

- A. if statement (1) *ALONE* is sufficient but statement (2) alone is not sufficient to answer the question asked,
- B. if statement (2) *ALONE* is sufficient but statement (1) alone is not sufficient to answer the question asked,
- C. if *BOTH* statements (1) and (2) *TOGETHER* are sufficient to answer the question asked, but *NEITHER* statement *ALONE* is sufficient,
- D. if *EACH* statement is sufficient by itself to answer the question asked,
- E. if statements (1) and (2) *TOGETHER* are *NOT* sufficient to answer the question asked and additional data specific to the problem are needed.

1. In a four-volume work, what is the weight of the third volume?

    2. The four-volume work weighs 8 pounds.
    3. The first three volumes together weigh 6 pounds.

EXPLANATION

From and (2), it is apparent that the fourth volume weighs 2 lbs. However, there is insufficient information to determine the weight of any of the first three volumes. Thus, the answer is E.

2. Pump Q takes how many minutes longer than pump P to remove all the water from tank T?
   1. Working together, pump P and pump Q can remove all the water from tank T in 16 minutes.
   2. Pump P can remove all the water from tank T in 25 minutes.

   ### EXPLANATION
   From (2), we can determine only the rate of removal for pump P.
   From (1), we can determine only the rate of removal of both pumps working together.
   Using both (1) and (2), then, we can determine the relative rates of P and Q.
   Thus, the answer is C.

3. Is X greater than Y?
   1. $3X = 2K$, $4Y - 3K$, K is positive.
   2. $X + Y = 5$

   ### EXPLANATION
   From (1), $X = 2/3K$ and $Y = 3/4K$. Therefore, X is less than Y. From (2), the relative size of X and Y cannot be determined. Thus, the answer is A.

4. What is the size of angle P in △ PQR?
   (1) PQ = PR
   (2) Angle Q = 40°

   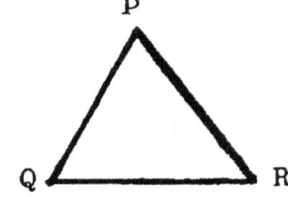

   ### EXPLANATION
   Since PQ = PR from (1), PQR is isosceles. Therefore $\angle Q = \angle R$.
   Since $\angle Q - 40°$ from (2), $\angle R = 40°$. Since the sum of the angles of a triangle is 180°, angle P can now be found. Since both (1) and (2) are needed, the answer is C.

5. What is the length of a certain cube's diagonal?
   1. The volume of the cube is 8.
   2. The diagonal of one face of the cube is $2\sqrt{2}$.

   ### EXPLANATION
   From (1), each edge of the cube is 2. The square of the diagonal of a rectangular solid = $1^2 + w^2 + h^2$. Since $1 = w = h = 2$, we can find the diagonal.
   From (2), the side of the square face is 2. Again we have all the edges of the cube, and the diagonal can be found. Hence, the answer is D.

6. If x is a whole number, is x a two-digit number?
   1. x^2 is a three-digit number.
   2. $10x$ is a three-digit number.

   ### EXPLANATION
   (1) is sufficient alone because the square root of any three-digit square of a whole number is a two-digit whole number.

(2) is sufficient alone because whenever a three-digit multiple of 10 is divided by 10, the result is a two-digit number.

Thus, the correct answer is D.

7. In △RST, is angle R greater than angle S?
   1. Angle T is somewhere between 50° and 65°.
   2. ∠P = ∠S

   ### EXPLANATION
   From (1) alone or (2) alone, we cannot determine the relative size of R and S.

   From both (1) and (2), S may vary from 50° to 60°, and T from 80° to 50°, respectively. Thus, the answer is E.

8. John may sell a certain candy bar at 5 cents or 6 cents. If he wants to sell at a single price, at which price would his total receipts be higher?
   1. He can sell twice as many bars at 5 cents as at 6 cents.
   2. He can sell 30 bars a day at 6 cents.

   ### EXPLANATION
   From (1), if he sells n bars at 6 cents each, his receipts would be 6n cents; but he would sell 2n bars at 5 cents each and his receipts would be 10n cents.

   Fact (2) alone does not indicate the receipts if he sells bars at 5 cents each.

   Thus, the problem can be done with (1) alone, and the answer is A.

9. Is the average price of 24 items greater than 15 cents?
   1. 1/2 of the items cost 20 cents per item.
   2. 1/3 of the items cost 20 cents per item.

   ### EXPLANATION
   By knowing only the cost of a fraction of the items, it is impossible in either case to determine the average price of all 24 items, or whether this average price is greater than 15 cents.

   Thus, the answer is E.

10. If R and S are points on line segment PQ and R lies between P and S, how long is RP + SQ?
    1. PQ = 8 inches
    2. RS = 1/4 PQ

    ### EXPLANATION
    From (1) alone or (2) alone the length of RP and SQ cannot be determined.
    Using both facts, RS = 1/4 PQ = 2 and RP + SQ = 6. Thus, the answer is C.

EXAMINATION SECTION
TEST 1

DIRECTIONS: See DIRECTIONS under Sample Questions and Answers on Page 1.

1. In triangle ABC, how many degrees are there in Angle A? 1.____
   1. AB = AC
   2. Angle B = 40 degrees

2. There are 12 pencils in a box. How many have *both* erasers and dull points? 2.____
   1. 9 have erasers
   2. 3 have dull points

3. How many hours will it take some boy scouts and some scout-masters to put up a tent? 3.____
   1. The boys can put it up in 4 hours alone and the scout-masters in 2 hours alone.
   2. There are 3 scout-masters and 5 boy scouts.

4. Find the area of parallelogram ABCD. 4.____
   1. AB = 12 inches
   2. AD = 20 inches

5. How many nickels does John have in his pocket? 5.____
   1. He has 52 cents in coins in his pocket.
   2. Only one of the coins in his pocket is a quarter.

6. Find the number of degrees in an exterior angle of a regular polygon. 6.____
   1. The apothegm of the polygon is 6 inches.
   2. The polygon has eight sides.

7. Write an equation of the straight line. 7.____
   1. The line passes through the point (2, 3).
   2. The line is perpendicular to the x-axis.

8. Find the radius of a circle. 8.____
   1. The area of the circle is 36 π.
   2. The circumference of the circle is 12 π.

9. How many degrees in a base angle of an isosceles triangle? 9.____
   1. The vertex angle contains $70°$.
   2. The area of the triangle is 14 sq. in.

10. Are two triangles congruent? 10.____
    1. They have equal bases and equal altitudes drawn to these bases.
    2. The triangles are isosceles.

SOLUTIONS TO TEST #1

1. Answer (C)
   From (1), angle B = angle C, but this is not enough to determine angle A.
   (2) alone is not enough to determine A.
   If we use (1) and (2) together, B and C are each 40 degrees, and A is determined.
   Thus, the answer is C.

2. Answer (E)
   Since the facts in (1) and (2) are not mutually exclusive, there is no way of determining how many pencils have both erasers and dull points. Thus, the answer is E.

3. Answer (A)
   Using (1) alone, we can determine how long it takes them all to put up the tent.
   If it takes x hours, we may then solve the equation, $x/4 + x/2 = 1$.

   The information in (2) is irrelevant to the time it takes the group working together.
   Hence, the correct answer is A.

4. Answer (E)
   Finding the area of a parallelogram requires knowing the base and altitude. Either AB or AD may be used as base, but the altitude cannot be determined from the information given. The answer is, therefore, E.

5. Answer (E)
   Statement (2) merely tells us that the remaining 27 cents may be in nickels, dimes, or pennies, but there is not enough information to determine how many nickels. The answer is E.

6. Answer (B)
   Statement (1) is irrelevant to finding the exterior angle.
   The sum of the exterior angles is $360°$. Hence, from (2), we can divide by 8 to determine each of the exterior angles.
   The answer is B.

7. Answer (C)
   From (2), we see that the line is vertical.
   From (1), we see that the abscissa of every point on the line is 2.
   Thus, its equation is $x = 2$ from both facts.
   The answer is C.

8. Answer (D)
   Using the formula, $A = \pi r^2$, we can determine r from (1).
   Using the formula, $C = 2 \pi r$, we can determine r from (2).
   Hence, the answer is D.

9. Answer (A).
   Statement (2) has no bearing on the size of the angles of the triangle. From statement (1), we can determine the number of degrees in both base angles and, then, divide by 2.
   The answer is A.

10. Answer (C)
    Statement (1) merely establishes that the triangles are equal in area. If, however, the triangles are isosceles, then they are also congruent. Thus, the answer is C.

TEST 2

1. Find the value of x. 1.____

    1. $x + y = 5$
    2. $x - y - 1$

2. The tax rate is 3%. Find the property tax. 2.____

    1. Property is assessed at 70% of its true value.
    2. This property is assessed for $6000.

3. How far is A from C? 3.____

    1. A is 20 miles from B.
    2. B is 20 miles from C.

4. Two angles A and B are complementary. Find A. 4.____

    1. The ratio of A to B is 2:1.
    2. The difference of A and B is 30 degrees.

5. What are the dimensions of a rectangle? 5.____

    1. The perimeter is 14.
    2. The diagonal is 5.

6. How many pennies does a boy have? 6.____

    1. He has 47 cents in coins in his pocket.
    2. One of the coins in his pocket is a nickel.

7. Find three numbers. 7.____

    1. The three numbers are in the ratio 5:7:9.
    2. The middle number is equal to half the sum of the first and third numbers.

8. Find three consecutive even integers. 8.____

    1. Their sum is 66.
    2. The largest is 4 more than the smallest.

9. If $4x - 8y = 4$, find the value of y. 9.____

    1. $x - 2y = 0$
    2. $x = 5$

10. In triangle RST, find angle R. 10.____

    1. $\dfrac{RS}{ST} = 1$
    2. $\dfrac{RS}{TR} = 1$

SOLUTIONS TO TEST #2

1. Answer (C)
   The value of x cannot be determined from either (1) or (2) alone. By adding the two equations and solving the resulting equation, x can be found. Thus, the answer is C.

2. Answer (B)
   The information given in (1) is irrelevant to the problem.
   The tax can be determined from (2) by taking 3% of $6000.
   Thus, the answer is B.

3. Answer (E)
   The information in (1) and (2) gives us two sides of a triangle. This is not enough to determine the third side. Thus, the answer is E.

4. Answer (D)
   Using fact (1), we see that $A = 2B$; this equation solved with $A + B = 90$ will yield A.
   Using fact (2), we see that $A - B - 30$; this equation solved with $A + B = 90$ will yield A.
   Thus, the answer is D.

5. Answer (C)
   From (1), we see that $1 + w = 7$.
   From (2), we see that $1^2 + w^2 = 25$.
   We can solve these equations together for 1 and w. Each, by itself, is not solvable.
   Thus, the answer is C.

6. Answer (E)
   Both facts together do not supply enough information to answer the question. The remaining 42 cents may be in pennies, dimes, nickels, or any combination of these. Thus the answer is E.

7. Answer (E)
   There are many possible sets of three numbers that satisfy condition (1). Fact (2) gives us no additional information since any three numbers satisfying condition (1) also satisfy condition (2). Thus, the answer is E.

8. Answer (A)
   Statement (2) says nothing more than the fact that the three even integers are consecutive.
   Fact (1) yields an equation which is solvable to yield all three numbers; i.e., denote the numbers by $x, x + 2, x + 4$ and let their sum be 66.
   Thus, the answer is A.

9. Answer (B)
   Fact (2) can be substituted in the original equation to yield y. Equation (1) is inconsistent with the original equation and, as a result, they have no common solution. Thus, the answer is B.

10. Answer (C)
    From (1) and (2), we see that $RS = ST = TR$ and the triangle is, therefore, equilateral. Angle R is, then, $60°$. Thus, the answer is C.

TEST 3

1. There are 75 people in the town that attend either meeting X or meeting Y or both. How many attend each meeting?

    1. 30 people attend meeting X only.
    2. 45 people attend meeting Y.

2. In triangle RST, angle S is 90 and SR = ST. Find the area of triangle RST.

    1. SR = 5
    2. RT = $5\sqrt{2}$

3. How many degrees in each angle of a triangle?

    1. One of the angles is 30 degrees more than another.
    2. The triangle is a right triangle.

4. Find the height of a flagpole.

    1. The shadow of a yardstick is 6 ft. long.
    2. At the same time and place, the shadow of the flagpole is 54 ft. long.

5. Find the side of a square.

    1. The area of the square is 36 square inches.
    2. The square is equal in area to an equilateral triangle.

6. What is the relationship of the fathers of two girls?

    1. The girls are good friends.
    2. The girls are first cousins.

7. Find the area of a parallelogram.

    1. Two adjacent sides are 20 and 12.
    2. One angle is 60 degrees.

8. Is a parallelogram a rectangle?

    1. Its diagonals bisect each other.
    2. Its diagonals are equal.

9. A cylindrical glass 6 inches high is full of water. How many pints of water does it contain?

    1. A cubic foot of water weighs 62.5 pounds.
    2. The diameter of the glass is 4 inches.

10. The bases of an isosceles trapezoid are 6 and 10. Find its area.

    1. The diagonals of the trapezoid are each 9.
    2. The lower base angles are acute.

SOLUTIONS TO TEST #3

1. **Answer (E)**
   The 30 people in (1) and the 45 people in (2) are not mutually exclusive. Any of the 45 people in (2) may also attend meeting X. Hence, we cannot determine the number of people attending each meeting. Thus, the answer is E.

2. **Answer (D)**
   This is a right, isosceles triangle. If we are given any one side, we can find the other sides and, therefore, the area of the triangle. Thus, the answer is D.

3. **Answer (C)**
   (1) or (2) by itself is insufficient to determine the angles. Call the angles x and x + 30. From (2), these add up to 90 degrees and can, thus, be determined. The answer is C.

4. **Answer (C)**
   The two facts in (1) and (2) produce similar triangles. By setting up a proportion of the corresponding sides, the height of the flagpole can be found. Thus, the answer is C.

5. **Answer (A)**
   From (1), the side of the square is the square root of the area and can thus be determined.
   (2) yields inadequate information to determine the square.
   Thus, the answer is A.

6. **Answer (E)**
   (1) gives no evidence of any relationship.
   (2) fixes no definite relationship of the fathers since the girls may be related through their mothers.
   Thus, the answer is E.

7. **Answer (C)**
   From (1), we cannot determine the altitude of the parallelogram, which is needed for the area.
   From (1) and (2) together, we can determine the altitude to either one of the sides, and thus calculate the area.
   The correct answer is, therefore, C.

8. **Answer (B)**
   (1) is true of all parallelograms.
   If (2) is true of a parallelogram, the figure is a rectangle. Thus, the answer is B.

9. **Answer (B)**
   We do not need (1) since we are finding only the volume of the water and not its weight.
   Fact (2) gives us the radius, which is needed to find the volume. Thus, the answer is B.

10. **Answer (A)**
    By using (1) and the values of the bases, we can determine the altitude of the trapezoid and, thereby, its area.
    Statement (2) has no particular bearing on the area. Thus, the answer is A.

TEST 4

1. Find the height to which each end of a seesaw can rise. 1.____

    1. The seesaw is 14 feet long.
    2. The board is supported at its center by a block 4 feet high.

2. Find the speed of a locomotive. 2.____

    1. The drive wheels are each 50 inches in diameter.
    2. The wheels make 140 revolutions per minute.

3. John has 5 coins in his pocket. Does he have a quarter? 3.____

    1. He has 45 cents in his pocket.
    2. One of the coins is a nickel.

4. A table is 30 inches long and 9 inches wide. It is covered by three overlapping napkins, each 9 inches wide. How long is each of the napkins? 4.____

    1. All three napkins are of equal length.
    2. If the table were 1 1/2 times as long as it is now, the napkins would just cover the table without overlapping.

5. Find x and y 5.____

    1. $2x + y = 10$
    2. $3x - y = 15$

6. Is a quadrilateral a square? 6.____

    1. It is equilateral.
    2. The diagonals are perpendicular to each other.

7. G and S go on a 300-mile trip by car. They take turns driving, each driving for 8 hours. Find the average rate of each. 7.____

    1. G drove 48 miles more than S.
    2. G averaged 6 miles an hour faster than S.

8. Find the area of a trapezoid. 8.____

    1. The bases of the trapezoid are 8 and 12.
    2. One of the lower base angles is 45°.

9. The distance to Bill's house is 40 miles from his college. Bill went to school Friday but then returned home. How long did the entire trip take? 9.____

    1. If Bill went 40 miles per hour faster, it would have taken him half the time.
    2. He traveled at a uniform rate, both going and coming, of 40 miles per hour.

10. Can a salesman compute his earnings for the entire week? 10.____

    1. He knows his sales for each day of the week.
    2. He works on a commission basis, which is 10% of his total sales.

SOLUTIONS TO TEST #4

1. Answer (B)
   It is not necessary to know statement (1).
   Fact (2) alone tells us that one end may rise to a height of 8 feet, since the support is at the center.
   Thus, the answer is B.

2. Answer (C)
   From (1), we can find the circumference of each drive wheel.
   Using (1) together with (2), we can find the distance traveled by each drive wheel per minute, thus giving the speed.
   The correct answer is, therefore, C.

3. Answer (E)
   (2) tells us that he has 4 coins besides the nickel.
   (1) tells us further that the 4 coins must add up to 40 cents. These might be 4 dimes. Hence, we cannot conclude that John definitely has a quarter. Thus, the correct answer is E.

4. Answer (C)
   Fact (1) alone does not determine each napkin since they may overlap. Using (2) as well, we see that 3 napkins of equal length would just cover a 45-inch table. Thus, the answer is C.

5. Answer (C)
   Neither equation by itself can determine x or y. However, the two equations can be solved simultaneously for x and y. The answer is C.

6. Answer (E)
   Both of these properties of a square are also the properties of a rhombus. Hence, there is not enough information here to determine whether the quadrilateral is a square. The answer is E.

7. Answer (D)
   Using (1) alone, we can determine the distances traveled by G and S. Since they each traveled 8 hours, their rates can be determined.
   Using (2) alone, let r = the rate of S and $r + 6$ = the rate of G. Then $8r + 8(r + 6) = 300$, and r can be determined.
   Thus, the correct answer is D.

8. Answer (E)
   Since the trapezoid is not necessarily isosceles, we cannot determine its altitude from all the given information. (The area of a trapezoid equals half the altitude times the sum of the bases.) Hence, the area cannot be determined. The answer is E.

9. Answer (D)
   From (2), it is apparent that it would take Bill one hour to go each way, so that his total time is determined.
   Using (2), let r = Bill's original rate; then $(r + 40) = 80$, and r can be found, and, therefore, the time for the round trip. The correct answer is D.

10. Answer (C)
    From (1), he can determine his total sales for the week.
    From (2), he can take 10% of his total sales to determine his earnings.
    Thus, the correct answer is C.

TEST 5

1. Is a trapezoid isosceles?

    1. One base is twice the other.
    2. The diagonals are equal.

2. Find the value of p.

    1. $p + q = 5$
    2. p and q are rational numbers.

3. What were Jim's marks on his last two tests?

    1. His average for the last three tests is 80%.
    2. He received 80% on his first test.

4. Find the area of a regular hexagon.

    1. One side is 8.
    2. The apothegm is $4\sqrt{3}$.

5. Is Florium the best toothpaste?

    1. It contains 10% iridium.
    2. Many professional baseball pitchers use Florium.

6. Is John a member of the Arista?

    1. John is a senior.
    2. Only seniors are eligible to join the Arista.

7. Are the diagonals of a parallelogram perpendicular to each other?

    1. The parallelogram is a rectangle.
    2. The parallelogram is equilateral.

8. Find the area of a right isosceles triangle.

    1. The hypotenuse of the triangle is 10 inches.
    2. The median to the hypotenuse is equal to half the hypotenuse.

9. Two cars are traveling toward each other on the same highway. In how many hours will they meet?

    1. They are now 217 miles apart.
    2. One is traveling at 27 miles per hour and the other at 35 miles per hour.

10. At what time will the passenger train overtake the freight train?

    1. An eastbound freight train left Buffalo traveling at the rate of 40 miles per hour.
    2. Two hours later, an eastbound passenger train left the same station, traveling 60 miles per hour.

SOLUTIONS TO TEST #5

1. **Answer (B)**
   (1) has no bearing on whether the trapezoid is isosceles.
   (2) alone is sufficient to establish that the trapezoid is isosceles. Thus, the answer is B.
2. **Answer (E)**
   The values of p and q cannot be determined from (1) and (2) or both. Thus, the correct answer is E.
3. **Answer (E)**
   From both (1) and (2), we can determine that the average of the last two tests was 80%. However, this is not sufficient to determine the grade on each test. The correct answer is E.
4. **Answer (D)**
   The side of a regular hexagon forms with two of its radii an equilateral triangle. Hence, from (1) we can determine the apothegm. Likewise, from (2), we can reverse the process and find the side. Since the area of the hexagon is six times the area of the triangle, it is determined by (1) or (2). Thus, the correct answer is D.
5. **Answer (E)**
   From the information in (1), we have no idea what effect iridium has on the teeth.
   The fact in (2), that pitchers use Florium, has no bearing on its quality as a toothpaste.
   The correct answer is E.
6. **Answer (E)**
   Both (1) and (2) together do not determine whether John is a member of the Arista. Thus, the answer is E.
7. **Answer (B)**
   From (1), the diagonals of a rectangle need not be perpendicular. From (2), the figure is a rhombus whose diagonals are perpendicular. Thus, the answer is B.
8. **Answer (A)**
   From (1), each leg of the triangle can be determined by the Pythagorean Theorem. Thus the area can be obtained.
   Fact (2) is true of all right triangles and has no bearing on determining the area.
   The correct answer is A.
9. **Answer (C)**
   (1) alone indicates the distance between them but does not state how fast they are approaching each other.
   (2) alone indicates the rate of approach but fails to state the distance apart. Using both (1) and (2), let t = the number of hours it takes them to meet; then, the equation $27t + 35t = 217$ leads to the desired result.
   The answer is C.
10. **Answer (E)**
    From all the given information, it is possible to determine how long it will take for the passenger train to overtake the freight train. If it takes t hours, we may solve the equation, $60t = 40(t + 2)$. However, we do not know at what time either train started and, therefore, we cannot answer the desired question.
    Hence, the correct answer is E.

TEST 6

1. Find the height of a tree. 1.____
   1. At 10 A.M., the tree casts a shadow 35 feet long.
   2. At the same time and place, a yardstick casts a shadow 2 feet long.

2. The circumference of circle P is how many times that of circle Q? 2.____
   1. The diameter of circle P is twice that of circle Q.
   2. The area of circle P is 4 times that of circle Q.

3. How many 2-cent stamps did a woman buy? 3.____
   1. She spent 60 cents for stamps.
   2. Some of the stamps were 2-cent stamps and some were 3-cent stamps.

4. What is a boy's average speed for a round trip to school and back? 4.____
   1. He rides to school at 30 mph and returns home at 20 mph.
   2. The distance from home to school is 10 miles.

5. Into how many right triangles can a rectangular sheet of paper be cut? 5.____
   1. The sheet of paper is 6 inches by 8 inches.
   2. Each triangle is to be 2 square inches in area.

6. What is the original price of a book? 6.____
   1. The book was sold for $3.80.
   2. A discount of 40% was granted on the sale.

7. In how many seconds will an armature turn through 360? 7.____
   1. The armature is 4 inches in diameter.
   2. The armature turns at 120 revolutions per minute.

8. How many boys in the senior class? 8.____
   1. There are 140 pupils in the class.
   2. The ratio of boys to girls is 4:3.

9. Find the area of an equilateral triangle. 9.____
   1. A side of the triangle is 10.
   2. An altitude of the triangle is $5\sqrt{3}$.

10. Find each angle of a triangle. 10.____
    1. The triangle is scalene.
    2. The three angles of the triangle are in the ratio 2:5:8.

SOLUTIONS TO TEST #6

1. **Answer (C)**
   Using both facts (1) and (2), we can set up similar triangles that will permit us to solve for the height of the tree. Thus, the answer is C.

2. **Answer (D)**
   From the formula $C = 2\pi r$, we can find C when given r. From (1), r = 1/2 of the diameter. From (2), we can obtain r from the formula, $A = \pi r^2$
   Hence, we can use either (1) or (2). The answer is D.

3. **Answer (E)**
   Using statements (1) and (2), there are many possible answers to the equation that is formed, $2x + 3y = 60$. To get a unique solution, we would have to know the total number of stamps purchased. The answer is E.

4. **Answer (A)**
   The average speed can be computed from (1) alone.
   The datum in (2) is irrelevant. Choose any distance from home to school, and the average rate will be the same.
   The answer is A.

5. **Answer (C)**
   Using both (1) and (2), the sheet can be cut into rectangles, each 4 sq. in. in area. Each of these rectangles can then be cut into 2 right triangles. The answer is C.

6. **Answer (C)**
   From statement (2), the book was sold for 60% of its original price. From (1), form the equation, $6x = 3.80$, and solve to obtain the original price.
   Both (1) and (2) are needed.
   The answer is C.

7. **Answer (B)**
   Statement (1) is irrelevant to the problem.
   From (2), we can see that the armature does 1 revolution in 1/2 minute. The answer is B.

8. **Answer (C)**
   From (2), we can designate the number of boys and girls as 4x and 3x, respectively.
   From (1), we can form the equation, $4x + 3x = 140$.
   Both facts are needed to obtain a solution.
   The answer is C.

9. **Answer (D)**
   From the formula, $A = \frac{s^2}{4}\sqrt{3}$ we can find the area from (1).
   Using (2) and the formula $h = \frac{s}{2}\sqrt{3}$, we can find s and then determine the area.
   Either (1) or (2) can, thus, be used. The answer is D.

10. **Answer (B)**
    (1) is irrelevant to finding the angles of the triangle. Using (2), form the equation, $2x + 5x + 8x = 180$. Thus (2) is needed but not (1).
    The answer is B

DIAGNOSING THE CAUSES OF AUTOMOTIVE TROUBLES

CONTENTS

	Page
INTROUCTION	1
A. ENGINE TROUBLES	1
1. Engine Fails to Start	1
2. Engine Starts But Misses	1
3. Engine Starts But Will Not Pull	1
4. Engine is Hard to Start	2
5. Engine Overheats	2
6. Engine Stalls	2
7. Engine Knocks	2
8. Engine Backfires	3
9. Engine Keeps Running With Switch Off	3
B. STARTING MOTOR TROUBLES	3
1. Starting Motor Does Not Operate	3
2. Starting Motor Operates, But Not Enough to Turn Over	3
C. ENGINE LUBRICATION TROUBLES	3
1. High Oil Consumption	3
2. Low Oil Consumption	3
3. High and Low Oil Pressures	3
4. Oil Gauge Hand Flutters	3
D. CLUTCH TROUBLES	4
1. Clutch Slips	4
2. Clutch Drags	4
3. Clutch Spins	4
4. Clutch Grabs	4
E. COOLING SYSTEM TROUBLES	4
F. BATTERY TROUBLES	4
G. CARBURETOR TROUBLES	5
1. Mixture Too Rich	5
2. Mixture Too Lean	5
H. REAR AXLE TROUBLES	5
1. Wheels Do Not Turn	5
2. Axle Bucks or Clashes	5
I. STEERING TROUBLES	5
1. Shimmy	5
2. Pulling to One Side	6
3. Wandering or Weaving	6
4. Hard Steering	6
J. TIRE TROUBLES	6
K. BRAKE TROUBLES	6
L. TROUBLES INDICATED BY THE EXHAUST SMOKE	

DIAGNOSING THE CAUSES OF AUTOMOTIVE TROUBLES

The number of possible difficulties encountered with an automobile is endless, and no attempt will be made to present them all. Diagnosing auto troubles requires thought and reasoning. If the principles and construction of the various parts of the care are understood, and one of the hundreds of possible troubles occurs, then simply reason it out. Determine what the trouble is, learn what might cause that trouble, and why the trouble is present. Decide whether it is in the ignition, fuel system, lubrication system, or just where it is, and then track it down by a process of elimination. Following is a list of various common troubles, each one of which is directly followed by its possible causes.

A. ENGINE TROUBLES

1. Engine fails to start
   a. Lack of gasoline - empty tank or trouble in fuel system
   b. Carburetor needs priming
   c. Poor quality of gasoline - may contain water or be old and stable
   d. Too much gasoline - cylinder may be flooded; spark plugs may be soaked; gasoline needle valve not working
   e. No pressure in fuel tank
   f. Lack of ignition current may be due to exhausted battery or broken or loose wiring
   g. Spark plugs may be sooted from over-lubrication, or the point may be burnt or corroded

2. Engine Starts But Misses
   (The missing cylinder or cylinders may be located by short circuiting each spark plug with a screwdriver. When the plug in the missing cylinder is short-circuited, no difference will be noticed in the engine. Short-circuiting a good cylinder will cause another miss and slow the engine.)
   a. Defective spark plugs
   b. Wet spark plugs, wiring or distributor
   c. Defective or dirty or wet distributor
   d. Improper or broken wiring connections
   e. Weak battery
   f. Incorrect fuel mixture
   g. Defective condenser
   h. Engine cold on a cold day
   i. Valve leakage, which might be due to
      (1) Valves adjusted too tightly
      (2) Need for grinding
      (3) Broken spring or seat
      (4) Carbon deposit

3. Engine Starts But Will Not pull
   a. Brakes dragging or hand brake set
   b. Low oil supply
   c. Defective lubrication system
   d. Water supply low, or defect in cooling system
   e. Mixture too lean or too rich

f. Leady valves or rings, causing loss of compression
g. Spark retarded or improperly timed
h. Slipping clutch
i. Trouble in the ignition system

4. Engine is Hard to Start
   a. Stiff engine due to cold weather or improper lubrication
   b. Choke not functioning properly
   c. Incorrect throttle setting
   d. Lean mixture; leaky valves; weak battery

5. Engine Overheats
   a. Water or oil supply low
   b. Defective or dirty cooling or lubrication system
   c. Spark retarded or improperly timed
   d. Mixture too rich or engine badly carbonized
   e. Too much running on low gear

6. Engine Stalls
   a. If it stops suddenly without warning, either the ignition switch was turned off accidentally or there is trouble in the ignition system.
   b. If permanent stalling is preceded by intermittent missing or stalling, look for ignition trouble.
   c. If the engine "peters out" as though through the throttle were suddenly closed all the way, look for carburetor trouble (usually dirt).
   d. If petering out is preceded by loss of power, backfiring, or missing (without muffler explosions) the trouble is most probably due to dirt in the fuel system.
   e. List of possible causes
      (1) Lack of gasoline
      (2) Dirt or water in the fuel system
      (3) Failure of fuel feed system
      (4) Defects, improper connections, dirt or water in the ignition system
      (5) Valves adjusted too tightly
      (6) Mixture too rich
      (7) Incorrect timing of valves

7. Engine Knocks
   a. Carbon knock: Most noticeable when the car climbs in a steep grade in high gear. Usually not heard when engine is warming up.
   b. Spark too far advanced: Noticeable with the throttle open and the engine pulling hard.
   c. Loose connecting-rod bearing: Heard when the engine is running idly down hill, or when it is allowed to decelerate after speeding up.
   d. Loose main bearing: Noticeable when running fast with the spark advanced
   e. Loose flywheel: Noticed when the ignition is shut off with the engine running, and then switched on when the engine has almost stopped.
   f. Loose pistons: Most noticeable when the engine is speeded up while the car is standing.
   g. Loose piston pin
   h. Lean mixture

i. Engine too hot or lacks oil
   j. Valves stuck or need adjusting

8. Engine Backfires (This is always accompanied by missing.)
   a. Cold engine
   b. Spar too far retarded
   c. Fuel heating device not working
   d. Lean mixture
   e. Dirt in the carburetor
   f. Intake valve leaks, or too much clearance on exhaust valve

9. Engine Keeps Running With Switch Off
   (This is caused by overheating, which may be due to:)
   a. Ignition system - defective switch
   b. Poor oil - deposits carbon on the cylinder, and this carbon becomes red-hot, causing pre-ignition

B. STARTING MOTOR TROUBLES

1. Starting Motor Does Not Operate
   a. Battery may be weak or exhausted, or a connection may be loose
   b. Bendix drive or starting mechanism out of order
   c. Open circuit in the wiring: broken or loose wiring connections

2. Starting Motor Operates, But Not Enough to Turn Over
   a. Weak battery
   b. Engine may be unusually stiff
   c. Poor contact at battery terminals
   d. Trouble in the starting motor mechanism

C. ENGINE LUBRICATION TROUBLES

1. High Oil Consumption
   a. Leakage past pistons, or in the lubricating system
   b. Oil too light or of poor quality
   c. Pump pressure too high
   d. High engine speeds

2. Low Oil Consumption
   a. Dilution of oil by fuel
   b. Leakage of water into the oil

3. High and Low Oil Pressures

4. Oil Gauge Hand Flutters
   a. Low oil supply
   b. Leak in the piping
   c. Pump strainer dirty
   d. Intermittent clogging in the lubrication system

D. CLUTCH TROUBLES

1. Clutch Slips (Engine runs too fast in relation to car speed)
   a. Too much oil on a lubricated clutch; oil present on a dry clutch
   b. Clutch needs adjusting
   c. Weak clutch
   d. Badly worn clutch facings

2. Clutch Drags (Fails to release fully when thrown out)
   a. Adjustment too tight
   b. Rivets in the facing are protruding
   c. Clutch bearing worn or broken
   d. Clutch out of alignment

3. Clutch Spins (The drive member of the clutch fails to come to rest quickly when the clutch is thrown out)
   a. Oil on clutch brake
   b. Clutch adjusted too tightly

4. Clutch Grabs (A tendency of the clutch to take hold too suddenly)
   a. Gummed oil on clutch faces
   b. Adjustment too tight
   c. Rivets protruding from clutch facing
   d. Glazed lining

E. COOLING SYSTEM TROUBLES (Any defect in this system results in overheating the engine)

1. Not enough water in the system
2. Core passages of the radiator clogged: Cleaned by flushing with a mixture of salsoda and water
3. Faulty water in the radiator
4. Frozen water in the radiator
5. Anti-freeze in the system in hot weather
6. Leaks in the system
7. Fan belt not working properly

F. BATTERY TROUBLES

1. Defective generator or circuit breaker
2. Open circuits or poor connections
3. Low electrolyte
4. Sulphated or corroded battery terminals
5. Battery does not hold charge
   a. Car not run enough in the daytime, or not a high enough speed, for the generator to charge the battery and replace the current consumed by the lights, tarter, etc.
   b. Generator output not properly adjusted
   c. Circuit breaker not operating properly
   d. Overload on the electrical system, due to too many appliances (radio, lighters, etc.)
   e. Plates are sulphated

f. Active material of the plate grids is loose

G. **CARBURETION TROUBLES**

1. Mixture too rich
   a. Air cleaner dirty or clogged
   b. Improper choke adjustment
   c. Fuel pump pressure too high
   d. Nozzle oversize or improperly adjusted
   e. Leaking float, with not enough buoyancy to close the valve
   f. Float level too high; this is one of the most common causes for incorrect carburetion
   g. Leaking float valve
   h. Changing from heavy to light fuel, with the carburetor adjusted for the heavier fuel
   i. Cold intake manifold
   j. Excessive back pressure due to clogged muffler or partly clogged exhaust pipe

2. Mixture too lean
   a. Air leaks between the carburetor and the cylinders
   b. Float level set too low
   c. Fuel nozzle clogged or undersized
   d. Low pressure from fuel pump
   e. Incorrect valve timing, causing the inlet valves to close before allowing a full charge of gas into the cylinder
   f. Change from light to heavy fuel, with the carburetor adjusted to light fuel
   g. Excessively high temperatures of intake manifold or cooling system

H. **REAR AXLE TROUBLES**

1. Wheels do not turn
   a. Key holding the wheel may be broken
   b. Ring gear rivets sheared on differential housing
   c. Broken axle shaft, or pinion shaft coupling
   d. Broken universal joint or propeller shaft

2. Axle bucks or clashes
   a. Worn pinion shaft thrust bearing or drive gear or pinion
   b. Worn universal joint or differential pinion
   c. Broken teeth or ring gear

I. **STEERING TROUBLES**

1. Shimmy: Excessive vibration of the front wheels from side to side or up and down, causing a jerky motion of the steering wheel
   a. Excessive caster, or incorrect toe-in
   b. Low or unequal tire pressures
   c. Unbalanced front wheels
   d. Shock absorbers not acting properly
   e. Springs that are weak or have broken leaves
   f. Loose wheels or steering connections

2. Pulling to one side
   a. Unequal camber or caster, or one rear wheel cambered
   b. Unequal tire inflation
   c. Dragging brakes or tight wheel bearings

3. Wandering or weaving – gradual swinging of the car to one side or the other of the road
   a. Insufficient or reversed caster
   b. Excessive tightness or looseness in the steering system
   c. Unequal camber or caster
   d. Incorrect toe-in
   e. Underinflation of rear tires

4. Hard steering, especially in making turns
   a. Excessive caster or tightness in steering system
   b. Twisted axle, or improper camber
   c. Low or unequal tire inflation

J. TIRE TROUBLES

1. Tire scuffing – abrasion of the tread as it is dragged over the road surface instead of rolling on it. Caused by incorrect toe-in, or incorrect turning radius.
2. Excessive wear on one side of the tread caused by incorrect camber.
3. Several worn spots are caused by a wobbly wheel or consistently making abrupt stops.
4. Uneven wear may be caused by springs that are too flexible, allowing variations in camber, caster, or toe-in.
5. Excessive wear of the center of the tread may be due to improper alignment of the wheels or over-inflation.
6. Greater wear on the outer edges of the tread than in the center is usually due to under-inflation.

K. BRAKE TROUBLES

The most common brake trouble is slipping, which may be caused by oil, water or grease on the lining; by poor adjustment; by worn brakes linings. Sometimes the car tends to skid to one side when the brakes are applied. This means the brake on one wheel is dragging or binding, and is due to improper adjustment. Where all brakes tighten suddenly, the cause is most probably a broken near spring. Since the brakes control the safe operation of the car, they should be kept in the best possible condition. Any troubles in the brake system should be remedied immediately, and it should be kept in mind that "taking up" the brakes is sometimes a poor substitute for replacing the lining.

L. TROUBLES INDICATED BY THE EXHAUST SMOKE
1. Black and foul-smelling smoke is caused by too rich a mixture.
2. White or blue smoke means too much oil in the engine.
3. Gray smoke indicates too much fuel as well as excess oil.

GLOSSARY OF ELECTRONIC TERMS

TABLE OF CONTENTS

	Page
Acorn Tube ... Bias	1
Biasing Resistor ... Coefficient of Coupling (K)	2
Condenser ... Dielectric	3
Dielectric Constant ... Electrostatic Field	4
Equivalent Circuit ... Henry (h)	5
Helmholts Coil ... Klystron	6
Lag ... Neutralisation	7
Node ... Plate Resistance (r_p)	8
Positive Feedback ... Relaxation Oscillator	9
Reluctance ... Solenoid	10
Space Charge ... Unbalanced Line	11
Unidirectional ... Z	12

ELECTRONICS SYMBOLS	
Amplifier ... Cell, Photosensitive	13
Circuit Breaker ... Discontinuity	14
Electron Tube ... Inductor	15
Key, Telegraph ... Meter, Instrument	16
Mode Transducer ... Semiconductor Device	17
Squib ... Transformer	18
Vibrator, Interrupter ... Visual Signaling Device	19

TRANSISTOR SYMBOLS	19

TUBE SYMBOLS	20

GLOSSARY OF ELECTRONIC TERMS

Acorn tube. An acorn-shaped vacuum tube designed for ultra-high-frequency circuits. The tube has short electron transit time and low inter-electrode capacitance because of close spacing and small size electrodes.

Align. To adjust the tuned circuits of a receiver or transmitter for maximum signal response.

Alternation. One-half of a complete cycle.

Ammeter. An instrument for measuring the electron flow in amperes.

Ampere (amp). The basic unit of current or electron flow.

Amplification (A). The process of increasing the strength of a signal.

Amplification factor (ft). The ratio of a small change in plate voltage to a small change in grid voltage, with all other electrode voltages constant, required to produce the same small change in plate current.

Amplifier. A device used to increase the signal voltage, current, or power, generally composed of a vacuum tube and associated circuit called a stage. It may contain several stages in order to obtain a desired gain.

Amplitude. The maximum instantaneous value of an alternating voltage or current, measured in either the positive or negative direction.

Amplitude distortion. The changing of a waveshape so that it is no longer proportional to its original form. Also known as harmonic distortion.

Anode. A positive electrode; the plate of a vacuum tube.

Antenna. A device used to radiate or absorb r-f energy.

Aquadag. A graphite coating on the inside of certain cathode-ray tubes for collecting secondary electrons emitted by the screen.

Array (antenna). An arrangement of antenna elements, usually di-poles, which results in desirable directional characteristics.

Attenuation. The reduction in the strength of a signal.

Audio frequency (a-f). A frequency which can be detected as a sound by the human ear. The range of audio frequencies extends approximately from 20 to 20,000 cycles per second.

Autodyne circuit. A circuit in which the same elements and vacuum tube are used as an oscillator and as a detector. The output has a frequency equal to the difference between the frequencies of the received signal and the oscillator signal.

Automatic gain control (age) A method of automatically regulating the gain of a receiver so that the output tends to remain constant though the incoming signal may vary in strength.

Automatic volume control (avc). See Automatic gain control.

Autotransformer. A transformer in which part of the primary winding is used as a secondary winding, or vice versa.

Azimuth. The angular measurement in a horizontal plane and in a clockwise direction, beginning at a point oriented to north.

Ballast resistance. A self-regulating resistance, usually connected in the primary circuit of a power transformer to compensate for variations in the line voltage.

Ballast tube. A tube which contains a ballast resistance.

Band of frequencies. The frequencies existing between two definite limits.

Band-pass filter. A circuit designed to pass with nearly equal response all currents having frequencies within a definite band, and to reduce substantially the amplitudes of currents of all frequencies outside that band.

Bazooka. See Line-balance converter.

Beam-power tube. A high vacuum tube in which the electron stream is directed in concentrated beams from the cathode to the plate. Variously termed beam-power tetrode and beam-power pentode.

Beat frequency. A frequency resulting from the combination of two different frequencies. It is numerically equal to the difference between or the sum of these two frequencies.

Beat note. See Beat frequency.

Bias. The average d-c voltage maintained between the cathode and control grid of a vacuum tube.

Biasing resistor. A resistor used to provide the voltage drop for a required bias.

Blanking. See Gating.

Bleeder. A resistance connected in parallel with a power-supply output to protect equipment from excessive voltages if the load is removed or substantially reduced; to improve the voltage regulation, and to drain the charge remaining in the filter capacitors when the unit is turned off.

Blocking capacitor. A capacitor used to block the flow of direct current while permitting the flow of alternating current.

Break-down voltage. The voltage at which an insulator or dielectric ruptures, or at which ionization and conduction take place in a gas or vapor.

Brilliance modulation. See Intensity modulation.

Buffer amplifier. An amplifier used to isolate the output of an oscillator from the effects produced by changes in voltage or loading in following circuits.

Buncher. The electrode of a velocity-modulated tube which alters the velocity of electrons in the constant current beam causing the electrons to become bunched in a drift space beyond the buncher electrode.

Bypass capacitor. A capacitor used to provide an alternating current path of comparatively low impedance around a circuit element.

Capacitance. The property of two or more bodies which enables them to store electrical energy in an electrostatic field between the bodies.

Capacitive coupling. A method of transferring energy from one circuit to another by means of a capacitor that is common to both circuits.

Capacitive reactance (X_c). The opposition offered to the flow of an alternating current by capacitance, expressed in ohms.

Capacitor. Two electrodes or sets of electrodes in the form of plates, separated from each other by an insulating material called the dielectric.

Carrier. The r-f component of a transmitted wave upon which an audio signal or other form of intelligence can be impressed.

Catcher. The electrode of a velocity-modulated tube which receives energy from the bunched electrons.

Cathode (K). The electrode in a vacuum tube which is the source of electron emission. Also a negative electrode.

Cathode bias. The method of biasing a tube by placing the biasing resistor in the common cathode return circuit, making the cathode more positive, rather than the grid more negative, with respect to ground.

Cathode follower. A vacuum-tube circuit in which the input signal is applied between the control grid and ground, and the output is taken from the cathode and ground. A cathode follower has a high input impedance and a low output impedance.

Characteristic impedance (Z_0). The ratio of the voltage to the current at every point along a transmission line on which there are no standing waves.

Choke. A coil which impedes the flow of alternating current of a specified frequency range because of its high inductive reactance at that range.

Chopping. See Limiting.

Clamping circuit. A circuit which maintains either amplitude extreme of a waveform at a certain level of potential.

Class A operation. Operation of a vacuum tube so that plate current flows throughout the entire operating cycle and distortion is kept to a minimum.

Class AB operation. Operation of a vacuum tube with grid bias so that the operating point is approximately halfway between Class A and Class B.

Class B operation. Operation of a vacuum tube with bias at or near cut-off so that plate current flows during approximately one-half cycle.

Class C operation. Operation of a vacuum tube with bias considerably beyond cut-off so that plate current flows for less than one-half cycle.

Clipping. See Limiting.

Coaxial cable. A transmission line consisting of two conductors concentric with and insulated from each other.

Coefficient of coupling (K). A numerical indication of the degree of coupling existing between two circuits, expressed in terms of either a decimal or a percentage.

Condenser. See Capacitor.

Conductance (G). The ability of a material to conduct or carry an electric current. It is the reciprocal of the resistance of the material, and is expressed in *ohms.*

Continuous waves. Radio waves which maintain a constant amplitude and a constant frequency.

Control grid (G). The electrode of a vacuum tube other than a diode upon which the signal voltage is impressed in order to control the plate current.

Control-grid-plate transconductance. See Transconductance.

Conversion transconductance (gc). A characteristic associated with the mixer function of vacuum tubes, and used in the same manner as transconductance is used. It is the ratio of the i-f current in the primary of the first i-f transformer to the r-f signal voltage producing it.

Converter. See Mixer.

Converter tube. A multielement vacuum tube used both as a mixer and as an oscillator in a superheterodyne receiver. It creates a local frequency and combines it with an incoming signal to produce an intermediate frequency.

Counting circuit. A circuit which receives uniform pulses representing units to be counted and produces a voltage in proportion to their frequency.

Coupled impedance. The effect produced in the primary winding of a transformer by the influence of the current flowing in the secondary winding.

Coupling. The association of two circuits in such a way that energy may be transferred from one to the other.

Coupling element. The means by which energy is transferred from one circuit to another the common impedance necessary for coupling.

Critical coupling. The degree of coupling which provides the maximum transfer of energy between two resonant circuits at the resonant frequency.

Crystal (Xtal). (1) A natural substance, such as quartz or tourmaline, which is capable of producing a voltage stress when under pressure, or producing pressure when under an applied voltage. Under stress it has the property of responding only to a given frequency when cut to a given thickness.

(2) A nonlinear element such as gelena or silicon, in which case the piezo-electric characteristic is not exhibited.

Crystal mixer. A device which employs the nonlinear characteristic of a crystal (nonpiezo-electric type) and a point contact to mix two frequencies.

Crystal oscillator. An oscillator circuit in which a piezoelectric crystal is used to control the frequency and to reduce frequency instability to a minimum.

Current (J). Flow of electrons; measured in amperes.

Cut-off (c.o.). The minimum value of negative grid bias which prevents the flow of plate current in a vacuum tube.

Cut-off limiting. Limiting the maximum output voltage of a vacuum-tube circuit by driving the grid beyond cut-off.

Cycle. One complete positive and one complete negative alternation of a current or voltage.

Damped waves. Waves which decrease exponentially in amplitude.

Decoupling network. A network of capacitors and chokes, or resistors, placed in leads which are common to two or more circuits to prevent unwanted interstage coupling.

Deflection sensitivity (CRT). The quotient of the displacement of the electron beam at the place of impact by the change in the deflecting field. It is usually expressed in millimeters per volt applied between the deflection electrodes, or in millimeters per gauss of the deflecting magnetic field.

Degeneration. The process whereby a part of the output signal of an amplifying device is returned to its input circuit in such a manner that it tends to cancel the input.

De-ionization potential. The potential at which ionization of the gas within a gas-filled tube ceases and conduction stops.

Demodulation. See Detection.

Detection. The process of separating the modulation component from the received signal.

Dielectric. An insulator; a term applied to the

insulating material between the plates of a capacitor.

Dielectric constant. The ratio of the capacitance of a capacitor with a dielectric between the electrodes to the capacitance with air between the electrodes.

Differentiating circuit. A circuit which produces an output voltage substantially in proportion to the rate of change of the input voltage.

Diode. A two-electrode vacuum tube containing a cathode and a plate.

Diode detector. A detector circuit employing a diode tube.

Dipole antenna. Two metallic elements, each approximately one quarter wavelength long, which radiate r-f energy fed to them by the transmission line.

Directly heated cathode. A filament cathode which carries its own heating current for electron emission, as distinguished from an indirectly heated cathode.

Director (antenna). A parasitic antenna placed in front of a radiating element so that r-f radiation is aided in the forward direction.

Distortion. The production of an output waveform which is not a true reproduction of the input waveform. Distortion may consist of irregularities in amplitude, frequency, or phase.

Distributed capacitance. The capacitance that exists between the turns in a coil or choke, or between adjacent conductors or circuits, as dis- tinguished from the capacitance which is concentrated in a capacitor.

Distributed inductance. The inductance that exists along the entire length of a conductor, as distinguished from the self-inductance which is concentrated in a coil.

Doorknob tube. A doorknob-shaped vacuum tube designed for ultra-high-frequency circuits. This tube has short electron transit time and low interelectrode capacitance, because of the close spacing and small size of electrodes.

Dropping resistor. A resistor used to decrease a given voltage to a lower value.

Dry electrolytic capacitor. An electrolytic capacitor using a paste instead of a liquid electrolyte. *See* Electrolytic capacitor.

Dynamic characteristics. The relation between the instantaneous plate voltage and plate current of a vacuum tube as the voltage applied to the grid is moved; thus, the characteristics of a vacuum tube during operation.

Dynatron. A negative resistance device; particularly, a tetrode operating on that portion of its i_p vs. e_p characteristic where secondary emission exists to such an extent that an increase in plate voltage actually causes a decrease in plate current, and, therefore, makes the circuit behave like a negative resistance.

Eccles-Jordan circuit (trigger circuit). A direct coupled multivibrator circuit possessing two conditions of stable equilibrium. Also known as a flip-flop circuit.

Effective value. The equivalent heating value of an alternating current or voltage, as compared to a direct current or voltage. It is 0.707 times the peak value of a sine wave. It is also called the rms value.

Efficiency. The ratio of output to input power, generally expressed as a percentage.

Electric field. A space in which an electric charge will experience a force exerted upon it.

Electrode. A terminal at which electricity passes from one medium into another.

Electrolyte. A water solution of a substance which is capable of conducting electricity. An electrolyte may be in the form of either a liquid or a paste.

Electrolytic capacitor. A capacitor employing a metallic plate and an electrolyte as the second plate separated by a dielectric which is produced by electrochemical action.

Electromagnetic field. A space field in which electric and magnetic vectors at right angles to each other travel in a direction at right angles to both.

Electron. The negatively charged particles of matter. The smallest particle of matter.

Electron emission. The liberation of electrons from a bo]difference.

Electronic switch. A circuit which causes a start-and-stop action or a switching action by electronic means.

Electronic voltmeter. *See* Vacuum tube voltmeter.

Electrostatic field. The field of influence

between two charged bodies.

Equivalent circuit. A diagrammatic arrangement of coils, resistors, and capacitors, representing the effects of a more complicated circuit in order to permit easier analysis.

Farad (f). The unit of capacitance.

Feedback. A transfer of energy from the output circuit of a device back to its input.

Field. The space containing electric or magnetic lines of force.

Field intensity. Electrical strength of a field.

Filament. See Directly heated cathode.

Filter. A combination of circuit elements designed to pass a definite range of frequencies, attenuating all others.

Firing potential. The controlled potential at which conduction through a gas-filled tube begins.

First detector. See Mixer.

Fixed bias. A bias voltage of constant value, such as one obtained from a battery, power supply, or generator.

Fixed capacitor. A capacitor which has no provision for varying its capacitance.

Fixed resistor. A resistor which has no provision for varying its resistance.

Fluorescence. The property of emitting light as the immediate result of electronic bombardment.

Fly-back. The portion of the time base during which the spot is returning to the starting point. This is usually not seen on the screen of the cathode-ray tube, because of gating action or the rapidity with which it occurs.

Free electrons. Electrons which are loosely held and consequently tend to move at random among the atoms of the material.

Free oscillations. Oscillatory currents which continue to flow in a tuned circuit after the impressed voltage has been removed. Their frequency is the resonant frequency of the tuned circuit.

Frequency (f). The number of complete cycles per second existing in any form of wave motion; such as the number of cycles per second of an alternating current.

Frequency distortion. Distortion which occurs as a result of failure to amplify or attenuate equally all frequencies present in a complex wave.

Frequency modulation. See Modulation.

Frequency stability. The ability of an oscillator to maintain its operation at a constant frequency.

Full-wave rectifier circuit. A circuit which utilizes both the positive and the negative alternations of an alternating current to produce a direct current.

Gain (A). The ratio of the output power, voltage, or current to the input power, voltage, or current, respectively.

Gas tube. A tube filled with gas at low pressure in order to obtain certain desirable characteristics.

Gating (cathode-ray tube). Applying a rectangular voltage to the grid or cathode of a cathode-ray tube to sensitize it during the sweep time only.

Grid current. Current which flows between the cathode and the grid whenever the grid becomes positive with respect to the cathode.

Grid detection. Detection by rectification in the grid circuit of a detector.

Grid leak. A high resistance connected across the grid capacitor or between the grid and the cathode to provide a d-c path from grid to cathode and to limit the accumulation of charge on the grid.

Grid limiting. Limiting the positive grid voltage (minimum output voltage) of vacuum-tube circuit by means of a large series grid resistor.

Ground. A metallic connection with the earth to establish ground potential. Also, a common return to a point of zero r-f potential, such as the chassis of a receiver or a transmitter.

Half-wave rectification. The process of rectifying an alternating current wherein only one-half of the input cycle is passed and the other half is blocked by the action of the rectifier, thus producing pulsating direct current.

Hard tube. A high vacuum electronic tube.

Harmonic. An integral multiple of a fundamental frequency. (The second harmonic is twice the frequency of the fundamental or first harmonic.)

Harmonic distortion. Amplitude distortion.

Heater. The tube element used to indirectly heat a cathode.

Henry (h). The basic unit of inductance.

Helmholts coil. A variometer having horizontal and vertical balanced coil windings, used to vary the angle of phase difference between any two similar waveforms of the same frequency.

Heterodyne. To beat or mix two signals of different frequencies.

High-frequency resistance. The resistance presented to the flow of high-frequency current. See Skin effect.

Horn radiator. Any open-ended metallic device for concentrating energy from a waveguide and directing this energy into space.

Hysteresis. A lagging of the magnetic flux in a magnetic material behind the magnetizing force which is producing it.

Image frequency. An undesired signal capable of beating with the local oscillator signal of a superheterodyne receiver which produces a difference frequency within the bandwidth of the i-f channel.

Impedance (Z). The total opposition offered to the flow of an alternating current. It may consist of any combination of resistance, inductive reactance, and capacitive reactance.

Impedance coil. See Choke.

Impedance coupling. The use of a tuned circuit or an impedance coil as the common coupling element between two circuits.

Impulse. Any force acting over a comparatively short period of time, such as a momentary rise in voltage.

Indirectly heated cathode. A cathode which is brought to the temperature necessary for electron emission by a separate heater element. Compare *Directly heated cathode.*

Inductance (L). The property of a circuit which tends to oppose a change in the existing current.

Induction. The act or process of producing voltage by the relative motion of a magnetic field across a conductor.

Inductive reactance (X_1). The opposition to the flow of alternating or pulsating current caused by the inductance of a circuit. It is measured in ohms.

Inductor. A circuit element designed so that its inductance is its most important electrical property; a coil.

Infinite. Extending indefinitely; having innumerable parts, capable of endless division within itself.

In phase. Applied to the condition that exists when two waves of the same frequency pass through their maximum and minimum values of like polarity at the same instant.

Instantaneous value. The magnitude at any particular instant when a value is continually varying with respect to time.

Integrating circuit. A circuit which produces an output voltage substantially in proportion to the frequency and amplitude of the input voltage.

Intensify. To increase the brilliance of an image on the screen of a cathode-ray tube.

Intensity modulation. The control of the brilliance of the trace on the screen of a cathode-ray tube in conformity with the signal.

Interelectrode capacitance. The capacitance existing between the electrodes in a vacuum tube.

Intermediate frequency (i-f). The fixed frequency to which r-f carrier waves are converted in a superheterodyne receiver.

Inverse peak voltage. The highest instantaneous negative potential which the plate can acquire with respect to the cathode without danger of injuring the tube.

Ion. An elementary particle of matter or a small group of such particles having a net positive or negative charge.

Ionization. Process by which ions are produced in solids, liquids, or gases.

Ionization potential. The lowest potential at which ionization takes place within a gas-filled tube.

Ionosphere. A region composed of highly ionized layers of atmosphere from 70 to 250 miles above the surface of the earth.

Kilo (k). A prefix meaning 1,000.

Kilocycle (kc). One thousand cycles; conversationally used to indicate 1,000 cycles per second.

Klystron. A tube in which oscillations are generated by the bunching of electrons (that is, velocity modulation). This tube utilizes the transit time between two given electrodes to deliver pulsating energy to a cavity resonator in order to sustain oscillations within the cavity.

Lag. The amount one wave is behind another in time; expressed in electrical degrees.

Lead The opposite of *lag.* Also, a wire or connection.

Leakage. The electrical loss due to poor insulation.

Lecher line. A section of open-wire transmission line used for measurements of standing waves.

Limiting. Removal by electronic means of one or both extremities of a waveform at a predetermined level.

Linear. Having an output which varies in direct proportion to the input.

Line-balance converter. A device used at the end of a coaxial line to isolate the outer conductor from ground.

Load. The impedance to which energy is being supplied.

Local oscillator. The oscillator used in a superheterodyne receiver the output of which is mixed with the desired r-f carrier to form the intermediate frequency.

Loose coupling. Less than critical coupling; coupling providing little transfer of energy.

Magnetic circuit. The complete path of magnetic lines of force.

Magnetic field (H). The space in which a magnetic force exists.

Magnetron. A vacuum-tube oscillator containing two electrodes, in which the flow of electrons from cathode to anode is controlled by an externally applied magnetic field.

Matched impedance. The condition which exists when two coupled circuits are so adjusted that their impedances are equal.

Meg (mega) (m). A prefix meaning one million.

Megacycle (M_c). One million cycles. Used conversationally to mean 1,000,000 cycles per second.

Metallic insulator. A shorted quarter-wave section of a transmission line which acts as an electrical insulator at a frequency corresponding to its quarter-wave length.

Mho. The unit of conductance.

Micro (μ). A prefix meaning one-millionth.

Microsecond (μs). One-millionth of a second.

Milli (m). A prefix meaning one-thousandth.

Milliampera (ma). One-thousandth of an ampere.

Mixer. A vacuum tube or crystal and suitable circuit used to combine the incoming and local-oscillator frequencies to produce an intermediate frequency. *See* Beat frequency.

Modulation. The process of varying the amplitude (amplitude modulation), the frequency (frequency modulation), or the phase (phase modulation) of a carrier wave in accordance with other signals in order to convey intelligence. The modulating signal may be an audiofrequency signal, video signal (as in television), or electrical pulses or tones to operate relays, etc.

Modulator. The circuit which provides the signal that varies the ampli- tude, frequency, or phase of the oscillations generated in the transmitter tube.

Multielectrode tube. A vacuum tube containing more than three electrodes associated with a single electron stream.

Multiunit tube. A vacuum tube containing within one envelope two or more groups of electrodes, each associated with separate electron streams.

Multivibrator. A type of relaxation oscillator for the generation of nonsinusoidal waves in which the output of each of its two tubes is coupled to the input of the other to sustain oscillations.

Mutual conductance (g_m). *See* Transconductance.

Mutual inductance. A circuit property existing when the relative position of two inductors causes the magnetic lines of force from one to link with the turns of the other.

Negative feedback. *See* Degeneration.

Neon bulb. A glass bulb containing two electrodes in neon gas at low pressure.

Network. Any electrical circuit containing two or more interconnected elements.

Neutralisation. The process of nullifying the voltage fed back through the interelectrode capacitance of an amplifier tube, by providing an equal voltage of opposite phase; generally necessary only with triode tubes.

Node. A zero point; specifically, a current node is a point of zero current and a voltage node is a point of zero voltage.

Noninductive capacitor. A capacitor in which the inductive effects at high frequencies are reduced to the minimum.

Noninductive circuit. A circuit in which inductance is reduced to a minimum or negligible value.

Nonlinear. Having an output which does not vary in direct proportion to the input.

Ohm (ω). The unit of electrical resistance.

Open circuit. A circuit which does not provide a complete path for the flow of current.

Optimum coupling. See Critical coupling.

Oscillator. A circuit capable of converting direct current into alternating current of a frequency determined by the constants of the circuit. It generally uses a vacuum tube.

Oscillatory circuit. A circuit in which oscillations can be generated or sustained.

Oscillograph. See Oscilloscope.

Oscilloscope. An instrument for showing, visually, graphical representations of the waveforms encountered in electrical circuits.

Overdriven amplifier. An amplifier designed to distort the input signal waveform by a combination of cut-off limiting and saturation limiting.

Overload. A load greater than the rated load of an electrical device.

Parallel feed. Application of a d-c voltage to the plate or grid of a tube in parallel with an a-c circuit so that the d-c and a-c components flow in separate paths. Also called shunt feed.

Parallel-resonant circuit. A resonant circuit in which the applied voltage is connected across a parallel circuit formed by a capacitor and an inductor.

Paraphase amplifier. An amplifier which converts a single input into a push-pull output.

Parasitic suppressor. A resistor in a vacuum-tube circuit to prevent un-wanted oscillations.

Peaking circuit. A type of circuit which converts an input to a peaked output waveform.

Peak plate current. The maximum instantaneous plate current passing through a tube.

Peak value. The maximum instantaneous value of a varying current, voltage, or power. It is equal to 1.414 times the effective value of a sine wave.

Pentode. A five-electrode vacuum tube containing a cathode, control, grid, screen grid, suppressor grid, and plate.

Phase difference. The time in electrical degrees by which one wave leads or lags another.

Phase inversion. A phase difference of 180 between two similar waveshapes of the same frequency.

Phase-splitting circuit. A circuit which produces from the same input waveform two output waveforms which differ in phase from each other.

Phosphorescence. The property of emitting light for some time after excitation by electronic bombardment.

Piezoelectric effect. The effect of producing a voltage by placing a stress, either by compression, by expansion, or by twisting, on a crystal, and, conversely, the effect of producing a stress in a crystal by applying a voltage to it.

Plate (P). The principal electrode in a tube to which the electron stream is attracted. See Anode.

Plate circuit. The complete electrical circuit connecting the cathode and plate of a vacuum tube.

Plate current (i_p). The current flowing in the plate circuit of a vacuum tube.

Plate detection. The operation of a vacuum-tube detector at or near cutoff so that the input signal is rectified in the plate circuit.

Plate dissipation. The power in watts consumed at the plate in the form of heat.

Plate efficiency. The ratio of the a-c power output from a tube to the average d-c power supplied to the plate circuit.

Plate impedance. See Plate resistance.

Plate-load impedance (R_L or Z_L). The impedance in the plate circuit across which the output signal voltage is developed by the alternating component of the plate current.

Plate modulation. Amplitude modulation of a class-C r-f amplifier by varying the plate voltage in accordance with the signal.

Plate resistance (r_p). The internal resistance to

the flow of alternating current between the cathode and plate of tube. It is equal to a small change in plate voltage divided by the corresponding change in plate current, and is expressed in ohms. It is also called a-c resistance, internal impedance, plate impedance, and dynamic plate impedance. The static plate resistance, or resistance to the flow of *direct current* is a different value. It is denoted by R_p.

Positive feedback. See Regeneration.

Potentiometer. A variable voltage divider a resistor which has a variable contact arm so that any portion of the potential applied between its ends may be selected.

Power. The rate of doing work or the rate of expending energy. The unit of electrical power is the watt.

Power amplification. The process of amlifying a signal to produce a gain in power, as distinguished from voltage amplification. The gain in the ratio of the alternating power output to the alternating power input of an amplifier.

Power factor. The ratio of the actual power of an alternating or pulsating current, as measured by a wattmeter, to the apparent power, as indicated by ammeter and voltmeter readings. The power factor if an inductor, capacitor, or insulator is an expression of the losses.

Power tube. A vacuum tube designed to handle a greater amount of power than the ordinary voltage-amplifying tube.

Primary circuit. The first, in electrical order, of two or more coupled circuits, in which a change in current induces a voltage in the other or secondary circuits; such as the primary winding of a transformer.

Propagation. See Wave propagation.

Pulsating current. A unidirectional current which increases and decreases in magnitude.

Push-pull circuit. A push-pull circuit usually refers to an amplifier circuit using two vacuum tubes in such a fashion that when one vacuum tube is operating on a positive alternation, the other vacuum tube operates on a negative alternation.

Q. The figure of merit of efficiency of a circuit or coil. Numerically it is equal to the inductive reactance divided by the resistance of the circuit or coil.

Radiate. To send out energy, such as r-f waves, into space.

Radiation resistance. A fictitious resistance which may be considered to dissipate the energy radiated from the antenna.

Radio frequency (r-f). Any frequency of electrical energy capable of propagation into space. Radio frequencies normally are much higher than sound-wave frequencies.

Radio-frequency amplification. The amplification of a radio wave by a receiver before detection, or by a transmitter before radiation.

Radio-frequency choke (RFC). An air-core or powdered iron core coil used to impede the flow of r-f currents.

Radio-frequency component. See Carrier.

Ratio. The value obtained by dividing one number by another, indicating their relative proportions.

Reactance (X). The opposition offered to the flow of an alternating current by the inductance, capacitance, or both, in any circuit.

Reciprocal. The value obtained by dividing the number 1 by any quantity.

Rectifier. A device used to change alternating current to unidirectional current.

Reflected impedance. See Coupled impedance.

Reflection. The turning back of a radio wave caused by reradiation from any conducting surface which is large in comparison to the wavelength of the radio wave.

Reflector. A metallic object placed behind a radiating antenna to prevent r-f radiation in an undesired direction and to reinforce radiation in a desired direction.

Regeneration. The process of returning a part of the output signal of an amplifier to its input circuit in such a manner that it reinforces the grid excitation and thereby increases the total amplification.

Regulation (voltage). The ratio of the change in voltage due to a load to the open-circuit voltage, expressed in per cent.

Relaxation oscillator. A circuit for the generation of nonsinusoidal waves by gradually storing and quickly releasing energy either in the electric field of a capacitor or in the magnetic field of an inductor.

Reluctance. The opposition to magnetic flux.

Resistance (R). The opposition to the flow of current caused by the nature and physical dimensions of a conductor.

Resistor. A circuit element whose chief characteristic is resistance; used to oppose the flow of current.

Resonance. The condition existing in a circuit in which the inductive and capacitive reactances cancel.

Resonance curve. A graphical representation of the manner in which a resonant circuit responds to various frequencies at and near the resonant frequency.

Rheostat. A variable resistor.

Ripple voltage. The fluctuations in the output voltage of a rectifier, filter, or generator.

rms. Abbreviation of root mean square. See Effective value.

Saturation. The condition existing in any circuit when an increase in the driving signal produces no further change in the resultant effect.

Saturation limiting. Limiting the minimum output voltage of a vacuum-tube circuit by operating the tube in the region of plate-current saturation (not to be confused with emission saturation).

Saturation point. The point beyond which an increase in either grid voltage, plate voltage, or both produces no increase in the existing plate current.

Screen dissipation. The power dissipated in the form of heat on the screen grid as the result of bombardment by the electron stream.

Screen grid (S_c). An electrode placed between the control grid and the plate of a vacuum tube to reduce interelectrode capacitance.

Secondary. The output coil of a transformer. See Primary circuit.

Secondary emission. The emission of electrons knocked loose from the plate, grid, or fluorescent screen of a vacuum tube by the impact or bombardment of electrons arriving from the cathode.

Selectivity. The degree to which a receiver is capable of discriminating between signals of different carrier frequencies.

Self-bias. The bias of a tube created by the voltage drop developed across a resistor through which either its cathode current or its grid current flows.

Self-excited oscillator. An oscillator depending on its resonant circuits for frequency determination. See Crystal oscillator.

Self-induction. The production of a counter-electromotive force in a conductor when its own magnetic field collapses or expands with a change in current in the conductor.

Sensitivity. The degree of response of a circuit to signals of the frequency to which it is tuned.

Series feed. Application of the d-c voltage to the plate or grid of a tube through the same impedance in which the alternating current flows. Compare *Parallel feed.*

Series resonance. The condition existing in a circuit when the source of voltage is in series with an inductor and capacitor whose reactances cancel each other at the applied frequency and thus reduce the impedance to a minimum.

Series-resonant circuit. A resonant circuit in which the capacitor and the inductor are in series with the applied voltage.

Shielding. A metallic covering used to prevent magnetic or electrostatic coupling between adjacent circuits.

Short-circuit. A low-impedance or zero-impedance path between two points.

Shunt. Parallel. A parallel resistor placed in an ammeter to increase its range.

Shunt feed. See Parallel feed. *Sine wave.* The curve traced by the projection on a uniform time scale of the end of a rotating arm, or vector. Also known as a sinusoidal wave.

Skin effect. The tendency of alternating currents to flow near the surface of a conductor, thus being restricted to a small part of the total cross-sectional area. This effect increases the resistance and becomes more marked as the frequency rises.

Soft tube. A vacuum tube the characteristics of which are adversely affected by the presence of gas in the tube; not to be confused with tubes designed to operate with gas inside them.

Solenoid. A multiturn coil of wire wound in a

*uniform layer or layerson a hollow cylindrical form.

Space charge. The cloud of electrons existing in the space between the cathode and plate in a vacuum tube, formed by the electrons emitted from the cathode in excess of those immediately attracted to the plate.

Space current. The total current flowing between the cathode and all the other electrodes in a tube. This includes the plate current, grid current, screen-grid current, and any other electrode current which may be present.

Stability. Freedom from undesired variation.

Standing wave. A distribution of current and voltage on a transmission line formed by two sets of waves traveling in opposite directions, and characterized by the presence of a number of points of successive maxima and minima in the distribution curves.

Static. A fixed nonvarying condition; without motion.

Static characteristics. The characteristics of a tube with no output load and with d-c potentials applied to the grid and plate.

Superheterodyne. A receiver in which the incoming signal is mixed with a locally generated signal to produce a predetermined intermediate frequency.

Suppressor grid (Su). An electrode used in a vacuum tube to minimize the harmful effects of secondary emission from the plate.

Surge. Sudden changes of current or voltage in a circuit.

Surge impedance (Co). See Characteristic impedance.

Sweep circuit. The part of a cathode-ray oscilloscope which provides a time-reference base.

Swing. The variation in frequency or amplitude of an electrical quantity.

Swinging choke. A choke with an effective inductance which varies with the amount of current passing through it. It is used in some power-supply filter circuits.

Synchronous. Happening at the same time; having the same period and phase.

Tank circuit. See Parallel-resonant circuit.

Tetrode. A four-electrode vacuum tube containing a cathode, control grid, screen grid, and plate.

Thermionic emission. Electron emission caused by heating an emitter.

Thermocouple ammeter. An ammeter which operates by means of a voltage produced by the heating effect of a current passed through the junction of two dissimilar metals. It is used for r-f measurements.

Thyratron. A hot-cathode, gas-discharge tube in which one or more electrodes are used to control electrostatically the starting of an unidirectional flow of current.

Tight coupling. Degree of coupling in which practically all of the magnetic lines of force produced by one coil link a second coil.

Trace. A visible line or lines appearing on the screen of a cathode-ray tube in operation.

Transconductance (G_m). The ratio of the change in plate current to the change in grid voltage producing this change in plate current, while all other electrode voltages remain constant.

Transformer. A device composed of two or more coils, linked by magnetic lines of force, used to transfer energy from one circuit to another.

Transient. The voltage or current which exists as the result of a change from one steady-state condition to another.

Transit time. The time which electrons take to travel between the cathode and the plate of a vacuum tube.

Transmission lines. Any conductor or system of conductors used to carry electrical energy from its source to a load.

Triggering. Starting an action in another circuit, which then functions for a time under its own control.

Triode. A three-electrode vacuum tube, containing a cathode, control grid, and plate.

Tuned circuit. A resonant circuit.

Tuning. The process of adjusting a radio circuit so that it resonates at the desired frequency.

Unbalanced line. A transmission line in which the voltages on the two conductors are not equal with respect to ground; for example, a coaxial line.

Unidirectional. In one direction only.

Vacuum-tube voltmeter (VTVM). A device which uses either the amplifier characteristic or the rectifier characteristic of a vacuum tube or both to measure either d-c or a-c voltages. Its input impedance is very high, and the current used to actuate the meter movement is not taken from the circuit being measured. It can be used to obtain accurate measurements in sensitive circuits.

Variable-u tube. A vacuum tube in which the control grid is irregularly spaced, so that the grid exercises a different amount of control on the electron stream at different points within its operating range.

Variocoupler. Two independent inductors, so arranged mechanically that their mutual inductance (coupling) can be varied.

Variometer. A variocoupler having its two coils connected in series, and so mounted that the movable coil may be rotated within the fixed coil, thus changing the total inductance of the unit.

Vector. A line used to represent both direction and magnitude.

Velocity modulation. A method of modulation in which the input signal voltage is used to change the velocity of electrons in a constant-current electron beam so that the electrons are grouped into bunches.

Video amplifier. A circuit capable of amplifying a very wide range of frequencies, including and exceeding the audio band of frequencies.

Volt (V). The unit of electrical potential.

Voltage amplification. The process of amplifying a signal to produce a gain in voltage. The voltage gain of an amplifier is the ratio of its alternating-voltage output to its alternating-voltage input.

Voltage divider. An impedance connected across a voltage source. The load is connected across a fraction of this impedance so that the load voltage is substantially in proportion to this fraction.

Voltage doubter. A method of increasing the voltage by rectifying both halves of a cycle and causing the outputs of both halves to be additive.

Voltage regulation. A measure of the degree to which a power source maintains its output-voltage stability under varying load conditions.

Watt (w). The unit of electrical power.

Wave. Loosely, an electromagnetic impulse, periodically changing in intensity and traveling through space. More specifically, the graphical representation of the intensity of that impulse over a oeriod of time.

Waveform. The shape of the wave obtained when instantaneous values of an a-c quantity are plotted againsi: time in rectangular coordinates.

Wavelength (A). The distance, usually expressed in meters, traveled by a wave during the time interval of one complete cycle. It is equal to the velocity divided by the frequency.

Wave propagation. The transmission of r-f energy through space.

Wien-bridge circuit. A circuit in which the various values of capacitance and resistance are made to balance with each other at a certain frequency.

X. The symbol for reactance.

Z. The symbol for impedance.

ELECTRONICS SYMBOLS

AMPLIFIER (2)

general

with two inputs

with two outputs

with adjustable gain

with associated power supply

with associated attenuator

with external feedback path

Amplifier Letter Combinations (amplifier-use identification in symbol if required)

- BDG Bridging
- BST Booster
- CMP Compression
- DC   Direct Current
- EXP Expansion
- LIM Limiting
- MON Monitoring
- PGM Program
- PRE Preliminary
- PWR Power
- TRQ Torque

ANTENNA (3)

general

dipole

loop

counterpoise

ARRESTER, LIGHTNING (4)

general

carbon block

electrolytic or aluminum cell

horn gap

protective gap

sphere gap

valve or film element

multigap

ATTENUATOR, FIXED (see PAD) (57)
(same symbol as variable attenuator, without variability)

ATTENUATOR, VARIABLE (5)

balanced

unbalanced

AUDIBLE SIGNALING DEVICE (6)

bell, electrical; ringer, telephone

buzzer

horn, electrical; loudspeaker; siren; underwater sound hydrophone, projector or transducer

Horn, Letter Combinations (if required)

- *HN   Horn, electrical
- *HW   Howler
- *LS   Loudspeaker
- *SN   Siren
- ‡EM   Electromagnetic with moving coil
- ‡EMN Electromagnetic with moving coil and neutralizing winding
- ‡MG   Magnetic armature
- ‡PM   Permanent magnet with moving coil

identification replaces (*) asterisk and (‡) dagger)

sounder, telegraph

BATTERY (7)

generalized direct current source; one cell

multicell

CAPACITOR (8)

general

polarized

adjustable or variable

continuously adjustable or variable differential

phase-shifter

split-stator

feed-through

CELL, PHOTOSENSITIVE (Semiconductor) (9)

asymmetrical photoconductive transducer

symmetrical photoconductive transducer

ELECTRONICS SYMBOLS

photovoltaic transducer; solar cell

CIRCUIT BREAKER (11)

general

with magnetic overload

drawout type

CIRCUIT ELEMENT (12)

general

Circuit Element Letter Combinations (replaces (*) asterisk)

EG	Equalizer
FAX	Facsimile set
FL	Filter
FL-BE	Filter, band elimination
FL-BP	Filter, band pass
FL-HP	Filter, high pass
FL-LP	Filter, low pass
PS	Power supply
RG	Recording unit
RU	Reproducing unit
DIAL	Telephone dial
TEL	Telephone station
TPR	Teleprinter
TTY	Teletypewriter

Additional Letter Combinations (symbols preferred)

AR	Amplifier
AT	Attenuator
C	Capacitor
CB	Circuit breaker
HS	Handset
I	Indicating or switch board lamp
L	Inductor
J	Jack
LS	Loudspeaker
MIC	Microphone
OSC	Oscillator
PAD	Pad
P	Plug
HT	Receiver, headset
K	Relay
R	Resistor
S	Switch or key switch
T	Transformer
WR	Wall receptacle

CLUTCH; BRAKE (14)

disengaged when operating means is de-energized

engaged when operating means is de-energized

COIL, RELAY and OPERATING (16)

semicircular dot indicates inner end of wiring

CONNECTOR (18)

assembly, movable or stationary portion; jack, plug, or receptacle

→ or ⊰

jack or receptacle

plug

separable connectors

two-conductor switchboard jack

two-conductor switchboard plug

jacks normalled through one way

jacks normalled through both ways

2-conductor nonpolarized, female contacts

2-conductor polarized, male contacts

waveguide flange

plain, rectangular

choke, rectangular

engaged 4-conductor; the plug has 1 male and 3 female contacts, individual contact designations shown

coaxial, outside conductor shown carried through

coaxial, center conductor shown carried through; outside conductor not carried through

mated choke flanges in rectangular waveguide

COUNTER, ELECTROMAGNETIC; MESSAGE REGISTER (26)

general

with a make contact

COUPLER, DIRECTIONAL (27)
(common coaxial/waveguide usage)

(common coaxial/waveguide usage)

E-plane aperture-coupling, 30-decibel transmission loss

COUPLING (28)

by loop from coaxial to circular waveguide, direct-current grounds connected

CRYSTAL, PIEZO-ELECTRIC (62)

DELAY LINE (31)

general

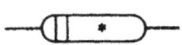

tapped delay

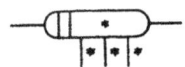

bifilar slow-wave structure (commonly used in traveling-wave tubes)

(length of delay indication replaces (*) asterisk)

DETECTOR, PRIMARY; MEASURING TRANSDUCER (30)
(see HALL GENERATOR and THERMAL CONVERTER)

DISCONTINUITY (33)
(common coaxial/waveguide usage)

equivalent series element, general

capacitive reactance

inductive reactance

inductance-capacitance circuit, infinite reactance at resonance

ELECTRONICS SYMBOLS

inductance-capacitance circuit, zero reactance at resonance

resistance

equivalent shunt element, general

capacitive susceptance

conductance

inductive susceptance

inductance-capacitance circuit, infinite susceptance at resonance

inductance-capacitance circuit, zero susceptance at resonance

ELECTRON TUBE (34)

triode

pentode, envelope connected to base terminal

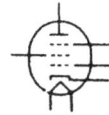

twin triode, equipotential cathode

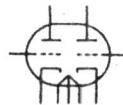

typical wiring figure to show tube symbols placed in any convenient position

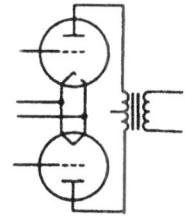

rectifier; voltage regulator (see LAMP, GLOW)

phototube, single and multiplier

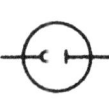 

cathode-ray tube, electrostatic and magnetic deflection

mercury-pool tube, ignitor and control grid (see RECTIFIER)

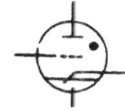

resonant magnetron, coaxial output and permanent magnet

reflex klystron, integral cavity, aperture coupled

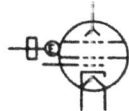

transmit-receive (TR) tube gas filled, tunable integral cavity, aperture coupled, with starter

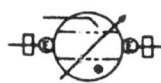

traveling-wave tube (typical)

forward-wave traveling-wave-tube amplifier shown with four grids, having slow-wave structure with attenuation, magnetic focusing by external permanent magnet, rf input and rf output coupling each E-plane aperture to external rectangular waveguide

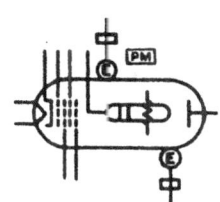

FERRITE DEVICES (100)

field polarization rotator

field polarization amplitude modulator

FUSE (36)

high-voltage primary cutout, dry

high-voltage primary cutout, oil

GOVERNOR (Contact-making) (37)

contacts shown here as closed

HALL GENERATOR (39)

HANDSET (40)

general

operator's set with push-to talk switch

HYBRID (41)

general

junction (common coaxial/waveguide usage)

circular

(E, H or HE transverse field indicators replace (*) asterisk)

rectangular waveguide and coaxial coupling

INDUCTOR (42)

general

ELECTRONICS SYMBOLS

magnetic core

tapped
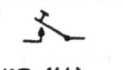

adjustable, continuously adjustable

KEY, TELEGRAPH (43)
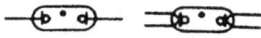

LAMP (44)

ballast lamp; ballast tube

lamp, fluorescent, 2 and 4 terminal

lamp, glow; neon lamp
a-c

d-c

lamp, incandescent

indicating lamp; switchboard lamp
(see VISUAL SIGNALING DEVICE)

LOGIC (see 806B and Y32-14) (including some duplicate symbols; left and right-hand symbols are not mixed)

AND function
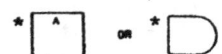

OR function
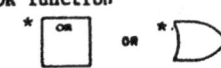

EXCLUSIVE-OR function

((*) input side of logic symbols in general)

condition indicators

state (logic negation)
○

a Logic Negation output becomes 1-state if and only if the input is not 1-state

an AND func. where output is low if and only if all inputs are high
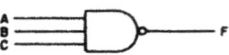

electric inverter
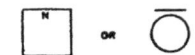

(elec. invtr. output becomes 1-state if and only if the input is 1-state) (elec. invtr. output is more pos. if and only if input is less pos.)

level (relative)

1-state is less +   1-state is more +

(symbol is a rt. triangle pointing in direction of flow)

an AND func. with input 1-states at more pos. level and output 1-state at less pos. level

single shot (one output)
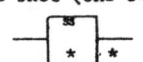

(waveform data replaces inside/outside (*))

schmitt trigger, waveform and two outputs
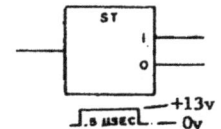

flip-flop, complementary
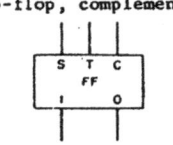

flip-flop, latch
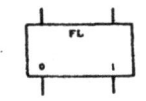

register
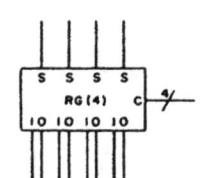

(binary register denoting four flip-flops and bits)

amplifier (see AMPLIFIER)

channel path(s) (see PATH, TRANSMISSION)

magnetic heads (see PICK-UP HEAD)

oscillator (see OSCILLATOR)
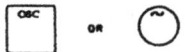

relay, contacts (see CONTACT, ELECTRICAL)
relay, electromagnetic (see RELAY COIL RECOGNITION)

signal flow (see DIRECTION OF FLOW)

time delay (see DELAY LINE)
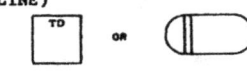

time delay with typical delay taps:
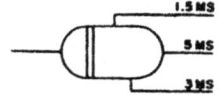

functions not otherwise symbolized
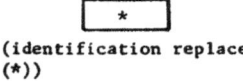

(identification replaces (*))

Logic Letter Combinations

S	set
C	clear (reset)
T	toggle (trigger)
(N)	number of bits
BO	blocking oscillator
CF	cathode follower
EF	emitter follower
FF	flip-flop
SS	single shot
ST	schmitt trigger
RG(N)	register (N stages)
SR	shift register

MACHINE, ROTATING (46)

generator

motor

METER, INSTRUMENT (48)

(*)

identification replaces (*) asterisk)

Meter Letter Combinations

A	Ammeter
AH	Ampere-hour
CMA	Contact-making (or breaking) ammeter
CMC	Contact-making (or breaking) clock
CMV	Contact-making (or breaking) voltmeter
CRO	Oscilloscope or cathode-ray oscillograph
DB	DB (decibel) meter
DBM	DBM (decibels referred to 1 milliwatt) meter
DM	Demand meter
DTR	Demand-totalizing relay
F	Frequency meter
G	Galvanometer
GD	Ground detector
I	Indicating
INT	Integrating
µA or UA	Microammeter
MA	Milliammeter
NM	Noise meter
OHM	Ohmmeter
OP	Oil pressure

ELECTRONICS SYMBOLS

MODE TRANSDUCER (53)

(common coaxial/waveguide usage)

transducer from rectangular waveguide to coaxial with mode suppression, direct-current grounds connected

MOTION, MECHANICAL (54)

rotation applied to a resistor

(identification replaces (*) asterisk)

NUCLEAR-RADIATION DETECTOR, gas filled; IONIZATION CHAMBER; PROPORTIONAL COUNTER TUBE; GEIGER-MULLER COUNTER TUBE (50) (see RADIATION-SENSITIVITY INDICATOR)

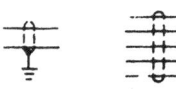

PATH, TRANSMISSION (58)

cable; 2-conductor, shield grounded and 5-conductor shielded

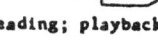

PICKUP HEAD (61)

general

writing; recording

reading; playback

erasing

writing, reading, and erasing

stereo

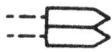

RECTIFIER (65)

semiconductor diode; metallic rectifier; electrolytic rectifier; asymmetrical varistor

mercury-pool tube power rectifier

fullwave bridge-type

RESISTOR (68)

general

tapped

heating

symmetrical varistor resistor, voltage sensitive (silicon carbide, etc.)

(identification marks replace (*) asterisk)

with adjustable contact

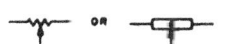

adjustable or continuously adjustable (variable)

(identification replaces (*) asterisk)

RESONATOR, TUNED CAVITY (71)

(common coaxial/waveguide usage)

resonator with mode suppression coupled by an E-plane aperture to a guided transmission path and by a loop to a coaxial path

tunable resonator with direct-current ground connected to an electron device and adjustably coupled by an E-plane aperture to a rectangular waveguide

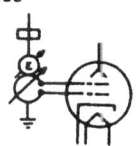

ROTARY JOINT, RF (COUPLER) (72)

general; with rectangular waveguide

(transmission path recognition symbol replaces (*) asterisk)

coaxial type in rectangular waveguide

circular waveguide type in rectangular waveguide

SEMICONDUCTOR DEVICE (73)
(Two Terminal, diode)

semiconductor diode; rectifier

capacitive diode (also Varicap, Varactor, reactance diode, parametric diode)

breakdown diode, unidirectional (also backward diode, avalanche diode, voltage regulator diode, Zener diode, voltage reference diode)

breakdown diode, bidirectional and backward diode (also bipolar voltage limiter)

tunnel diode (also Esaki diode)

temperature-dependent diode

photodiode (also solar cell)

semiconductor diode, PNPN switch (also Shockley diode, four-layer diode and SCR).

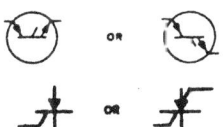

(Multi-Terminal, transistor, etc.)

PNP transistor

NPN transistor

unijunction transistor, N-type base

ELECTRONICS SYMBOLS

unijunction transistor, P-type base

field-effect transistor, N-type base

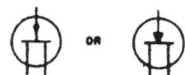

field-effect transistor, P-type base

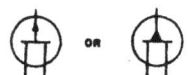

semiconductor triode, PNPN-type switch

semiconductor triode, NPNP-type switch

NPN transistor, transverse-biased base

PNIP transistor, ohmic connection to the intrinsic region

NPIN transistor, ohmic connection to the intrinsic region

PNIN transistor, ohmic connection to the intrinsic region

NPIP transistor, ohmic connection to the intrinsic region

SQUIB (75)

explosive

igniter

sensing link; fusible link operated

SWITCH (76)

push button, circuit closing (make)

push button, circuit opening (break)

nonlocking; momentary circuit closing (make)

nonlocking; momentary circuit opening (break)

transfer

locking, circuit closing (make)

locking, circuit opening (break)

transfer, 3-position

wafer

(example shown: 3-pole 3-circuit with 2 non-shorting and 1 shorting moving contacts)

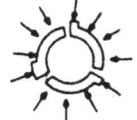

safety interlock, circuit opening and closing

2-pole field-discharge knife, with terminals and discharge resistor

(identification replaces (*) asterisk)

SYNCHRO (78)

Synchro Letter Combinations
CDX Control-differential transmitter
CT   Control transformer
CX   Control transmitter
TDR Torque-differential receiver
TDX Torque-differential transmitter
TR   Torque receiver
TX   Torque transmitter
RS   Resolver
B   Outer winding rotatable in bearings

THERMAL ELEMENT (83)

actuating device

thermal cutout; flasher

thermal relay

thermostat (operates on rising temperature), contact)

thermostat, make contact

thermostat, integral heater and transfer contacts

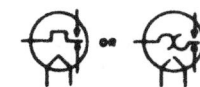

THERMISTOR; THERMAL RESISTOR (84)

with integral heater

THERMOCOUPLE (85)

temperature-measuring

current-measuring, integral heater connected

current-measuring, integral heater insulated

temperature-measuring, semiconductor

current-measuring, semiconductor

TRANSFORMER (86)

general

magnetic-core

one winding with adjustable inductance

separately adjustable inductance

adjustable mutual inductor, constant-current

ELECTRONICS SYMBOLS

autotransformer, 1-phase adjustable

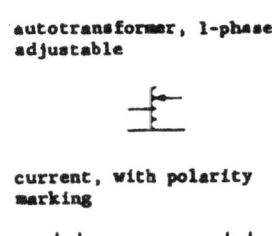

current, with polarity marking

potential, with polarity mark

with direct-current connections and mode suppression between two rectangular waveguides

(common coaxial/waveguide usage)

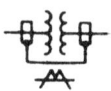

shielded, with magnetic core

with a shield between windings, connected to the frame

VIBRATOR; INTERRUPTER (87)

typical shunt drive (terminals shown)

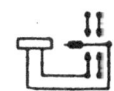

typical separate drive (terminals shown)

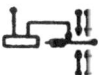

VISUAL SIGNALING DEVICE (88)

communication switchboard-type lamp

indicating, pilot, signaling, or switchboard light (see LAMP)

(identification replaces (*) asterisk)

indicating light letter combinations

A   Amber
B   Blue
C   Clear
G   Green
NE Neon
O   Orange
OP Opalescent
P   Purple
R   Red
W   White
Y   Yellow

jeweled signal light

TRANSISTOR SYMBOLS

Semiconductor, General
BV .... Breakdown voltage
TA .... Ambient temperature
T_{ep} .... Operating temperature

Transistor
B, b .... Base electrode
C, c .... Collector electrode
C_{ib} .... Input capacitance (common base)
C_{ie} .... Input capacitance (common emitter)
C_{ob} .... Output capacitance (common base)
C_{oe} .... Output capacitance (common emitter)
E, e .... Emitter electrode
I_B .... Base current (dc)
i_b .... Base current (instantaneous)
I_C .... Collector current (dc)
i_c .... Collector current (instantaneous)
I_{CBO} .... Collector cutoff current (dc) emitter open
I_{CEO} .... Collector cutoff current (dc) base open
I_E .... Emitter current
R_B .... External base resistance
r_b .... Base spreading resistance
r_i .... Input junction resistance
V_{BB} .... Base supply voltage
V_C .... Collector voltage (with respect to ground or common point)
V_{BE} .... Base to emitter voltage (dc)
V_{CB} .... Collector to base voltage (dc)
V_{CE} .... Collector to emitter voltage (dc)
V_{ce} .... Collector to emitter voltage (rms)
v_{ce} .... Collector to emitter voltage (instantaneous)
$V_{CE(sat)}$ ...... Collector to emitter saturation voltage
V_{EBO} .... Emitter to base voltage (static)
V_{CC} .... Collector supply voltage
V_{EE} .... Emitter supply voltage

TUBE SYMBOLS

A_{hf} .... High frequency gain
A_{lf} .... Low frequency gain
A_v .... Voltage gain
C_c .... Coupling capacitor
C_d .... Distributed capacitance
C_{gk} .... Grid-to-cathode capacitance
C_{gp} .... Grid-to-plate capacitance
C_i .... Input capacitance
C_K .... athode bypass capacitor
C_O .... Output capacitance
C_{pk} .... Plate-to-cathode capacitance
C_s .... Shunt capacitance ($C_d + C_i + C_o$)
E_b .... Plate volts (dc)
E_{bb} .... Supply volts (dc)
E_{bo} .... Quiescent plate voltage
E_{c1} .... Control grid voltage
E_{c2} .... Screen grid voltage
E_{cc} .... Control grid supply voltage
E_f .... Filament terminal voltage
e_b .... Instantaneous total plate volts (ac and dc)
e_{c1} .... Instantaneous total control grid volts (ac and dc)
e_{c2} .... Instantaneous total screen grid volts (ac and dc)
e_{g1} .... Instantaneous value of ac control grid volts
e_{g2} .... Instantaneous value of ac screen grid volts
e_{po} .... Instantaneous value of plate voltage above and below the quiescent value
E_g .... RMS value of grid volts
E_p .... RMS value of plate volts
g_m .... Grid-plate transconductance (mutual conductance)

I_b .... DC value of plate volts
I_{bo} .... Quiescent value of plate current
I_{c1} .... DC value of control grid current
I_{C2} .... DC value of screen grid current
I_f .... Filament or heater current
I_{g1} .... RMS value of control grid current
I_{g2} .... RMS value of screen grid current
I_{gml} .... Crest values of ac current control grid
g_{m2} .... Crest values of ac current screen grid
I_p .... RMS' values of plate current
I_{pm} .... Crest value of plate current
I_s .... Total electron emission
i_b .... Instantaneous total value of plate current
i_{c1} .... Instantaneous total value of control grid current
i_{c2} .... Instantaneous total value of screen grid current
i_{g1} .... Instantaneous ac value of control grid current
i_{g2} .... Instantaneous ac value of screen grid current
i_p .... Instantaneous ac value of plate current
i_{po} .... Instantaneous values of plate current above and below the uiescent value
R_b .... DC plate resistance
R_g .... DC grid resistance
R_k .... DC cathode resistance
R_L .... Plate load resistance
r_p .... AC plate resistance
μ .... Amplification factor

www.ingramcontent.com/pod-product-compliance
Lightning Source LLC
Chambersburg PA
CBHW081758300426
44116CB00014B/2167